ISHMAEL MY BROTHER

Ishmael My Brother

A Christian Introduction to Islam

Compiled by
ANNE COOPER

MARC
Tunbridge Wells

First published 1985
This edition 1993

British Library Cataloguing in Publication Data
A catalogue record for this book is available
from the British Library.

ISBN: 1 85424 233 4

Produced by Bookprint Creative Services
P.O. Box 827, BN23 6NX, England for
MARC an imprint of Monarch Publications
P.O. Box 163, Tunbridge Wells, Kent TN3 0NZ
Printed in Great Britain

Contents

Introduction to the Second Edition

The title of this book is a reminder that both Christians and Muslims look back to Abraham as father. Abraham prayed in Genesis 17:18, 'If only Ishmael might live under your blessing!'. God answered that prayer by replying,

> And as for Ishmael, I have heard you: I will surely bless him; I will make him fruitful and will greatly increase his numbers. He will be the father of twelve rulers, and I will make him into a great nation. But my covenant I will establish with Isaac, whom Sarah will bear to you by this time next year. (Gen 17:20–21)

The children of Ishmael have certainly been fruitful and their numbers have greatly increased. There are now some billion Muslims and they continue to increase rapidly in many parts of the world.

Although Muhammad the Prophet of Islam seems to have known and learnt from both Jews and Christians, hostility began when they did not accept his teaching nor his prophethood. Since then, exacerbated by historical events like the Crusades and European colonial rule, the rifts between Christianity and Islam have grown deeper. During the twentieth century wars are still being fought which, although politically motivated, identify the two religions as opposing forces.

While in no way minimising the deep doctrinal differences between Christianity and Islam, this book tries to dispel some of the barriers and prejudices that negate the fostering of personal relationships between Muslims and Christians and exclude a real understanding of each other's faith. The aim of the book is to open up a better understanding, encourage better relationships and press on towards better communication.

In undertaking this revision, the structure of the book has not been altered but some new material has been introduced: the rise of Islamic fundamentalism, for example, now merits a separate chapter, and the case studies are more relevant to the global nature of Islam as it is today.

This revision would not have been possible without the help of a team too numerous to mention by name. Over the last six months many have responded to questionnaires or have commented, advised, or made suggestions in person. The team of writers has been vital to the whole project. Dr Elsie Maxwell has been responsible for chapters 3, 4, 5 and 6. The Revd Dr Bill Musk has contributed chapters 11 and 14, Dr David Burnett chapter 8, Ida Glaser section 2 of chapter 1, Vivienne Stacey the greater part of chapter 13 and Dr Paul Shepherd, section 1 of chapter 15. Each of these writers has also given valuable help concerning the book as a whole and Dr Chris Wright has advised on chapter 1, section 1. Grateful thanks go to them and to the team of case study writers, the Revd Bob Cutler, Ron George, Jeremy Hinds, Dr Howard Norrish, Ray Porter, the Revd Ronald Waine, and also the workers in 'a town in north-west England'. Finally, thank you to my friend Margaret Wellings for her invaluable secretarial help.

Christian witness to Muslims has been weak, with few outstanding missionaries and those lacking the support that they needed for a significant breakthrough. Few Muslims have a clear idea of the teaching of Christ, or of the good news of salvation through him. It is our prayer that this book will help us all to present a Biblical view and to share our faith with Muslims.

Unless otherwise stated, Biblical references are taken from the New International Bible and Qur'anic references from the *Meaning of the Glorious Qur'an* by Abdullah Yusuf Ali. Both Qur'an and Koran are acceptable Anglicised spellings. Qur'an is used in this book as being more phonetically correct. Koran occurs in a number of the quotations. While Biblical references use the names of the books of the Bible, Qur'anic references are prefixed Sura (chapter), to avoid additional Arabic words and translations.

PART I
Preparation

I

Christians and Other Faiths

Study guide

Welcome to this study book! May God bless you as you read it and make you a blessing to others.

In this first chapter a distinction is made between God—who reveals himself to humankind—and religions, which are a human response. The three main sections look at the theological, the Biblical and the experiential aspects of the Christian and other faiths. The book uses some 'distance learning' techniques which are designed for home study. One of the advantages of using such techniques is that you can select for detailed study the sections that interest you most. However, we hope that you will read the whole chapter and use it as a springboard to propel you forward into the rest of the book!

When you have completed the chapter we hope you will:

1 Have a foundation on which to develop a Christian attitude to those of other faiths;
2 Understand that there are differing views and interpretations of the subject; and
3 Be able to form your own opinion as a basis for meeting and relating to those of other faiths.

1

She was elderly and from a privileged family; she got into the railway compartment in which my friend and I were travelling, accompanied by the usual relations, servants and baggage. We were making the 800-mile journey up country to the city where my friend was to begin her teaching assignment.

It was late at night and we hardly noticed her until the next morning when, as my friend was reading her Bible, she said, 'It always makes me happy to see people reading their holy book.' Conversation followed, during which we all shared something of what our belief in God meant to us and she displayed such a sense of God's nearness that we were able to talk together as one might in a group of Christian friends. As we shared what Jesus meant to us, she spoke of him as a wonderful prophet whom she greatly revered. She encouraged us to speak of him as our Lord and Saviour, although she did not share this belief. Our conversation ended and she then spent some time performing her morning prayers.

As we arrived at our destination there were questions in my mind. How does God look upon someone like this? Is it possible to have a relationship with him without accepting the saving death of Jesus on the cross? How should a Christian witness in such a situation?

Later, my friend said, 'What a wonderful way to start my life and work in this country!' Indeed it was. It happened many years ago, but I still remember this 'chance' encounter. The questions it raised are still very real, and they form the basis of this first chapter. We do not so much attempt to answer them, as to clarify the issues and bring them out in the open.

Who do people say I am? (Mark 8:27)

This is the question with which we must start. We know Peter's answer: 'You are the Messiah, the Son of the living God' (Mt 16:16). This points clearly to the uniqueness of Jesus. In a world of multi-faith societies this is a very relevant question. But what do we mean by 'unique'? If we are thinking of Jesus as the founder of a religion, or as an example of a really good teacher, then he is not unique in that sense. He is unique because he fulfilled the purposes of God in a way no one else has ever done, or ever could do. He is unique because God is unique and he is God. God created us and worked out his purposes uniquely through the people of Israel. Deuteronomy 4:32–35 explains this very clearly:

Ask now about the former days, long before your time, from the
day God created man on the earth; ask from one end of the heavens
to the other. Has anything so great as this ever happened, or has
anything like it ever been heard of? Has any other people heard the
voice of God speaking out of fire, as you have, and lived? Has any
god ever tried to take for himself one nation out of another nation,
by testings, by miraculous signs and wonders, by war, by a mighty
hand and an outstretched arm, or by great and awesome deeds, like
all the things the Lord your God did for you in Egypt before your
very eyes?

You were shown these things so that you might know that
the Lord is God; besides him there is no other.

There is an important distinction between 'God' and 'religion'
which is not always made clear in discussion. Religion is a
human activity, an effort to reach out to and know God, which
at best leads us to find God and to worship him. At worst,
however, it can go horribly wrong and can be influenced by evil
and demonic powers. Religion reflects the dilemma of humankind, made in the image of God (Gen 1:26), but disobedient to
him (Gen 3:6). Someone as close to Jesus as the apostle Peter
illustrates this dilemma. Jesus commended Peter for proclaim-
ing him to be the long-awaited Messiah, but when Peter in the
next breath protested over his predicted suffering and death,
Jesus called him Satan and a stumbling-block. Like Peter we
may experience times of God-given insight, but we are also
prone to misunderstanding and error. We need to learn more
of humility and repentance, as the apostle Peter did. It is
important to remember this as we meet and relate to people of
other faiths.

We need to 'see' Jesus before we attempt to study religions.
We need to see that 'he taught as one who had authority, and
not as their teachers of the law' (Mt 7:29). We need to hear
him proclaim, 'Before Abraham was born, I am!' (Jn 8:58),
remembering that I AM (*yahweh*) meant 'God' to the Jews. If
we do this we will not only proclaim, 'THERE IS ONLY
ONE GOD', but we will go on to say that God, the only source
of salvation, has provided the only way to obtain salvation,
through the sacrificial death of his Son, Jesus the Messiah.

Christians proclaim categorically, 'THERE IS NO OTHER WAY' (cf Jn 14:6) and 'THERE IS NO OTHER NAME' (Acts 4:12).

This proclaimation is in sharp contrast to the secular thinking of our day. The French sociologist Michel Foucault taught that all ideologies consist of 'regimes of truth' which are not fixed but are relative to time, place and situation. This teaching that truth is not absolute has permeated into religious thinking and is responsible for the religious pluralism of our day. It is as if the different religions are on display as products to be chosen by consumers to suit their particular needs. The fact that people from different social, ethnic and religious backgrounds may live side by side with us and that we want to attempt to reach out to them 'does not', as Dr Chris Wright says in his book *What's so Unique about Jesus?*, 'simply dissolve the theological distinctions and conflicts that exist between the Christian faith and other beliefs' (Wright, 1990, p. 24).[1]

'And how can they hear without someone preaching to them?'
(Romans 10:14)

What about those who have never had the opportunity to respond to the gospel? There are millions of people in this category, some because they lived before Jesus came to this earth, some because they have lived in areas where the gospel has never been heard; others, such as young children and those with learning difficulties, are people to whom it is not possible to communicate it. Surely a just God cannot condemn them?

This is perhaps the point at which we should remind ourselves that it is God who saves, not our evangelistic skills. We must not be limited in our view of his grace, but at the same time we must be true to Scripture, as we believe God has revealed it to us. Wright asks, 'Does that necessarily mean salvation is only through actual knowledge of Jesus Christ and conscious faith in

---

1. Bibliographic details of books mentioned in the text are provided at the end of each chapter.

him?' (p. 36). Some would answer 'Yes' and point out that this gives a sense of urgency to our evangelistic efforts; but others would take a more agnostic view. In any case, it is just as well to remember that 'Now we see but a poor reflection as in a mirror; then we shall see face to face' (1 Cor 13:12). We must expect to 'know in part' in this life and to look forward to when we shall 'know fully'. We need to remember that 'the secret things belong to the Lord our God' and to concentrate on sharing 'the things revealed' (Deut 29:29).

The Bible gives a number of instances of outstanding men and women who could not have had specific knowledge of Jesus. Jews, Christians and Muslims all look back to Abraham. He lived before the time of Jesus; he lived before the law was given to Moses; yet the Bible tells us that 'Abraham believed God, and it was credited to him as righteousness' (Rom 4:3). Hebrews 11 goes even further, giving a list of those who were justified by faith, including some whose connection with God's plan and purpose in Jesus Christ seems remote. Enoch was a man who lived by faith and who consequently 'did not experience death; he could not be found, because God had taken him away. For before he was taken, he was commended as one who pleased God' (Heb 11:5).

It is clear from the parables of Jesus that there are going to be surprises; that there will be those who expected to be saved but are not, and those who were not expected to be saved yet who were accepted by God. It is obvious that we do not see as God does. The parable of the Pharisee and the tax collector is a good example. Who would have thought that it would be the tax collector who 'went home justified before God' (Lk 18:14)? Imagine the impact this story would have on those who heard it for the first time! The conclusions that such parables lead to is not that God is unfair, but that he is amazingly generous. This should in no way dampen our evangelistic zeal; rather it should make it spring from our deep gratitude. It would be strange if a doctor failed to treat a seriously ill person because the hospital possessed a life-support machine; it is strange if we do not pass on really good news because a person may possibly get by without it. Surely the extent we see the gospel as good news determines our desire to pass it on. If we truly perceive, nothing will stop us.

'What is truth?' (John 18:38)

We do not know how Pilate asked that question. With longing? With mockery? With disillusionment? With despair? We do know, however, that this is the central question as we consider the Christian and other faiths. The way we answer it will show the position we hold.

It is difficult to see how biblically-based Christians can hold pluralist views, which, as we have seen, present a relativist view of truth. Wright describes the pluralist position as follows:

> Even if the beliefs of one religion are diametrically contradictory to those of another, you don't need to decide which is true and which is false, for they can all be 'true' at some more profound level of reality which we do not yet understand. (p. 46)

Wright also points out that pluralists want to see God (*theos*) at the centre of the religious universe, not Christ or Christianity. He also distinguishes between pluralism and syncretism, which is 'the desire to blend and unite the best in all world religions into one future composite world faith' (p. 46).

Although there are those who believe they can be Christians and hold pluralist views, the real debate is between those who exclude any religion other than Christianity from possessing any revealed truth or way to salvation (who may be called exclusivists) and those who think other faiths may have some truth revealed to them but that they are not ways to salvation (who may be called inclusivists). Some inclusivists may also believe that 'although Christianity remains the highest and final truth, a non-Christian religion can contain supernatural elements of grace for a person (until the arrival of the gospel) as a free gift from God on account of Christ' (Wright, 1990, p. 41).

Between the exclusivist and inclusivist poles lie many Christian people, perhaps some of us. One of the most important aspects of these different views is that Christians should learn to live with them. Many inclusivists are deeply committed to Christ and exclusivists are not hard and unfeeling. Dick Dowsett has written a book called *God, That's Not Fair!*, which, through correspondence with a younger friend, presents the exclusivist view. Here is an extract:

Of course the agony of this is when you translate it into real people. It is easy to talk about theory, but I find it hard when I think of my [Muslim] neighbours . . . We would be callous in the extreme if we did not long to find some way whereby some of them at least could be saved.

But the biblical way to achieve this is not to look for hints in Scripture to encourage our wishful thinking. Rather, it is by loving and costly friendship and evangelism of committed Christians that [Muslims] will be won (p. 39).

Activity 1:1

Look at the diagram overleaf. Where would you place your own arrow on the spectrum? You might like to pencil it in. It will be interesting to come back later and see whether your position has changed at all as a result of reading this book and having discussion with Muslims.

2

What does the Bible say about other faiths?

Ida Glaser has prepared this Bible study to help us think through some of the material in the previous section. She has written it with Christians and Muslims particularly in mind.

How can we relate to each other as human beings? How do we know about God? Is Jesus the only way to him? The answers depend not only on a few particular verses, but on our whole view of who we are, of why we do not automatically know all about God, and of why we need a way to him. In other words — if we are going to get the medicine right, we need to

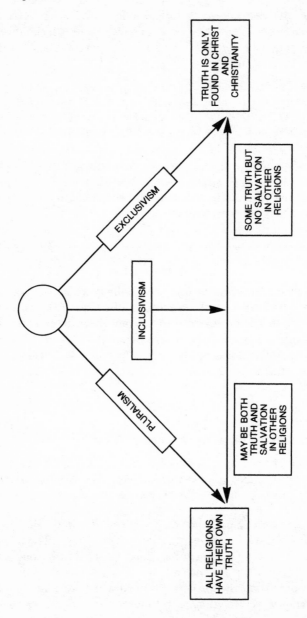

get the diagnosis right. A good starting place is the beginning of the Bible!

Read Genesis 1–12:3.

- What has gone wrong?
- Why has it gone wrong?
- What has God done about it?

Relationships have gone wrong: relationships between God and human beings, between humans and animals, humans and the planet, men and women, siblings, communities, nations . . .

They have gone wrong because of *deceit*, *disobedience* and *distortion*—listening to the wrong voice, deliberately disobeying God, directing efforts towards destruction of human beings and trying to usurp God's place.

God has *judged*, *preserved* and *chosen people*. He has chosen not to destroy humankind, but has chosen people—Noah and his family, then Abraham and his family, to bring the blessing that he has originally called mankind to receive.

As far as salvation is concerned, these chapters:

- Lay the foundation of our problems – the radical view of sin that means that Jesus is necessary.
- Lay down the principle of exclusion – God's sovereign choice of how he will save.

    The choice of Abel's sacrifice—we know not why.

    The choice of Noah—why was he the one to find grace?

    The choice of Abraham—again, no reason given.
- Lay down the principle of inclusivism—

    The choice of Noah's family was the choice of all mankind — that is the point of chapter 10, which traces all human beings to Noah and therefore includes them all in the covenant of chapter 9.

    The choice of Abraham was for the sake of all mankind— all the peoples of chapter 10 were the objects of the blessing which was the purpose of God's choice.

But the Genesis story does not only point us to God's chosen way of salvation: it also confronts us with the problem of relating to people. Islam is not just a system: it is *people* who practise it, and with whom we have to live in the world. If Jesus is the only way to God, we need to tell them about him. But we also need to relate to them as human beings, and to do this we need to recognise that we too are part of the world that has gone wrong.

In particular, Genesis 4 shows us *sibling rivalry*. One of the primal facts about the world is jealousy, hatred and revenge between brothers—Cain and Abel, Jacob and Esau, Joseph and the rest . . . and . . . Ishmael and Isaac. In fact, the Bible tells us that Ishmael was to have problems in relating with all his brothers (Gen 16:11–12).

Interpreting the Bible

People who hold these differing views all use the Bible. It is not simply that exclusivists believe in the Bible and pluralists reject it; people use it differently. For example, exclusivists often point to the very strong statement in John 14:6, where Jesus says, 'I am the way and the truth and the life. No-one comes to the Father, except through me.'

This seems to be very clear as well as very strong; but the Anglican discussion document, *Towards a Theology of Inter-Faith Dialogue* says:

> Taken like this out of context there can be little doubt that it appears to support such a [rigidly exclusivist] view. But again the text ought to be interpreted only within the development of thought in the discourse as a whole and then set within a wider framework of biblical thought. The context is that of Thomas' question about how the disciples can know where Jesus is going, and therefore how they can know the way. The answer is that Jesus is going to the Father, and since they know him they have no need to demand as Philip did, 'Show us the Father'; indeed to have seen Jesus was to have seen the Father. John is here trying to assure the disciples that to have seen Jesus is indeed to have seen nothing less than God, for God is perfectly reflected in Jesus, as indeed the prologue to this gospel is at pains to show. Again, in the words of John Robinson, 'the Father is perfectly reflected in him, he is God, all through'. There is no suggestion in the context that Jesus is claiming

to be 'the whole of God', that outside him there is no truth or life
to be found. The main thrust is that in him truth and life are to be
found, that same truth and life which belong to the Father. There
is no cause for fear. When we read the text this way there is no
need to suppose that it is claiming that apart from Jesus there is
neither truth nor life. That is indeed too limiting an interpretation
to fit in with the rest of John's Gospel. (pp. 23–24)

Pause for thought (1)

Why do you think that the writers of this discussion document
want to interpret John 14:6 in this way? Are there aspects of
the passage that they have ignored?

One of the main reasons for thinking this way is the desire
to relate to people of all faiths.

The writers are wanting to say that there is truth and life
outside Christ—that is, people can know about God and do
good things and perhaps even communicate with God without
knowing anything about Jesus. This has to do with:

> *The nature of human beings*—made in God's image (Gen
> 1:26)
> *Revelation*—all humans know something about God (Rom
> 1:18–20)

They have ignored the idea of Jesus as the only way—that is,
that people can only be saved through him.

Our shared human nature, access to revelation, the way of
salvation . . . these are the three themes that occur repeatedly
in discussion about other faiths. The Bible has much to say
about all of these, but we need to be careful not to confuse
them.

Pause for thought (2)

How well does the story of Cain and Abel describe relationships
between Muslims and Christians?

Muslim commentators see the Qur'anic version of the story
as a parable of relationships between Muslims and Jews:

> Israel rebelled against God, slew and insulted righteous men who
> did them no harm but on the contrary came in all humility. When

God withdrew His favour from Israel because of its sins and bestowed it on another nation, the jealousy of Israel plunged it deeper into sin. (Yusuf Ali, N. 737 on Sura 5:35)

What has all this to say about other faiths?

Not much! The problems of looking to the *Old Testament* to find a theology of other faiths are:

1. The Old Testament really is not interested in religions, but in God and how we relate to him. It tells us about what God has done, and how he has worked in and through Israel who are his chosen way of dealing with the human mess.

2. Before Jesus, God's chosen Way is linked with a particular people. Thus attitudes to other groups are not only to do with their religions, but also with the fact that they are not Israel—religion is linked with race. In Christ, race is not relevant for salvation. We need to be careful that ideas of exclusiveness about Israel are carried into thinking about the uniqueness of Christ, but *not* into thinking about the superiority of any group of human beings, nor indeed about the inferiority of any.

Thus, for example, there is much in the Old Testament against idolatry, and therefore against the kind of worship practised by the peoples around Israel. We can therefore conclude that idolatry is wrong. *But* it is Israel that receives most of the harsh words, when God's people go after idols.

Judgement on the surrounding nations is not usually because of wrong worship, but because of moral failure (cf Amos). Sometimes people who are not Israelites actually hear God more clearly than do even his prophets (see Gen 20, Jon 1).

When we come to the *New Testament*, the Jew/Gentile barriers are broken down, and we can more easily distinguish religion and race. But we still have a problem: Which people referred to in the New Testament are like the people of other faiths we meet today? In particular, which of them are like our Muslim friends?

Read John 4:1–26, Acts 10, Acts 17:16–34.

These passages all deal with people who are religious, but

are not Jews or Christians. What do the passages have in common?

- They all find positive things in the other faith and in the peoples' attempts to relate to God.
- They build on these positive things.
- They finish with the seekers coming to Jesus.

Are the Jews a special case?

Romans 9–11 tells us that they are. They have received revelation: in fact, it is through them that Christ has come, and they are the rightful inheritors of God's promises. They certainly worship the same God as Christians worship, although, like many at Jesus' time, they may not understand what he is like. They have a rich heritage in culture and tradition as well as in religion. *But* . . .

> They need Jesus if they are to be saved (Rom 10:1)
> The heritage is nothing beside Christ (Phil 3:4–9).

Are the Muslims a special case?

There are promises to Ishmael as well as to Isaac (Gen 21:13, 18); and Muslims claim to follow the faith given to his descendants—to be responding to the same message that came first to Adam and then to all the prophets after him. They reject all forms of idolatry, and worship the one God who created the heavens and the earth.

As you study Islam, you will want to ask yourself where Muslims fit into the pattern of the world we see in the Bible. Are they like the Samaritans? Like Cornelius? Like the Athenians? By the end of your studies, you may have come to some conclusions.

But beware!

Muslims are human beings—in the end, each individual as well as each group is different. Their standing before God and the way we can best relate to them may have more to do with their humanity than with their Islam.

We can fall into sibling rivalry as easily as Cain did. Jesus expounded the Old Testament teaching on relationships with human beings by telling a story about a person of a different race and faith, the Good Samaritan (Lk 10:25–37).

Whether or not we are relating as descendants of Isaac to descendants of Ishmael—as Jews to Arabs—we are all related, because we are all in the family of Noah. Whether person to person or community to community, we are in danger of reverting to the rivalry and violence between the original brothers. As in the case of those brothers, the rivalry is very likely to be over a religious issue—which sacrifice is acceptable to God. However strong our understanding of the unique sacrifice of Christ, we need to be aware of this.

The more we are sure that we have the right sacrifice, the more we need to heed Jesus' parable of the lost son (Lk 15:11– 32).

Read this—

● as a comment on the Cain and Abel story;
● as an account of God's love for Muslim people;
● as a question about how the elder brother will respond.

Activity 1:2

In the light of what Ida Glaser has shown in this section, read John 4:4–26 again and jot down the points you think might help you in meeting Muslims.

There are some suggestions in the notes on activities at the end of the chapter.

3

Attitudes to other faiths

Important as it is to have a good Biblical understanding, it is equally important to have the right attitudes. We need to

*make a distinction between Islam the religion, and Muslims the
people—as, indeed, we need to distinguish between Christianity and
Christians. As the themes of this book develop, the distinctions
will become clearer.*

*Vivienne Stacey has written this section which enlarges on
some of the points already covered, as well as introducing new
ones.*

Some Afghan friends report that woven into a carpet in
the United Nations building in New York are words from the
famous Persian poet Saadi, who was one of the poets of the
lovely city of Shiraz. The English translation of the Persian
verse is:

> All men are members of the same body,
> Created from one essence. If fate brings suffering to one member
> The others cannot stay at rest.
> You who remain indifferent to the burden of pain of others
> Do not deserve to be called human . . .

God has created of one blood all nations of the earth (cf Acts
17:26). We are all created in the image of God. The Lord Jesus
Christ became man. These facts remind us of our common
humanity. We approach men and women of other faiths not so
much as Hindus, Muslims, Buddhists, Jains, Sikhs, Parsees,
Jews and Communists, but as fellow human beings. We are not
to be so engrossed with their religious systems that we forget
that they, like us, are human and deserve the respect that must
surely be given to those who are created in God's image and
beloved by God himself. Our recognition of the love and
purposes of God for mankind will shape our attitudes to those
who have not yet come to see the glory of God in the face of
our Lord Jesus Christ. When we become too absorbed by
religious systems we begin to see our own faith as a system,
rather than in terms of relationships. In seeking to share the
gospel in appropriate ways, Christians necessarily try to understand the worldviews and belief systems of people of other
faiths. In our effort to understand, several things will shape our
attitudes.

1. The sovereignty of God and our humility. Sometimes we forget that God is Lord over all. A heathen king like Nebuchadnezzar is described by the prophet Jeremiah as God's servant (Jer 43:10). It follows that God is master not only of Nebuchadnezzar, but also of his gods. Cyrus, King of Persia, is called by the prophet Isaiah God's shepherd and God's anointed (Is 44:28 and 45:1). God is lord of these rulers and of the systems, both religious and political, that they represent. If we share the view of the prophets we will not regard as totally evil and irredeemable all that is involved in other worldviews and faiths. God can and does use them for his own purposes. In our arrogance we sometimes see things as black or white, forgetting that God is master of all.

2. The work of the Holy Spirit and our faith. Do we lack faith in the power of God the Holy Spirit to convince people of sin and to bring them to himself? Many have laboured in unresponsive and difficult fields and have lost confidence in the power of the Spirit of God. Preaching correct doctrine is not enough. He who sows must sow in faith that a harvest will come. What then of those devout neighbours around us who pray so regularly to a God whom they do not know through Jesus Christ? Cornelius is a Biblical character who both encourages and warns us. He is very like a sincere Muslim, 'a devout man who feared God with all his household, gave alms liberally to the people, and prayed constantly to God'. The angel of God told him that his prayers and his alms had ascended as a memorial before God. God answered the prayers of this man. He and his household came to faith in Christ and were baptised (Acts 10:2,4,44,48). In the light of Scripture, should we not believe that when a person is devoutly seeking God he will find him? I have a Muslim friend whom I have known for over 30 years. She follows her faith as keenly as I do mine. I do not know her heart, but I believe that if she is truly seeking God then Jesus, who alone cleanses the heart and satisfies its hunger, will find her and bring her home.

3. The uniqueness of the Lord Jesus Christ and our assurance. Muslims generally regard a declaration of assurance of the forgiveness of sins as presumption. They hope and work for acceptance with God, but cannot ever be sure of it. This is partly because they have not understood that it is God's intention in redeeming man to forgive his sins and to give him the assurance of forgiveness. They have not understood the uniqueness and authority of the Christ who says, 'My son, your sins are forgiven' (Mk 2:5, RSV). They have also not understood the function of law in Christ's scheme of things. 'The law of Moses was in fact given to a redeemed people as a way of life not to an unredeemed people as a means of redemption' (Anderson, 1983, p. 21).

To the Muslim, God reveals his will in a book—the Qur'an. The Christian claims that God reveals himself in a Person, and therefore holds to the unique revelation of God in the unique person of his Son, the Lord Jesus Christ, the eternal Word. As Sir M. Monier-Williams said in 1887 at a Church Missionary Society meeting, speaking of the Bible: 'First, where else do we read of a sinless Man who was "made sin"? Secondly, where else do we read of a dead and buried Man who is "Life"?' Many Hindus seek the one God through the many or through philosophy. Among Hindus we may feel like Paul at Athens: 'I perceive that in every way you are very religious. For as I passed along, and observed the objects of your worship, I found also an altar with this inscription, "To an unknown god." What therefore you worship as unknown, this I proclaim to you' (Acts 17:22–23, RSV). Paul proclaimed the risen Christ—the unique Christ—in whom he had assurance of forgiveness of sins and of the gift of eternal life.

4. The power of the word of God and our use of it. If we believe in the unique Lord Jesus Christ as revealed in the Bible, we will present him through the words of the inspired writings even though we may adapt our method of presentation so that our hearers appreciate and understand the message. There is a tendency today to underestimate the power of Scripture. We do not memorise it as we ought. We do not quote it as we might. We sometimes think that if we have given some personal testimony to Jesus our Saviour, we have preached the gospel. However, we may have omitted the objective testimony of Scripture. We should seek to sit down with our Hindu or Buddhist or Muslim friend and study Scripture.

5. *The need of our fellow humans and our compassion.* What should motivate us as we live among people of other faiths? Should not the love of Christ constrain us, as it did Paul? What of hell and damnation? Knowing that our God is a consuming fire (Heb 12:29) we should plead with people to be reconciled to God and to flee from the wrath to come. When I have wept for the salvation of others, I have seen the Lord work and bring some to himself. We must seek this balance between love and compassion, and the knowledge of judgement. How often Jesus was moved with compassion! How little I am moved with compassion, or moved to tears for the lost!

Or *are* they lost? Is there any hope of salvation for a godly person of any religion who does not know or follow the Lord Jesus Christ?

Paul in his letter to the Romans shows that God will judge men and women by what they have known of the truth and how they have responded to it (Rom 1:20–21). Certainly there is a mystery here. There is no salvation except by virtue of what Christ has wrought. Like Abraham we can bring our questions to God and still declare in faith: 'Shall not the judge of all the earth do right?' (Gen 18:25, rsv).

Activity 1:3

The apostle Paul has a great deal to teach us through his evangelistic methods. Read Acts 17:1–9 and 16:34. It is interesting to compare these two passages. In the first Paul is speaking to a Jewish audience, in the second to those who have a Greek religious background. In Athens he uses the altar to the 'unknown God' as a starting point. What do you think might be a useful starting point in sharing with Muslims?

4

Here are four principles to keep before us as we move on into the rest of the book:

- Our attitudes and relationships must be firmly based on Biblical truth.
- Any activity of reaching out to others should be expected to deepen our own spiritual understanding.
- We must listen to and learn from those of other faiths and establish a meaningful relationship with them, reading their writings and listening to what they have to say.
- We relate to a person, not a religion. Evangelism should be part of personal communication, interest, friendship, caring and understanding.

A concluding thought

It is important to distinguish between recognising that we as Christians have something to learn from people of other faiths, and thinking that God's revelation and salvation itself needs to be corrected or supplemented by other faiths. We should be humble enough to be challenged in many ways by other religions, but at the same time convinced and confident in the adequacy and finality of the biblical witness to God and Christ (Goldsmith & Wright, Anglican Evangelical Assembly paper, 1992).

Notes

Look back to the three suggested goals in the study guide at the beginning of the chapter. How far do you think you have gone towards achieving them? We hope you feel you have a foundation on which to study another religion.

The Biblical passage in Activity 1:2 was chosen because it was an occasion when Jesus, himself, was talking to someone of another faith. The Samaritans had, and still have, a mixed form of worship, abhorrent to Orthodox Jews. You probably thought of the following three basic points, and related them to meeting those of other faiths:

1 Jesus makes it quite clear that it is the water he gives which permanently quenches thirst, and which 'will become [for the person who drinks it] a spring of water welling up to eternal life' (v. 14).

2 Although the water is available for everyone, it is only those who actually drink it who will benefit from it (v. 14).

3 There is a right way and a wrong way to worship God. The Jews have knowledge which is linked to salvation. The time has now come when 'true worshippers' will worship 'in spirit and in truth' (v. 23).

It is interesting to note, too, that Jesus uses different levels of conversation in this dialogue. He moves from the physical: 'Will you give me a drink?' (v. 7), through the moral: 'Go, call your husband and come back' (v. 16), to the spiritual: 'God is spirit, and his worshippers must worship in spirit and in truth' (v. 24). It may be helpful to be aware of these different levels of dialogue in your own discussions.

Books referred to in the chapter

Ali, Abdullah Yusuf, *The Holy Qur'an: Test, Translation and Commentary* (Islamic Foundation: Leicester, 1975).

Anderson, Norman, *God's Law and God's Love: An Essay in Comparative Religion* (Collins: Glasgow, 1981).

Anglican Inter-Faith Consultative Group of the Board of Mission and Unity, *Towards a Theology for Inter-Faith Dialogue* (Church Information Office: London, 1984).

Dowsett, Dick, *God, That's Not Fair!* (OMF/STL: Sevenoaks/Bromley, 1982).

Wright, Christopher, *What's So Unique About Jesus?* (Monarch: Eastbourne, 1990).

For further reading

Wright, Christopher, *What's So Unique About Jesus?* (Monarch: Eastbourne, 1990). Wright sets out to answer this question clearly and concisely. He also explains current social and theological thinking.

Goldsmith, Martin, *What About Other Faiths?* (Hodder & Stoughton: London, 1989). A more detailed treatment of the subject. It includes brief explanations of other religious concepts of God, revelation and salvation. There are chapters on the Bible and other faiths, and questions such as 'Are other faiths demonic?' are discussed.

Committee for Relations with People of Other Faiths, *In Good Faith: the Four Principles of Inter-Faith Dialogue* (CCBI: London, 1992).

2

Making Muslim Friends

Study guide

*Having thought about Christian attitudes to those of other faiths
in Chapter 1, we turn now to the practical preparation needed
for making Muslim friends. Another distinction is helpful at this
point: the difference between Islam the religion and Muslims, the
followers of Islam. In this chapter we concentrate on the people.
It is important even at this early point in the book to begin to
meet Muslims and relate to them.*

When you have completed the chapter we hope you will:

1 *Have met some Muslims and have formed some understanding
   of the things in life which are important to them;*
2 *Have become aware of some of the strengths and weaknesses
   both in your own outlook and in that of the Muslims you have
   met; and*
3 *Have started to think about how you might begin to share your
   faith with your Muslim friends.*

1

Making Muslim friends

The prayer meeting had finished and people were chatting
together. Someone turned to Jamila and said, 'How did
you become a Christian?' Without a moment's hesitation she
answered, 'It was because of Mr and Mrs Smith. They really

loved me. They invited me into their home and treated me like one of their daughters.'

Time and time again this is the testimony: 'They really loved me.' This is not only true of Muslims, of course. How did you and I take that first step towards belief? Both experience and statistics tell us that many, many of us come to know Christ through the witness of our friends. Friendship is, however, specially important for those who come to believe in Jesus as Lord and Saviour from a Muslim background. This is an enormous step for them to take and it is almost always met with severe opposition, with the probable consequence that they are cut off from family and friends, and even in some cases have to face death.

Muslims in all walks of life need the support which friendship gives. Roger Malstead tells of a Turkish man with whom he was speaking, who had come to truly know Christ from a Muslim background. He is a graduate of a university. He asked him what it was that influenced him. He told him simply that it was someone in Turkey who had shown love to him; not a 'professional' missionary, but someone who simply showed his Turkish friend the love of Christ.

Professor J. N. D. Anderson once said, 'You don't need to know a lot about Islam to be able to talk to Muslims. The more you know the better, but you don't need to know a lot to tell them that Jesus loves them.' We must grasp the fact that the need today is for Christian people who will show genuine love, concern and respect for Muslim people, young, old, men or women, educated or not, whether they are in Islamic countries or ethnic minority groups.

What should our attitude be? We must respect Muslims as fellow human beings. We need to remember the principle stated in Chapter 1, 'We relate to people, not to a religion.' We can all learn from one another. Getting to know people of another culture is an exciting and mind-stretching activity. It makes us question our own attitudes and—yes—our prejudices as well. As Islamic religion and culture are so bound up together, we should not try to separate them. We are going to learn much more about both in the chapters which lie ahead.

But at this point we should be observing and questioning on a personal level, sharing our own customs and beliefs as occasions arise without any sense of superiority; being ready to give help and to receive it, as it is needed.

Finding Muslim friends

Now is the time to start looking for friends who are Muslims. You may be living in a Muslim country, in which case almost all the people you meet will be Muslims. If however you live in your own country, you will need to look more carefully. There may be Muslims working with you, or students in college with you or your children. There may be a Muslim family living near you, even next door. Perhaps you meet Muslims when you buy your newspaper, or go to your local supermarket.

What should you do when you meet them? Perhaps the first thing to remember is that life is more leisurely in countries where most Muslims originate, and it will be polite just to 'pass the time of day' before making your purchase or getting down to what you really want to say. One way to start a conversation is to ask about the country from where they, or their families originate. It is genuinely interesting to find out about different ways of life. Don't forget to share your experiences as well! Sometimes as the friendship develops and you both share more deeply, you will be surprised at how much you have in common.

In many Muslim areas there are coffee-houses or tea-houses where Muslim men come together to sit and talk. They will most probably be speaking their own language, but you will no doubt be able to meet them and begin to develop acquaintances. It might even be a good way for you to begin to learn their language. Your efforts may sometimes cause amusement, but will be appreciated as a sign of respect for their culture. (This may be a good place to stress the importance of learning the language of those with whom we wish to relate. It is a formidable task, but not an impossible one; there are now new and challenging methods of learning other languages. Especially helpful, not least because it is so closely linked with the significance of culture, is the LAMP method developed by the Brewsters.)

For women, the most likely place of contact is the home, although activities such as learning English or another foreign language from native speakers can meet a real need and can lead to lasting friendships. Just how much of value can come from this activity is seen in Marion Molteno's book, *A language in common.*

One of the important aspects of meeting Muslims is to find out what they think of us. Some of their off-the-cuff remarks can be very revealing. Here is a comment from a lady during Ida Glaser's first visit to her home:

> There are some differences between your religion and ours. For example, we don't believe in unmarried mothers and that sort of thing.

Activity 2:1

What would you say in answer to the above comment?

It is important to remember that both friendship and voluntary help are valuable in themselves, not just as evangelistic tools. We must also be aware of two possible dangers in looking for Muslim friends:

1. It would be easy while doing this course to use your friend merely as a kind of 'guinea pig' to help you in your study of Islam. This must be a genuine friendship; your friend will not be happy if he feels he is essentially a target of evangelism. It may be that you will not find deep friendship developing with the first Muslim you meet. We do not automatically 'click' with a person. If this is so, look for someone else. However, give time for a friendship to develop first; there are enormous barriers of language and culture to overcome.

2. Your friend may not know very much about his or her religion. Did you know much about the Christian religion before you found faith in Christ and the guidance of the Holy Spirit? If you are an average Christian, you will agree that it is still quite difficult to explain our beliefs. It may be that your friend knows a lot and sincerely practises his faith, but he or she is not able to express himself easily in a second language. He may well be grateful for help with this, particularly if you are interested in learning some of his language at the same time.

2

Muslim family life

In *Worlds of Faith*, John Bowker has compiled statements by adherents of six main religions about their faith. Here is what a Muslim, Mohammad Hassan, says about family life:

> The family is one of the stones of the whole building—indeed it's the whole building: without these stones of family life, you can't build the house—the whole society. (Bowker, 1983, p. 184)

Most Muslims do not come from Western, industrialised societies, so they do not have a Western cultural background. Many of the differences that we note are due to this, rather than to specifically Muslim differences. At the same time, it is important to realise at this point that Islam is a complete way of life, not simply a religion. Cultural differences are of religious significance in Islam.

Nuclear and extended families

Although families may have been split up due to migration of some members, the extended family is the norm in Islam. As sons marry they bring their wives into their parents' home, where their children are born and grow up. Daughters, on the other hand, marry into another extended family and only return to their parents for occasional visits. The extended family is the unit. All important decisions are made by the head of the family, in consultation with other members. Muslims living in other countries may live as nuclear families, parents and their adult children living separately, but there is still a strong bond between those who have migrated and members of the extended family remaining in the country of origin. Children who have professional careers, even responsible positions in society, may refer back to their father, or elder brother before making decisions which affect the family. Sometimes, one after another, a whole extended family may have uprooted itself and may now be settled in another country.

Hospitality

This is very important, and is a sign that a friendly relationship is accepted. It will be more formal than we are used to and the food will be elaborately prepared. Some women members of the family will remain in the kitchen, only appearing to serve the meal, eating later themselves. Never arrive too early—ten or fifteen minutes later than the stated time will be best. It is quite usual to be left alone in the front room after arriving. The meal is the highlight of the entertainment. It may be served quite late and last a long time; it is customary to leave after it is finished. It is also polite to ask if you may leave. It will also be appreciated if you show your appreciation of the food and the hospitality in general; this is not difficult, it is usually delicious! Customs vary, of course, and it is important to be alert and sensitive and to ask guidance from your hosts if in trouble.

Apart from formal invitations, as friendship develops it is quite in order to 'drop in' from time to time—perhaps to bring something with you, or return something that has been lent. You will almost always be invited to have a cup of tea or a snack; it is important to accept this and to stay for a relaxed chat, so don't go unless you have time to spare.

Of course you too will want to entertain your Muslim friends. Some care is needed over this, as they have very strict dietary rules. Most Muslims do not take alcohol in any form; if it is your custom to do so, it will be best to refrain and to remove all traces, such as bottles and cans, before they arrive. Muslims abhor any product from the pig. Don't forget that this includes lard—they may refuse cakes and fried food in case it has been used in the cooking, so you could reassure them that it has not been. Shellfish, too, are prohibited, so don't start with prawn cocktail. In fact, the best plan is to ask what food they like, and to arrange the menu with the wife. Sometimes people ask the wife to help prepare the food, at least on the first occasion. Always use your right hand for preparing, serving and eating food; it is the 'clean' hand.

Sometimes we will be invited to attend specific occasions, such as celebrating the birth of a boy, or one of their religious festivals. Especially with religious festivals, it is best to find out beforehand what one is expected to do rather than find oneself in embarrassing situations which would compromise one's own faith. If we are tactful, this may become an opportunity to explain something of our Christian beliefs. It is hardly surprising if our friends think that anything is acceptable for 'Christians'; after explanation, they will respect our hesitations.

One occasion when we can show our desire for friendship is when a death occurs in the family. Muslims like to bury their dead as soon as possible, but they have a lengthy mourning period. If we visit before the funeral has taken place, we may be shown the body. It is the custom of those who are bereaved to look as dishevelled as possible and there may be some noisy mourning going on. On arriving to offer condolences we do not need to say anything. One can hold a hand if it is offered, but just to sit quietly with the family will convey more than words.

Arranged marriages

Most of us in the West are horrified at the thought of parents choosing whom we should marry! This is, however, the normal procedure in some other cultures. It is not only accepted but expected, and on the whole it works well. In Muslim families the bride and groom may not have met before the marriage ceremony. Marriage, like the rest of living, is a family matter, and great efforts are made by the family to find the right partners for their children. The contract is between the families, not between the individuals.

Here are some comments from Muslims on the subject of marriage. The first is from Mrs Khan, a Muslim wife:

> In a country like England, where people are free to marry after a long courtship, they are really very unsuccessful—eight or five or six out of ten marriages are ended in divorce. But in our country, our marriages, Muslim marriages, are usually successful. It's really bad if we have divorce; we don't have divorce. (Bowker, p. 192)

Hajji Cassim Mohammad, who comes from Trinidad, comments:

> Asian girls and Muslim girls, especially among the Muslim community, are not allowed to mix freely with the boys. So what chances have the boys to get to meet them, if you left it only on a meeting together to choose a husband, when they don't meet? Now parents obviously would want the best for their children. There are very, very few who will just want to get rid of their children, get rid of the daughters and marry them to anyone. But the majority of families I know would always like the best for their children. A father would like the best husband for his daughter and the same thing for his son. (pp. 192–193)

A young Muslim put it this way:

> Of course the families will be involved: I'll bring the girl and show her to the parents. They've got a lot more wisdom than me. If they say no they can give their reasons and I'm sure they will be right. (p. 199)

It is not always quite so easy, as the number of court cases where girls are claiming they were forced into marriage shows. However, it is still the accepted pattern for the majority of Muslim young people.

Activity 2:2

What Do I Say to my Muslim Friends? by Margaret Burness is a series of conversations between Beth, a Western Christian and her Asian Muslim next-door neighbour Razia. In one conversation, they are discussing an arranged marriage which has recently taken place. Beth says,

(Continued over)

(Continued)

'The parents found the boy? How strange! What about the bride? Is *she* happy?'

Razia replies,

'Of course she is happy with the man her parents chose, just as her mother was, and I was, and *our* daughter will be when the time comes. A girl doesn't know enough to be able to choose—she might not choose the right family, or the right man. We think parents know best. Won't you and your husband choose the man for Mary?

What is Beth to say? (p. 36)

The place of women

Speaking on the subject of divorce, the Qur'an says,

> And women shall have rights
> Similar to the rights
> Against them, according
> To what is equitable;
> But men have a degree
> (of advantage) over them.
> And Allah is Exalted in Power, Wise. (Sura 2:228)

Many see Islam as giving an inferior status to women. Muslims point out that it is a difference of role rather than status. Sura 2:282 of the Qur'an says,

> And get two witnesses,
> Out of your men,
> And if there are not two men
> Then a man and two women,
> Such as ye choose,
> For witnesses,
> So that if one of them errs,
> The other can remind her. (Sura 2:282)

The financial dealings being discussed in this sura were not considered to be the sphere of women. This may have been why two were required in place of one man! The Muslim writer Ghulam Sarwar, in *Islam: Beliefs and Teachings*, says this:

Islam is a religion of common sense and is in line with human nature. It recognises the realities of life. This does not mean it has recognised equality of man and woman in every respect. Rather, it has defined their duties in keeping with their different biological make-up (2:228). Allah has not made man and woman identical, so it would be against nature to have total equality between a man and a woman. (Sarwar, 1984, pp. 167–168)

It is very important that Christian men and women understand the Muslim concept of the man as the head of the household and decision-maker, and the woman as the homemaker, the bearer and nurturer of children. This is particularly important when living and working in a Muslim country when we are called upon not only to understand but also to practise these roles.

Undoubtedly the average woman in Islam leads a very restricted life compared to her Western counterpart. This does not necessarily mean that Muslim women resent this; for many, the restrictions are looked upon as protection, rather than under-privilege. Christian women need to remember that Muslim women have attitudes and skills they can share with us.

The centre and focus of Asian life is the family, and it is the women who hold the family together and who teach the next generation to do the same. Though the male dominance in Asian society and the decision-making role of the male head of the family suggest that the women are of no importance, such is not the case. In fact they have a significant but different role—looking after the family life—even when, as in the case of some of my friends, they have long hours and demanding work in the world outside their family. With the concern about the break-up of family life in this country, Asian women may well have a contribution to make in arresting this trend of disintegration as they continue to make their role in the family a priority. (Cooper, in *Women to Women*, 1988, p. 160–161)

This is borne out by Mrs Qureshi:

To me my family is my priority, I go to work, I earn my living to be a support to my husband, to be a support to my children; but I don't want to ignore my family for the sake of my job. My priority is my children—and my home. (Bowker, 1983, p. 218)

The place of women in Islam is controlled by the importance of modesty and family honour. *Purdah*, the Persian
word for a curtain or veil, is the practice of women covering
their bodies when in the presence of men, other than near
relatives.

A family's decision as to whether its girls keep *purdah* does
not depend so much on whether they are educated as on
whether they hold traditional beliefs. In Muslim countries,
many highly educated women have professional careers while
remaining in *purdah*. In the West, *purdah* may be practised not
by women wearing veils, but by their never going out in public,
which is more restricting for them.

Marion Molteno describes how a friend of hers felt about
having to wear a *burqa* (a long garment covering the whole
body, with only a grid through which to see):

> A burqa—you know, a burqa is something a person *outside* sees.
> You are inside it, you don't see it or think it strange. It's there to
> stop others from seeing you, not you from watching them. You see
> everything. Inside it you feel free, all alone with yourself; you don't
> have any impertinent eyes coming in when you want to be left alone
> . . . (Molteno, 1987, p. 90)

Great sensitivity is necessary in relating to Muslims of the
opposite sex. When we look for Muslim friends they must be
of our own sex. Married couples may visit married couples, but
even then the sexes may become segregated, the wife going to
be with the other women and the husband staying with the men
of the household. Men must be particularly careful not to shake
hands with women or girls, nor should they sit next to them
on sofas or settees. Christian women too must be careful, in a
different way, remembering that Muslim men have had little
experience in coping with the freer relationship between the
sexes in Western culture; it is important that Western women
should do nothing that might be thought to be an encourage-
ment, such as looking a Muslim man full in the face. It
is difficult to remember not to do this, but it may prevent
embarrassing situations from happening!

Children

Large families are usual and children are welcomed and enjoyed. Childlessness is a shame and a tragedy. The gender of children is of considerable cultural significance. Boys will grow up to carry on the family and to work to support their parents in old age. They are greatly preferred to girls, who will leave the family on marriage and for whom expensive marriage arrangements will have to be made. From early childhood the children are taught their differing roles. Boys are encouraged to make decisions and to take the initiative, girls to stay in the background, looking after the younger children and helping with work in the home.

Allied to care of children is the question of education. In countries where Muslims are in the minority, most parents would like to have their children educated in separate Muslim schools, because of the difference in Muslim and Western ways of life. The freedom of women in the West is a traumatic issue for Muslims, and has led them to call for single-sex Islamic schools for their girls.

On the subject of separate schools, Mohammad Hassan, the caretaker of a mosque, thought, 'It's a very good idea; it should be done that way. But if you can't, you don't have to.' He also thought, 'There's more danger for boys than girls, in this society; how to be educated, how to bring them up.' He was thinking of gangs and riots which teach them how to fight against authority (Bowker, p. 234).

Hajji Cassim would certainly like separate schools. As he explained,

> The outlook on life is completely different from a Muslim parent's point of view, and a Western parent's point of view. We know, once upon a time, a Christian thought differently, but today he thinks differently again. Parents don't really like their daughters to practise permissiveness, but they do, they are forced into it, and they can't do otherwise. (p. 234)

A Shiite Muslim mother made this plea,

> Whatever religion they are, they should be taught whatever religion they are in. I don't mind whether it's separate schools or the same, but if they are Muslim they should be able to learn what Islam is. (p. 234)

Another scene in Margaret Burness' book *What do I Say to my Muslim Friends?* shows Beth's and Razia's daughters walking home from school together. They are joined by two of the boys in their class. One of the boys says something which makes Razia's daughter, Fatima, laugh; he also tries to put his hand on her arm, teasing her. Although Fatima quickly draws her arm away, this is totally unacceptable behaviour. Fatima's brother, who has seen the incident, dashes across the road, removes his sister and reports her to their father. As a result, their father makes arrangements to take Fatima away from the school.

In conversation afterwards, Beth cannot understand why Razia is so upset. It does not seem to her that Fatima has done anything wrong.

Razia replies that she has done something very wrong. 'She is beginning to forget what our religion teaches about modesty; and all this happened in the open street—it damaged the honour of our family before other Muslims.'

When Beth talks about the importance of education, Razia replies, 'But do Christians think education is more important than modesty and family honour?' (p. 40).

Activity 2:3

Well, what *do* Christians think? You might like to discuss the important question of children's education with your Muslim friends, making sure that you really find out what they think as well as telling them your views.

3

Some guidelines in talking with Muslims

Although looking to make friends with Muslims must be genuine and not just an evangelistic technique, you will probably find that conversations on religion start much more naturally than they do with Western friends. We end this chapter with some guidelines on how we, as Christians, may relate to our Muslim friends on a spiritual level. The first thing to say is that they will not distinguish between the spiritual and the secular in the same way that we do. Islamic culture and religion are one and the same thing.

We must always speak naturally and sincerely from the heart. Here is a quote from Martin Goldsmith's book, *Islam and Christian witness*:

> Since the realities and complexities of actual encounter with living Muslims do not allow for any neat pre-packaged evangelism, few of us will be in a position to engage in a witness closely related to Muslim backgrounds. But all of us can share what Jesus Christ means to us with joy and enthusiasm . . . While we may sometimes confess that we do not know all the theological answers or understand the deep mysteries of the Christian faith, our joyful testimony to what God has done for us in Christ and by his Spirit will remain real and attractive (p. 114).

The following are some points we should keep in mind as we go out to make friends with Muslims and to share the gospel with them.

1. Always show respect for your Bible, never placing it on the floor, nor in any other way showing disrespect. In fact, it might be good to have one New Testament or Bible which you have not marked, to take along with you as you speak to Muslims. They would never write in the Qur'an, and therefore, to show respect for God's word, it might be best not to take one with any markings in it. However, if they see your Bible in which you have marked, you can share with them that although we respect God's word, we really do want to honour him by studying it; and to mark it helps us to keep in mind some of God's teaching. Also, we can share with them that we believe the real Word of God is manifested in the Lord Jesus Christ.

2. Learn to use phrases such as 'Jesus the Messiah' rather than 'Jesus the Son of God', as this phrase is highly emotive and miscommunicates to Muslims. It is true that we believe Jesus is the Son of God, but we do not believe in any way that that implies any kind of physical relationship. So we do not believe, as some Muslims mistakenly think we do, that God had relations with Mary and their son is Jesus. We are as horrified as any Muslim at this blasphemous suggestion. We believe that the term 'Son of God' refers to a very special relationship. Jesus is called '*al Masih*' (the Messiah) eleven times in the Qur'an and no-one else, not even the Prophet Muhammad, is addressed in this way. It is a pity, perhaps, that Christians so frequently use the Greek word 'Christ', especially when talking to Muslims, 'Jesus Messiah' sounds so much nearer to 'Masih'. Other phrases describing Jesus that would be familiar and are acceptable to Muslims are, 'the Breath of God', 'the Spirit of God', or the 'Word of God'. Others that may be used in Muslim countries are, 'the Saviour, Jesus', or 'the Lamb of God'.

3. As mentioned earlier, be completely natural and genuine in the sharing of your faith as well as in questioning Muslims about their own beliefs and religious practices. Somehow Easterners have very keen insight into people who are not being honest and open and real with them.

4. Do not let yourself be drawn into heated arguments. There is a place, of course, for open and frank discussion, about our similarities and differences; but as the Bible says, 'The Lord's servant must not quarrel' (2 Tim 2:24). That is, we do not want to win an argument which might alienate our friends. If we see clearly that there are things with which we disagree, it is best to say something like, 'It's obvious that we don't agree on this point, so let's not argue over God or his truths, but let's learn to respect each other.' In this way, you are showing Muslims that you do respect them as people, as individuals, but you do not necessarily agree with their doctrines or teachings.

Remember not to speak ill of, or to degrade Muhammad or the Qur'an. I am sure you realise that this is not the way to win friends and witness to people. In the Gospels, following an incident where Jesus was slighted, the disciples asked if they could call down fire upon that town. Jesus rebuked them sternly for their judgemental and hostile attitudes (Lk 9:51–56). We must resist the tendency towards petty hostility and anger within us, that wants to condemn others for their religion. May we be the servants of Jesus, filled with graciousness and a winning and loving attitude towards those to whom we wish to witness. We never want, however, to say anything that will compromise the truth.

5. *Belief that the Old and New Testaments have been changed often arises in discussion.* There are many books which demonstrate that there is absolutely no proof that any change has been made in the Biblical texts, other than a few insignificant errors due to copying. In no way do these small discrepancies influence any major, or minor, doctrine.

One way in which some people handle this objection is to ask Muslim friends, 'Do you think the all-powerful God would ever allow little human beings to change his word? Even the Qur'an itself says, 'There is none that can alter the Words (and Decrees) of Allah' (6:34). So we as Christians simply believe that since God is all-powerful, he would not allow it to be changed by puny people.'

One book which discusses the accusation that the Bible has been changed in some detail is *In the Family of Abraham*. It also gives this piece of advice:

> Although we must understand the arguments used in Islamic teaching and be able to put forward points of our own to counter these arguments, it will be much more important to encourage Muslims to see for themselves what the Bible does say, and allow the Holy Spirit to reveal its truth and its authenticity. Only he can clear away unfounded prejudice and can convince anyone that the Bible is the inspired Word of God. (Cooper, 1989, p. 25)

6. *Another objection that may arise is that we are thought to believe in three Gods.* Of course, it is true that ultimately the doctrine of the Trinity is something that is very mysterious. I like to ask Muslims if they understand all about God themselves. It seems to me that if we understand every single thing about God, he must be very small. However, someone so great must be incomprehensible to our finite minds. We *can* understand all that he has revealed to us; that is why it is necessary to study the Bible, which is God's self-revelation. But some things we will not understand in this life.

7. Martin Goldsmith, in his book *Islam and Christian Witness* writes:

> In many cultures today we need to move away from teaching only through abstract concepts and begin to use vivid stories as a didactic means. The story should not be just an illustration which is subordinate to the actual point. The story is in itself the teaching. (Goldsmith, 1982, pp. 130–131)

Mr Goldsmith has many good suggestions on how to witness. He mentions that just as Jesus told stories or taught in parables, this may be a very useful way to present the gospel to Muslims. They love stories, as do many other people. Especially when working in villages and with children, it might be helpful to learn how to tell a good story. He also reminds us to be pictorial in our witness to Muslims—to use illustrations and draw pictures with our words just as Jesus did. We should avoid abstract reasoning and be prepared not to think logically, but to let ideas take off from one idea to another. Old Testament stories are useful; for example, the story of Abraham ready to sacrifice his son (but don't say 'Isaac' as Muslims believe the story was about Ishmael). Imagine what this sacrifice would mean to a father, especially after having waited so long for a son and in view of God's promises about him. We may then have opportunity to talk about God's own, even greater sacrifice.

8. *Jesus often asked questions.* Many times a well-placed question can stimulate people to think and can clarify arguments, helping them to draw inferences that will lead them to a truth of Scripture; perhaps ultimately to the Lord Jesus himself.

9. *In the book of Acts we see that the disciples took every opportunity to proclaim the resurrection of Jesus from the dead.* We should continue to proclaim his death and resurrection with boldness. I believe we should, as Peter says, 'Always be prepared to give an answer to everyone who asks you to give the reason for the hope that you have' (1 Pet 3:15). The hope that we have is in Jesus, who is alive.

10. *One of the most important things to remember as we witness is the need to be constantly in prayer.* Many, many

people who have witnessed to Muslims testify to the fact that as they prayed for their Muslim friends, God gave them specific answers to questions, or specific things they could do for their friends. So may we be, as Jesus and Paul were, constant in prayer, always remembering to pray for our Muslim friends.

A concluding thought

Reflections at a Muslim grave:

> Our dogmatic proclamation, our Western methodology, and our development projects must be permeated with the incarnate Christ. Let us draw near to share their grief and speak to them. We are not Christians preaching to Muslims; we are not Westerners trying to communicate with Easterners; we are not the developed seeking to lift the undeveloped. We are fallen men. We share their grief so they will share the joy of his presence. (Dard, 1984)

Notes

Do you feel you have made a start in relating to Muslims? Most people are dissatisfied with their efforts, especially at first. A more experienced friend with whom you can discuss your progress, or lack of it, will be invaluable.

How did you answer the comment in Activity 2:1? It is not easy to convince Muslim friends that all Westerners are not committed Christians and do not have Christian standards of behaviour. We must be positive in our witness, using Jesus' teaching and example, and his help in our efforts to follow him.

In the example from Margaret Burness' book used in Activity 2:2, the author goes on to remind her readers that choosing one's own partner is a comparatively recent practice in Western countries; for hundreds of years it was a family matter, as it is for Asians now. She also points out that this may be an opportunity to talk about Christian marriage and Christian attitudes towards divorce. In the same way, the discussion on education suggested in Activity 2:3 might lead on to thinking about how God is at work in our lives if we are committed to him, individually as well as in the family.

Mrs Khan's comment, '. . . we don't have divorce' (p. 43), is not legally correct. In Islamic countries divorce laws are framed by Islamic law. There may however be economic constraints; divorce may be too expensive to be considered. It is easier for men than women to initiate divorce proceedings.

Books referred to in the chapter

Bowker, John, *Worlds of Faith* (BBC Ariel: London, 1983). Extract used by permission of BBC Enterprises Limited.

Brewster, E. Thomas and Elizabeth S., *Language Acquisition Made Practical* (Lingua House: Toronto, 1976).

Burness, Margaret, *What Do I Say to my Muslim Friends?* (Church Missionary Society: London, 1989).

Cooper, Anne, Chapter 14 in: Keay, Kathy (ed.), *Women to Women* (MARC: Eastbourne, 1988).

Cooper, Anne (comp), *In the Family of Abraham* (People International: Tunbridge Wells, 1989).

Dard, H. M., 'Reflections at a Muslim Grave', *Evangelical Missions Quarterly*, April 1984.

Goldsmith, Martin, *Islam and Christian Witness* (Hodder & Stoughton/ STL: London/Bromley, 1982).

Molteno, Marion, *A Language in Common* (The Women's Press: London, 1987).

Sarwar, Ghulam, *Islam: Beliefs and Teachings* (Muslim Educational Trust: London, 3rd edn 1984).

For further reading

Burness, Margaret, *What Do I Say to my Muslim Friends?* (Church Missionary Society: London, 1989). These conversations are geared to women, though the customs and attitudes described relate to Muslims as a whole. Men may also find useful the suggestions on how a Christian perspective can be introduced.

Bowker, John, *Worlds of Faith* (BBC Ariel: London, 1983). This book is based on a BBC Radio 4 programme in which ordinary people were asked to explain their religion and what it meant to them in their everyday lives.

Molteno, Marion, *A Language in Common* (The Women's Press: London, 1987). Another book about women. Stories based on the years the author spent as an adult education worker, vividly and sympathetically told.

PART II
Islamic Beliefs and Practices

3

God: Muslim and Christian Conceptions

Study guide

We move on now to begin our study of Islam. The chapters 3–6 will give us an outline of the beliefs and practices of Islam. As it is good that readers understand the viewpoints of followers of the religion, references from the Qur'an (in the translation by Yusuf Ali) and from Muslim writers will be used and also the appropriate Biblical references.

In this chapter we begin to introduce a number of Arabic words. The language of Islam is Arabic, and it is important to understand these words. You may find it helpful to begin keeping a list of these special terms. There is a glossary at the end of the course. In this book we shall use the words 'God' (with a capital G) and Allah as synonymous. Allah is the Arabic word for God. Prior to Islam, some people in Mecca knew this word and worshipped Allah. Arabic-speaking Christians have no other word for God but Allah. This is not to deny that we need to explain the meaning of words we use. Words can have several meanings, and can be used differently in various contexts, as well as having various conceptional differences in different religions.

When you have completed this chapter we hope you will:

1 be able to understand the nature of God in Islam and compare it to the view of God in Scripture; and

2 begin to grapple with some Christian doctrinal issues such as Monotheism, Incarnation and the Trinity.

(Islam certainly challenges us as Christians to know what we believe, and to know how to give answers. 'Always be prepared to give an answer to everyone who asks you to give the reason for the hope that you have' (1 Pet 3:15).)

1

Introduction

When we desire to know about a particular faith, we must have the courage to collect information with a view to examining it critically for authenticity and correctness. For a deeper understanding and appreciation of that faith we need to try to find an 'inside' view of one who professes and practises that faith. Discussions with Muslim friends will therefore be valuable.

A Muslim's faith is firmly rooted in the belief that the source of Islam is God and that Muhammad is 'only' the last and final spokesman for this universal faith. Before going any further, we suggest you pause to consider what you already know about the origin and development of Islam. How would you answer the following questions?

    1 When did the religion of Islam arise?
    2 Where did it arise?
    3 Who founded the religion?
    4 How did Islam spread and develop?

As a Christian your answers may have been:
1 In the seventh century AD.
2 In what is today Saudi Arabia.
3 Muhammad.
4 By preaching

A Muslim would probably have answered:
1 It has always existed.
2 With God in heaven.
3 God.
4 By divine revelation and intervention.

No wonder Christians and Muslims have had a hard time communicating with each other!

Muslims hold that 'Islam' is not one religion among many, but *the* religion (better still, the 'Religion of Nature' or natural religion—in Arabic *din-al-fitrah*.) Islam is the religion of God. The Qur'an states: 'The Religion before God is Islam (submission to His Will)' (3:19).

2

What is the meaning of Islam?

The religion took the title Islam because God decreed it in the Qur'an. 'Lo the religion with God is AL ISLAM to His will and guidance' (3:19), and 'I have chosen for you as religion AL ISLAM' (5:3). *Islam* is an Arabic word and connotes submission, surrender and obedience. Other literal meanings from this root word of three letters (SLM)[1] are 'safe', 'secure' and 'peace'. Words formed from this word are used in greetings—'Peace be with you' (*salamalek*), and farewells 'Go in peace' (*bissalma, masalma*) which implies 'Have a safe journey'. Thus the word Islam is about a life of peace and a life preserved from harm through submission to the will of the Creator God, who is one, having no duality or trinity in his oneness; and a life lived in obedience to God's commands. The word MUSLIM (meaning the person who surrenders his life to the will of God) is also formed from the same root (SLM).

A Muslim is not following a religion but a complete way of life, with guidance provided by God which governs all aspects of individual and corporate living.

---

1. Arabic words are made up of three root letters. Each word can have various forms when an additional letter or vowel is added to the basic root. The basic root of ISLAM is the three letters S, L, M.
Thus some of the following forms are possible.

Verbs: *slm*,   1st form, 'safe and sound, unharmed'.
       tsslm,   2nd form, 'to keep from harm, to surrender'.
       salm,   3rd form, 'to keep peace'
       Islm,   4th form, 'to forsake, to surrender . . . to become a Muslim'

Noun   *salm* = peace   (*bis-salma* and *ma-salma*, 'with peace')
       islam = Islam the religion
       muslim = the person who surrenders

Under the heading, 'Islam—what does it mean?' Mawlana Mawdudi in *Towards Understanding Islam* writes:

> Ours is a law-governed universe and everything in it is following the course that has been ordained for it . . . As the whole of creation obeys the law of God, the whole universe, therefore, literally follows the religion of Islam—for Islam signifies nothing but obedience and submission to Allah, the Lord of the universe . . . Everything in the universe is 'Muslim' for it obeys God by submission to his laws. Even a man who refuses to believe in God, or offers his worship to someone other than Allah, has necessarily to be a 'Muslim' as far as existence is concerned. (Mawdudi, 1981, p. 18).

However, Mawdudi states that although man is completely caught in the grip of the law of nature and is bound to follow it, he has also been given the gift of a free will and can determine his own behaviour. As a result, although man's body is bound to submit to God's natural law, man can in the area of his will decide for himself whether or not to be a Muslim. How this freedom of choice is exercised determines whether one is a believer or an unbeliever. Of one who chooses to submit to God's law it can be said that:

> [He has] achieved completeness in his Islam by consciously deciding to obey God in the domain in which he was endowed with freedom of choice. He is a perfect Muslim. How his entire life has become one of submission to God and there is no conflict in his personality. (p. 19)

On the other hand, the unbeliever, having made a conscious decision to deny God, commits *kufr* (literally this means 'to cover or to conceal'. The unbeliever conceals what is inherent in his own nature by his unbelief and is a *kafir*—an unbeliever[1]). The one who commits *kufr* is in total rebellion to God. Mawdudi describes the unbeliever as follows:

---

1. The Arabic word is *kafara*, the root letters KFR.

Such a man destroys the calm and poise of life on earth. And in the life hereafter he will be held guilty for the crimes he committed against his nature. Every organ of his body—his very brain, eyes, nose, hands, and feet—will complain against the injustice and cruelty he has done unto them. Every tissue of his being will decry him before God whom, as the fountain of justice, will punish him as he deserves. This is the inglorious consequence of kufr. It leads to the blind alleys of utter failure, both here and hereafter. (pp 21–22)

In stark contrast, 'The life of a Muslim will always be filled with godliness, piety, righteousness and truthfulness . . .' (p. 25). Because the Muslim knows that God is ever-present, he will be fair and just in everything he does. In eternity, the believer will be showered with God's choicest blessings, 'for he will have discharged his duty ably, fulfilled his mission successfully, and emerged from his trial triumphantly' (p. 26). The Muslim 'is successful in life in this world and in the hereafter will live in eternal peace, joy and bliss' (p. 26).

Activity 3:1

How can you explain the meaning of 'Christian' to your Muslim friends?
Are Christians submitted to the will of God?
Is Christianity a total way of life? Is it a life of success?

3

Who is God?

In pre-Islamic times, God was described as having daughters:

. . . Has He (Allah) only daughters and ye have sons? (52:39)

Have ye seen (Al) Lat, and (Al) 'Uzza, and another the third [goddess], Manat? What! For you the male sex, and for Him, the female? (53:19–21)

These were the best-known pagan deities round about Mecca (see also Chapter 14, section 1, p. 266–268). There were some 360 idols established by the pagans, probably to represent the (inaccurately calculated) 360 days of the solar year. The idols were kept in the holiest shrine of the Black Stone, called the Ka'ba (a cube-shaped building in Mecca). This was a centre of worship, and life in Mecca revolved around the feast days and celebrations to its gods. But they also knew and worshipped Allah:

a. By giving him a tithe: 'Out of what Allah hath produced in abundance in tilth and in cattle, they assigned to Him a share: they say, according to their fancies: "This is for Allah and this is for Our 'partners!'" But the share of their "partners" reacheth not Allah' (6:136).

b. By praying to him for safety: 'Now if they embark on a boat, they call on Allah, making their devotion sincerely and exclusively to Him' (29:65).

God the creator

Muhammmad proclaimed God as Creator.

> Whatever is in the heavens and of earth, let it declare the Praises and Glory of God: For He is the Exalted in Might, the Wise.

> To Him belongs the dominion of the heavens and the earth: It is He Who gives Life and Death: and He has Power over all things.

> He is the First and the Last, the Evident, and the Immanent; and He has full knowledge of all things.

> He it is Who created the heavens and the earth in six Days, and is moreover firmly established on the Throne (of authority). He knows what enters within the earth and what comes forth out of it. (Sura 57:1–4)

> God is He, than Whom there is no other god; who knows (all things) both secret and open; He, Most Gracious, Most Merciful

God is HE, than Whom there is no other god: the Sovereign, The Holy One, the Sources of Peace (and Perfection), the Guardian of faith, the Preserver of Safety, the Exalted in Might, the Irresistible, the Supreme; Glory to God! (High is He) Above the partners they attribute to Him. He is God, the Creator, the Evolver, the Bestower of Forms (or Colours). To Him belong the Most Beautiful Names: whatever is in the heavens and on the earth, doth declare His Praises and Glory: And he is the Exalted in Might, the Wise. (Sura 59:22–24)

Beautiful names of God

'The most beautiful names belong to God: so call on him by them' 7:180 These beautiful names are found in the Qur'an and the Hadith (the Hadith, or 'Traditions', is explained in Chapter 7). There are ninety-nine names. The Hadith says that Paradise is the reward of those who recite them. This is often done with the use of rosary beads.

Some of the names follow:

AL RAHMAN	The Merciful	Sura 1:1
AL RAHIM	The Compassionate	Sura 1:1
AL MALIK	The King	Sura 1:3
AL KODDUS	The Holy	Sura 59:23
AS'SALAM	The Peace	Sura 58:23
AL'MUMIN	The Guardian of Faith	Sura 58:23
AL GHAFFAR	The Forgiver	Sura 2:225
AL RAZZAQ	The Provider	Sura 51:58
AL FATTAH	The Opener	Sura 34:26
AL AWWAL	The First	Sura 57:3
AL AKHIR	The Last	Sura 57:3
AL ZAHIR	The Evident One, Outwardly Manifest	Sura 57:3
AL BATIN	The Inward, Hidden One	Sura 57:3

Activity 3.2

Read the following passages from the Qur'an:
   16:3–12 4:58; 5:21; 35:44;
   3:26–27 and 2:28–29; 6:59

Note the qualities of God described, and consider how these are meaningful to Christians also.

Make a list of some of the names of God used in the Bible

Think how you could share this with your friend.

In Islam God expresses himself to man through his attributes: life, knowledge, power, will, hearing, seeing and speech. But these human terms are to be understood figuratively.

4

Tawhid

The first duty of a Muslim is to declare that God is One. THERE IS NO GOD BUT GOD. (*LA ILAH ILLA LLAH*). This profession of faith is found in the Qur'an, Sura 2:255, 28:88. Sura 112, helps us understand more fully the meaning of this declaration of *ONENESS*.

> In the name of God, Most Gracious, Most Merciful.
> Say: HE is God, the One and Only,
> God, the Eternal, Absolute;
> He begetteth not, nor is HE begotten;
> And there is none like unto Him.

Tawhid is the Arabic word used to express this concept of God's uniqueness in his unity. *Tawhid* for a Muslim means:

Firstly, we can speak of him using the word HE, as God is not an abstract conception of philosophy. Yusuf Ali comments that the best way in which we can realise him is to feel that He is a Personality, but that we should always be aware of the danger in conceiving God after our own patterns, as he is far beyond our limited conceptions. God in his unity and uniqueness is not like any other.

Secondly, God is One in essence, 'having no parts, no partners . . . He begetteth not . . . and has neither son or father (Sura 25:2)—He hath chosen no son nor hath He any partners in sovereignty').

Thirdly, he is eternal, ever-lasting, and absolute; one in his attributes, not having a multiplicity of powers or wills.

Fourthly, he is one in his works: no other being beside God has any influence on God at all.

This statement of belief in *Tawhid* marks him as a Muslim, declaring the special unity of God which pagans having many gods deny, and Christians who acknowledge a trinitarian God cannot affirm.

For Mawdudi, belief in the unity of God will give the believer a generous and broad-minded outlook on life.

Ghulam Sarwar said that belief in the *Tawhid* will produce in the believer a large degree of self-respect and confidence. He knows he can depend on Allah for the fulfilment of his needs. He can go forward in life without fear. A believer in *Tawhid* seeks the pleasure of Allah by making his belief and action go together. Belief without practice has no place in Islam. (Sarwar, pp 22–23). Nothing can happen without the will and knowledge of God. This aspect of belief about God pre-determining the course of the world and our lives is called *Al-Qadr*. Believing in this means we accept God as absolutely in control of the affairs of his world. He decides what is good and evil.

> He to whom belongs the dominion of the heavens and the earth: no son has He begotten, nor has He a partner in His dominion: It is He Who created all things, and ordered them in due proportions. (25:2)

> The command of God is a decree determined. (33:38).

> This is an admonition: Whosoever will, let him take a (straight) Path to his Lord. But ye will not, except as God wills; for God is full of Knowledge and Wisdom. (76: 29, 30)

And there is not a thing but its (sources and) treasures (inexhaustible) are with US; but We only send down thereof in due and ascertainable measures. (15:21).

But human beings do have responsibility for their actions.

Man is the Khalifah (agent) of God on this earth and is expected to obey Him. (2:30)

As for those who believe and work righteousness, verily we shall not suffer to perish the reward of any who do a (single) righteous deed. (18:30)

Activity 3.3

Who is God for the Christian?

Read Deuteronomy 6:4, 5: How must I understand God and how do I respond to him?

Think about how would you describe *your* God. Read Isaiah 40 and 44.

Shirk

The doctrine of the *Tawhid* of God (oneness) and *Al-Qadr* leads people to submit to him. But what of those who do not submit?

The controversy with Christians focuses on this issue, for Christians believe in a triune God. They are called *MUSHRIKUN* —those who associate others with God in his divinity, in particular Jesus Christ. This is to commit the grave sin of *shirk*, to make someone the associate or partner of God. Those who commit this sin are therefore *mushrikun*.

Pagan believers, idolators and polytheists would also be guilty of *shirk*. Quranic statements show what Muslims understand about the Christian belief of the Trinity.

Christ Jesus son of Mary was (no more than) an apostle of God, and His Word which He bestowed on Mary and a Spirit proceeding from Him: so believe in God and His apostles. Say not 'Trinity', desist; it will be better for you: For God is ONE GOD: . . . Christ disdaineth not to serve and worship God. (4: 171–172)

In blasphemy indeed are those that say that God is Christ. (5:19)

They do blaspheme who say: God is one of three in a Trinity . . . Christ the son of Mary was no more than an Apostle. (5:76, 77)

And behold! God will say 'O Jesus the son of Mary! Did'st thou say unto men, Worship me and my mother as gods in derogation of God?' (5:119)

The other point of controversy is that not only do Christians believe that Christ is God, violating the *tawhid*; but they also believe that Christ was crucified and rose again.

5

A Quranic view of Jesus

In the conclusion of his book *Jesus in the Qur'an*, Geoffrey Parrinder writes:

Jesus is mentioned in 15 suras of the Qur'an, but not in the other 99. 93 verses speak of him, but there are 6,226 (or 6,211) verses in the whole Qur'an. He receives many honourable names but he is placed in the succession of the prophets and teaching about the prophets is only one element in the Qur'an. (p 166)

The birth of Jesus the Messiah is found in Suras 3:35–51 and 19: 22–34:

Behold! the angels said: 'O Mary! God has chosen thee. O Mary! God giveth thee glad tidings of a Word from Him: his name will be Christ Jesus (Sura 3).

Mary is greatly honoured and Jesus is called 'son of Mary' 23 times in the Qur'an.

Jesus performed many different miracles, as a sign from the Lord. The Qur'an mentions this, though not in great detail. Sura 3:49, following on from his birth, says: 'And I heal those born blind, and the lepers, and I quicken the dead, by God's leave.'

One of the most remarkable references to Jesus in the Qur'an is 'So Peace is on me the day I was born, the day that I die, and the day that I shall be raised up to life again.' (19:34). The same words are spoken of John (*Yahya*), (19:15).

Although the words appear '. . . God if His Will were to destroy the Christ . . .', implying that God has the sovereign power to do so, despite such allusions to Christ the overriding interpretation is that Jesus was not crucified. The key passage for this view is Sura 4:157–158.

> That they said (in boast), 'We killed Christ Jesus the son of Mary, the Apostle of God'—But they killed him not, nor crucified him, but so it was made to appear to them, and those who differ therein are full of doubts, with no (certain) knowledge, but only conjecture to follow, for of a surety they killed him not—Nay, God raised him up unto Himself; and God is Exalted in Power, Wise.

The statement that Jesus was not crucified is followed by 'so it was made to appear to them'. This would seem to suggest that although Jesus was not crucified, God made it appear as if he was. This is interpreted by most Muslims to mean that God made someone else look like Jesus and allowed that person to be crucified instead. 'God raised him up unto Himself' is assumed to mean that God took Jesus into heaven without his having died first.

Crucifixion, which is central to the New Testament, seems to be of great repugnance to Muslims. Remember that Muhammad had suffered persecution and rejection by the Quraysh. Then after emigrating to Medina, he received acceptance and success. All the stories of prophets in the Qur'an are stories of success. A story of failure, of God allowing his servant to be defeated and not to hear his prayer for help and deliver him, seems an unacceptable model for a prophet.

In more recent years, an alternative theory has emerged concerning the crucifixion of Jesus which suggests that although Jesus was put on the cross, he was taken down before he was dead and in the cool of the tomb revived from his death-like swoon. This 'swoon theory' has been adopted and further embellished by the Ahmadiyyas, an Islamic group which has its origins in nineteenth-century India (see chapter 10, p. 189).

Activity 3:4

1 Think about how to answer the Muslim objection to the Trinity.
2 Think about how to share the life of Christ.
   Share his pre-existence, birth, miracles, words, and his uniqueness.
3 How do you answer the objections to the death of Christ? Remember to concentrate on not *how* he died, but *why*.

6

Apostacy

Christians living as minorities in Muslim countries may suffer for not submitting. There would seem to be tolerance in the Qur'an but also militant views. 'Let there be is no compulsion in religion' (2:256). 'Fight and slay the pagans wherever ye find them' (9:4). 'Fight them and God will punish them by your hands . . . help you to victory over them' (9:14). 'Fight those who believe not in God . . . even if they are of the People of the Book, until they pay the Jizya with willing submission and feel themselves subdued' (9:29).

Those who have submitted must remain Muslim and not embrace another religion. *RADDA* (renouncing or going back) makes a Muslim an apostate.

> Say: 'We believe
> In God, and in what
> Has been revealed to us
> And what was revealed
> To Abraham, Isma'il;
> Isaac, Jacob, and the Tribes,

And in [the Books]
Given to Moses, Jesus,
And the Prophets,
From their Lord:
We make no distinction
Between one and another
Among them, and to Allah do we
Bow our will (in Islam).'

If anyone desires
A religion other than
Islam (submission to Allah),
Never will it be accepted
Of him; and in the Hereafter
He will be in the ranks
Of those who have lost
(All spiritual good).

How shall Allah
Guide those who reject
Faith after they accepted it
And bore witness
That the Apostle was true
And that Clear Signs
Had come unto them?
But Allah guides not
A people unjust.

Of such the reward
Is that on them (rests)
The curse of Allah,
Of his angels,
And of all mankind;—

In that will they dwell;
Nor will their penalty
Be lightened, nor respite
Be their (lot);—

. . . For such
Is (in store) a penalty grievous
And they will find no helpers.

(Sur 3:84–88, 91; see also Sura 2:217)

Hadiths are cited which seem to give the right to practice the death penalty for *radda*, for men and women were to be imprisoned until they returned to the faith or to be executed. In many countries the penalty is imprisonment, and deportation.

Activity 3:5

Are you involved in praying for Muslims to come to Christ?

Request mission agencies and missionaries to begin sending prayer letters and news. Join a prayer group.

Get involved in praying for the persecuted believers. First, try to find out about them. Then it may be advisable to write to them, to Muslim embassies, or to your local government official.

7

Other beliefs

Belief in God's Angels
Belief in God's Books (See Chapter 4)
Belief in God's Prophets and Messengers (See Chapter 5)
Belief in life after death and the day of judgement

God's angels

Angels are a special creation of God. They are beings endued with bodies created from divine light. They neither eat nor drink. There is no distinction of sex among them.

Angels do not have free will, their chief characteristic being complete obedience to the will of God. Their time is spent praising God day and night and carrying out their given duties.

There has been a theological discussion in the history of Islam as to whether angels are to be regarded as superior in rank to human beings, in particular the prophets, because they do not deviate from God's law. However, the Qur'an says:

Behold! thy Lord said to the angels: 'I am about to create man from sounding clay from mud moulded into shape. When I have fashioned him (in due proportion) and breathed into him of My spirit fall ye down in obeisance unto him.' So the angels prostrated themselves, all of them together. Not so Iblis: he refused to be among those who prostrated themselves.' (15:28–30)

Prominent among the angels are the four archangels: Jibra'il (Gabriel), God's messenger and the Angel of Revelation because he brought God's revelation to Muhammad; Mika'il (Michael), who is said to have been the friend and protector of the Jews (Dan 12:1); Izra'il, who is considered the angel of death; and Israfil, who will blow the trumpet at the day of resurrection and judgement.

In addition to these archangels there are guardian angels, who protect humans from danger and calamities which are not decreed by God. Two recording angels attend everyone. The one on a person's right records his good deeds and words; the one on his left records all his sins. There are also the throne-bearers and the cherubin. Angels will receive the obedient believer in heaven and will throw the disobedient wrong-doer into hell. Two other angels are Munkar and Nakira. They are two huge, fierce-looking angels who visit every man in his grave immediately after the funeral is over to examine him as to his beliefs in God and in Muhammad, and to torture him if he cannot answer satisfactorily. A true believer will answer, 'Allah is my Lord, Islam is my religion and Muhammad is my prophet.' The angels will then assure him of the mercy of God and the delights of Paradise. His grave is made wide and comfortable and a window is put in, so that he can look into paradise and behold what is in store for him.

Belief in life after death

Muslims believe in life after death. The Qur'an says, in Sura 75 on the Resurrection:

'I do call to witness the Resurrection Day . . .
Does man think that We cannot assemble his bones: Nay, We are able to put together in perfect order the very tips of his fingers.' (75:1, 3)

God is the one who gives life and has appointed the hour for man to die. This belief in life after death (*akhira*) is an important belief. But this will happen in the end times, in the last days. 'And (Jesus) shall be a Sign (for the coming of) the Hour (of Judgment)' (43:61).

There are some signs which it is thought will inaugurate the last days. These are:

1 The sun will rise from the west instead of the east.
2 Antichrist will appear (some say from between Iraq and Syria), and will roam the world for 40 days, laying it waste, before he is slain by Jesus.
3 A Beast will appear and speak to them (27:82).
4 Jesus will return (43:61) and according to the traditions will kill the Antichrist, rule 40 years, kill the swine, forbid the eating of pork, marry and have children, preach Islam, destroy the cross, and then die and be buried in Medina, next to the grave of Muhammad.

'On that day, we shall gather together from every people . . . (before the Judgment-seat) (God) will say: 'Did ye reject My signs, though ye comprehended them not in knowledge, or what was it ye did?' . . . If any do good, good will (accrue) to them therefrom; and they will be secure from terror that Day. And if any do evil, their faces will be thrown headlong into the Fire: 'Do ye receive a reward other than that which ye have earned by your deeds?' (Sura 27:83, 83, 89, 90).

The book of deeds will be opened (18:49)

Those who reject Our Signs, We shall soon cast into the Fire: as often as their skins are roasted through, We shall change them for fresh skins, that they may taste the Penalty: for God is Exalted in Power, Wise. (4:56)

But those who believe and do deeds of righteousness we shall soon admit to Gardens, with rivers flowing beneath, their eternal home: therein shall they have companions pure and holy: we shall admit them to shades, cool and ever deepening. (4:57)

As to the Righteous, they shall be amid cool shades and springs (of water). And (they shall have) Fruits, all they desire. 'Eat ye and drink ye to your heart's content: For that ye worked (Righteousness).' (77:41)

Books referred to in the chapter

Ali, Abdullah Yusuf, *The Holy Qur'an: Text, Translation and Commentary* (Islamic Foundation: Leicester, 1975), notes on Sura 112.

Maududi, Sayyid Abul A'la, *Towards Understanding Islam* (Islamic Foundation: Leicester, 1980), pp 18–16.

Parrinder, Geoffrey, *Jesus in the Qur'an* (Sheldon Press: London, 1965) p. 166.

Sarwar, Ghulam, *Islam: Beliefs and Teachings* (Muslim Educational Trust: London, 3rd edn 1984), p. 23.

For further reading

Ali, Abdullah Yusuf, *The Holy Qur'an: Text, Translation and Commentary* (Islamic Foundation: Leicester, 1975).

Maududi, Sayyid Abdul A'la, *Towards Understanding Islam* (Islamic Foundation: Leicester, 1980).

Parrinder, Geoffrey, *Jesus in the Qur'an* (Sheldon Press, London, 1965).

Parshall, Phil, *The Cross and the Crescent* (1989: 1st edn, Scripture Press: Amersham, 1990).

Sarwar, Ghulam, *Islam: Beliefs and Teachings* (Muslim Educational Trust: London, 3rd edn 1984).

Shorrosh, Anis A., *Islam Revealed: A Christian Arab's View of Islam* (Nelson: Nashville, Tennessee, 1988).

Zwemer, Samuel M., *The Moslem Doctrine of God* (American Tract Society, NY, 1905) [repr. as *The Muslim Doctrine of God* (Darf: London, 1987)].

Zwemer, Samuel M., *The Muslim Christ* (Oliphant, Anderson & Ferrier: Edinburgh & London, 1912).

4

The Qur'an

Study guide

*God makes himself known through revelation, scriptures, and a
book; and God sends his messages by a prophet. Muslims
generally think it began with Adam, or more clearly with
Abraham, and followed on through the many prophets: Moses,
David, Jesus and then the final one Muhammad. Muhammad
was compelled to bring this message.*

*The Qur'an has a central place in Islam. This chapter will
discuss the Qur'an, how it came into being, how the book is
constructed, some of the main subjects of its teaching, and its
role in the faith of the followers.*

When you have completed this chapter we hope you will:

*1 Understand why Muslims hold the Qur'an in such high esteem
   and the role it has in formulating Muslim beliefs and practices;*
*2 Have seen why in Muslim eyes the Qur'an was necessary, and
   why it was written in Arabic;*
*3 Be able to relate the development of the Qur'an to events in
   the life of Muhammad and know how the text of the book was
   collected, understanding something of its style; and*
*4 Be aware of the crucial questions of what is the word of God,
   and Muslim views of the Christian Scriptures.*

1

Introduction

Iqraa means 'Read, Recite, or Proclaim aloud (the message)'.
Sura 96 Begins with this word *Iqraa* because the prophet

Muhammad was called by God and given the revelation. The word *Qur'an* is formed from the same Arabic word.[1]

The Qur'an is made up of 114 chapters known as SURAS (degrees, or steps by which we mount up) and 6666 verses known as AYA/AYAS. (Aya means a *SIGN* and each verse is a sign from God.) The Suras are known by a name or title, not by a number as it is in the English translation. The names come from the theme, person or event narrated and are sometimes, though not always, to be found in the opening Aya of that Sura.

Activity 4:1

Open the Qur'an and look at the form and the names.
The 1st Sura is called *FATIHAH* or the OPENING chapter.
The 2nd Sura is called *BAQARA* or Cow.
The 3rd Sura is *Al-i-'IMRAN* or the Family of Imran.
The 4th Sura is *NISAA* or the Women.
The 10th Sura is *YUNUS* or Jonah.
The 12th Sura is *YUSUF* or Joseph.
The 16th Sura is *NAHL* the Bee.
The 22nd Sura is *HAJJ* the Hajj.

Each Sura (except the ninth) begins with the words BISMILLAH RAHIMAN IRRAHIM—'In the Name of God, Most Gracious, Most Merciful'. *Rahiman* and *rahim* are words more intense than the superlative degree in English, and refer to different aspects of God's attribute of mercy.

---

1. *Qara'a*, to recite, to read; *IQRA'A*, to make to read, or to teach to recite; *AL QUR'AN*, the Qur'an, 'the recitation' (Probably from a Syrian word— *QERYANA*, the reading of the lesson, the scripture reading, in a church service. In Arabic the Qur'an has other names such as *AL KITAB* the book, *el furkan* (the distinction), *el mas'haf* (the scroll), *el dhikr* (the warning), and a few others.

The 114 Suras are divided mainly into two parts, the Meccan and the Medinan Suras. The prophet was commanded to start his mission in Mecca. The early messages which God sent down and the prophet recited in Mecca are known as Meccan, while those which he recited in Medina are called Medinan. The Meccan Suras are generally shorter and in excellent literary style, and the Medinan are longer as God-revealed discourses required for particular occasions. They were revealed over 23 years. There is general agreement that there are 86 Meccan and 28 Medinan Suras. But the order in the Qur'an is not chronological but rather in sequence from the longest to the shortest.

Unless you read Arabic you will have to be content with an 'interpretation', for the first important fact to recognise is that it is an Arabic Qur'an. The Arabic words are considered to be God's words, so the language itself is an intrinsic part of the revelation.

> We have made it a Qur'an in Arabic, That ye may be able to understand (and learn wisdom). (43:3)

> Qur'an in Arabic for people who understand (41:3)

> Had We sent this as a Qur'an (in a language) other than Arabic, they would have said: 'Why are not its verses explained in detail? What! (a Book) not in Arabic and (a Messenger) an Arab?' (41:44)

These and other Suras have led almost all Muslim commentators to agree that God willed the revelation to Muhammad to be an Arabic Qur'an. This doctrine applies both to its form and to its substance. If God willed it to be an Arabic Qur'an it is not part of 'submission' to translate it. In fact Muslims assert that it is untranslatable. So Pickthall (an English Muslim) calls his English translation *The Meaning of the Glorious Qur'an* and A.J. Arberry calls his *The Koran Interpreted*.

Activity 4:2

1 Consider this question: If Muhammad had had access to the Bible in Arabic during his lifetime, would there have been a Qur'an? (The Bible had not yet been translated into Arabic at that time.)

2 Consider the different style of the Bible. How would you introduce your Muslim friends to it? Where should they begin? What should they expect to find?

2

The original, the transmission and the miracle of the Qur'an

The Qur'an is divine in origin. The Mother of the book, or the preserved Eternal Tablet, is in heaven. From this fountain-head the message, the words were sent down.

> A Qur'an in Arabic . . . and verily, it is in the Mother of the Book in our Presence, high (in dignity), full of wisdom. (43:3,4)
> Nay, this is a Glorious Qur'an (Inscribed) in A Tablet Preserved. (85:21)

Muslims believe that the Qur'an is the miracle which authenticates Muhammad's claim to be a prophet. From the *aya* 'calling him an unlettered Prophet' (7:157), it is widely believed that Muhammad could neither read nor write; yet he was full of the highest wisdom and had a most wonderful knowledge of the previous Scriptures. This is the sign, the test, the proof of inspiration; illiteracy assures purity.

Every Muslim is to believe in the divinely inspired books which God has sent down from time to time, to various peoples, through his apostles or prophets. Ghulam Sarwar writes: 'Allah's greatest favour to mankind is his guidance contained in the books of revelation' (Sarwar, 1984, p. 29).

The number of books sent down is believed to be 104. Of these only five are named in the Qur'an. They are:

1. The Scrolls of Abraham (now lost).
2. The *Tawrat* (the Torah) given to the prophet Musa (Moses).
3. The *Zabur* (the Psalms) given to the prophet Dawud (David).
4. The *Injil* (the Gospel) given to the prophet Isa (Jesus).
5. The Qur'an revealed to the prophet Muhammad.

There are two terms used to explain the manner in which God communicated to Muhammad.

a. 'TANZIL'—what is sent down. This carries the idea that the Book was brought down from heaven and communicated to Muhammad by the angel Gabriel.

> It is We Who have sent down the Qur'an to thee by stages. (76:23)

> We have indeed revealed this (Message) in the Night of Power . . . therein come down the angels and the Spirit by God's permission. (97:1,4)

b. WAHY—a word for inspiration.

> It is not fitting for a man that God should speak to him except by inspiration, or from behind a veil, or by the sending of a Messenger. (42:51)

> To Gabriel—for he brings down the revelation to thy heart. (2:97)

Hadith list several ways that this experience came to the Prophet. Muhammad experienced suffocation and fits, his colour would change, sometimes he heard the sound of ringing bells, or dreams, or visions. He had been going to the cave Hira to pass his time in meditation. He perhaps wanted to find answers to his search for truth. It was during one of his retreats in the month of Ramadan, when Muhammad was forty years of age, that the angel appeared before him.

The angel said: 'Read.' Muhammad replied, 'I am not a reader.' At this the angel squeezed him so hard, Muhammad felt he would die of suffocation. He released him again and said: 'Read.' Muhammad again replied, 'I am not a reader.' And the angel squeezed him hard again and asked him a third time: 'Read!' After another crushing experience the Angel said:

> Proclaim! (or Read) in the name of thy Lord and Cherisher, who created
> Created man, out of a (mere) clot of congealed blood;
> Proclaim! (Read) And thy Lord is Most Bountiful.
> He Who taught (the use of) the Pen.
> Taught man that which he knew not. (96:1-5)

Thus in the year 610 the first visions began. He was greatly troubled at first. He rushed home and told his wife Khadijah who comforted him. Her cousin Waraqh Bin Hawfal, who was a Christian, thought God had come to him just as he used to come to Moses.

> Some months later he saw the angel again and he was shivering . . .
> The Angel said: 'O thou wrapped up (in a mantle)!
> Arise and deliver thy warning!' (74:1)

Summary

God speaks to Muhammad, who is a transmitter.
It is mechanical inspiration. There is no human element.
God gives the syntax, vocabulary, and word sequences . . .
Tanzil—the book, the Qur'an, comes down from heaven;
an eternal heavenly book becomes an earthly one . . . an incarnation of a book.

Activity 4:3

Consider how the Bible was revealed. Read 2 Peter 1:19–21; Jeremiah 1:9,10; 36:2; Ezekiel 3:17; Acts 1:16; 28:25; Hebrews 1:1,2; 2 Timothy 3:16,17.

3

The Qur'an around the life of Muhammad

'Muhammad's vocation initiates the Qur'an and his death closes it.'

These are the words that Kenneth Cragg uses in summarising the relationship between Muhammad and the Qur'an. Yet it must be remembered that for no Muslim is Muhammad ever seen as an author of the Qur'an; only a transmitter of the message.

But it is convenient, in this introductory study, to consider the Qur'an around the life of Muhammad (we shall be studying his life in more detail in the next chapter). His ministry began in the city of Mecca. Later in 622, he moved with his followers to Medina. It is customary to divide the 'revelations' according to three periods of the prophet's life:

> The First Meccan period (610–615);
> The Second Meccan period (616–622);
> The Medinan period (622–632).

The first Meccan period

During the first period Muhammad is mainly a warner, encouraging people to turn from idols to God, relating that there is a resurrection and judgment time when those who obey will be blessed and those who refuse will burn in the great fire.

Looking through one of these early suras you can pick out the main themes. For example, Sura 74:

1. O thou wrapped up (in a mantle)!
2. Arise and deliver thy warning!   A WARNER
3. And thy Lord do thou magnify!
4. And thy garments keep free from stain!

5. And all abomination
shun!

6. Nor expect, in giving, any
increase (for thyself)!

7. But, for thy Lord's
(Cause), be patient and
constant!

8. Finally, when the trumpet   The END TIMES
is sounded,

9. That will be—that Day—
a Day of Distress—

10. Far from easy for those
without Faith.

26. Soon will I cast him into   HELL
Hell-Fire!

27. And what will explain to
thee what Hell-Fire is?

28. Naught doth it permit to
endure, and naught doth
it leave alone!

29. Darkening and changing
the colour of man!

30. Over it are Nineteen.

31. And We have set none
but angels as guardians
Of the Fire; and We have
fixed their number

32. Nay, verily: by the Moon,   Literary or at
times more lyrical
33. And by the Night as it   (nature, moon, night,
retreateth,   dawn)

34. And by the Dawn as it
shineth forth—

35. This is but one of the
mighty (portents),

36. A Warning to mankind,

39. Except the Companions
of the Right Hand,

40. (They will be) in Gardens   GARDENS–PARADISE
(of delight).

The recitation of the oracle has a twofold purpose. It is a teaching method; and it enables men, by the use of the very words of Allah, to perform acceptable worship. The oracles declare God's goodness in creation.

> Then let man look at his Food (and how We provide it): For that We pour forth water in abundance, And We split the earth in fragments, And produce there in Corn, And Grapes and nutritious Plants, And Olives and Dates, And enclosed Gardens, dense with lofty trees. And Fruits and Fodder, For use and convenience to you and your cattle. (80:24-32)

And the oracles are a written revelation of Allah's will.

The suras from this period are mostly short and in a striking poetical style. The first revelation is Surah 96, and the following probably follow the chronological order: 74, 111, 106, 108, 104, 107, 102, 105, 92, 90, 94, 93, 97. You may wish to read a few of these to familiarise yourself with the style of the early suras.

Activity 4:4

1. Read one or two of the early suras and note the topics taught.
2. Read the Fatiha, the Opening Sura. List the Beliefs, then list the Petitions. How does it compare to the Lord's Prayer? This sura is used at the beginning of every formal time of prayer.

The second Meccan period

The first period ends with growing opposition to the new teaching which caused some Muslims to emigrate to Abyssinia. Muhammad seems to have thought that his movement would be free to develop under the patronage of the Christian emperor there. His hope was disappointed. Now the suras get longer. There is more discussion and more doctrine. Biblical material creeps in. Some suras are given names of Bible characters as titles, for example Noah, Mary, Joseph,

Abraham. 'Verily, this Brotherhood (Umma) of yours is a single Brotherhood' (21:92). (Yusuf Ali notes that all men and women of God form one united brotherhood, the earlier ones—Noah, David, Solomon, Job, Jonah, Zakariya and Mary—prefigure the final and perfected Brotherhood of Islam. (Comments on Sura 27:40).

The miraculous nature of the Qur'an is now affirmed and previous 'revelations' in the early suras are reiterated and confirmed. Suras from this period include 53, 43, 38, 39, 17, 23, 46, and 72.

The Medinan period

During this period, from the Hijra (622 AD) to his death, Muhammad the leader of the new community was based in Medina. The main thrust of the messages is now the divine approval and blessing of Muhammad's leadership. There are numerous references to historic events which emphasise his growing political authority.

Students have noted two leading features on the suras of this period. First, Muhammad changes from preacher to prince, or Prophet to Statesman (Mongomery Watt's terms). He begins to legislate in order to control the development of the new community. The times for prayer and the directions are fixed in more detail (2:142), and the fast is changed from the Day of Atonement to the month of Ramadan (2:183–185). Secondly, Muhammad also changes his attitude to the Jews and Christians who have refused to accept his claim to be the Apostle of Allah and his Prophet. See (33:40), where he is stated to be 'the Apostle of God, and the Seal of the Prophets'. The style of the earlier periods remains, but the subject matter changes. During this period some of the oracles seem to be included to justify his own family life. For example, he had married the divorced wife of his adopted son, Zaid, contrary to traditional custom. Sura 33:2, 23, 33, and 37 refer to this with approval.

Sura 2 The Heifer [Cow], *Baqara*

Perhaps the best known sura of this period is that with the unusual title 'The Heifer'. This sura sets forth in a kind of sequence some fundamental principles of Islam.

Extracts from Sura 2	Some of the Concepts of Islam
This is the Book; in it is guidance sure, without doubt to those who fear God;	The authority and divine origin of the Qur'an
It is He Who hath created for you All things that are on earth. (29)	God is creator of heaven and earth.
We said: 'O Adam! dwell thou and thy wife in the Garden; and eat of the bountiful things . . . but approach not this tree' . . . Then did Satan make them to slip. (36)	Satan caused Adam to sin
And remember We gave Moses the Scripture. (53)	God had given previous scriptures which the Qur'an confirms.
We gave Moses the book and followed him up with a succession of Apostles; We gave Jesus the Son of Mary clear signs and strengthened him with the holy spirit. (87)	
Gabriel—for he brings down the (revelation) to thy heart by God's will, a confirmation of what went before. (97)	

And none of Our revelations do we abrogate or cause to be forgotten
But We substitute something better. (106)

Later scriptures abrogate former where there is a difference. Even later verses of the Qur'an can replace earlier ones.

They say: 'God hath begotten a son'. (116)

Allah could not beget a son

Remember We made the House . . . of Abraham as a place of prayer (refers to Ka'ba)

Islam is the true faith of Abraham

Activity 4:5

Read through Sura 2 and find other themes that are also included in the Bible. Note how these are presented and compare the differences in the two books. A useful aid to the study of the Qur'an is *Topical Concordance to Qur'an*, translated by Aubrey Whitehouse from Muhammad al Araby al Azuzy, (2nd ed 1981).

Abraham in the Qur'an and the Bible

1. God took Abraham for a friend
(4:125 Khalilullah)

Is 41:8, 2 Chron 20:7; Jas 2:23

2. Father of true believers:
(2:124 Iman to the nations. 16:120, 3:67)
Not a Jew, not a Christian but UPRIGHT.

Gen 15:2
Gal 3:7–9; Rom 9:7, 8,

(NB Rom 4:23–25; 17)

3. Nature of his faith:
No idols, GOD only obey
3:95, 2:130–135, 6:161

Gal 3:6–9

4. Promises 11:70,71 a son	Gen 17:15–19
37:112 good news, Isaac	Rom 4:18–21
(NB the word wife—	
'*imra'ah* is used in the singular	
(Hagar is not a wife)	

5. Sacrifice 37:102ff; 2:260	Gen 22
What does Abraham	
believe about God?	
What does he believe about	
sacrifice?	
Why is this one special?	Jn 1:129 (the Passover)
It is celebrated yearly with a	
lamb being killed, and	
called *Eid Ul Adha*.	
Is this a substitution?	
How is Love shown? Is	Think about a loving
Abraham giving an only	suffering Father.
son? Costly love.	

'Only Son' notes

a. 37:100–113; no name is given for the son (Ishmael is not named, even though tradition identifies him).
b. 37: Isaac is used as the son of good news, in relation to what would seem to be the promise he had.
c. No mention of Hagar.
d. Early agreement in Judaism and Christianity for Isaac as the son.
e. 29:27 makes Isaac seem superior.

Autobiographical elements

The Qur'an is not an autobiography of Muhammad, but it contains some of the earliest and most reliable information we have on his life. Sura 93:6–8 reads 'Did he not find thee an orphan and give thee shelter (and care)? And HE found thee wandering and He gave thee guidance. And He found thee in need, and made thee independent'—a comment on his humble origins. Sura 9 recalls how Muhammad when leaving Mecca hid in a cave with Abu Bakr. References to the main battles are in Sura 8, Badr, Sura 3, Uhud and Sura 9, Hunayn. Reference to the Treaty of Hudaybiyah is in Sura 48. Sura 17:1–2 is a brief textual reference to the night journey to Jerusalem.

Sura 80:1–10 is an unusual passage, because it rebukes Muhammad for his neglect of a blind man.

Muhammad's name is used four times, which is an endorsement of his role and the message he received (47:2, 48:29, 3:144, 33:40).

4

How the text was collected and preserved

During Muhammad's lifetime some people recorded passages on leaves of date-palm, or bark of trees. The Companions of the Prophet committed these passages to memory, some of them knowing the entire Qur'an. It had not been put into book form.

Shortly after Muhammad's death many of these Companions, 'reciters' of the Qur'an, were killed in a battle. It was feared that the Qur'an would become irretrievably lost. So Abu Bakr commissioned Zayd-ibn-Thabit, who was one of Muhammad's secretaries, to collect the Qur'an. He carried out his task with great care. Tradition records that he collected 'not only from the hearts of men, but also from pieces of parchment or papyrus, flat stones, palm leaves, shoulder blades, ribs of animals, pieces of leather and wooden boards'. He checked that his written sources tallied with the memory of the Companions. It is said that he wrote all he collected on sheets of equal size, which after the death of Umar passed into the care of Hafsa, a widow of Muhammad.

Regarding the sequence, Yusuf Ali says that Zayd followed

the order that was followed by the prophet and would not have changed it. Since the Qur'an was recited twice before Gabriel during the last Ramadan of his life, this is proof of a clear existing order. Tradition says Zayd attended these last two recitals. Likewise the Companions would have memorised it in sequence. The Qur'an also speaks of itself as a BOOK (63:4).

The collection by Zayd was almost certainly the basis of a completion of the text ordered by Uthman. There is little doubt that the book we have today is the Uthmanic Qur'an. When disputes arose over the different readings, the dialect of the Quraysh (Muhammad's tribe) was preferred (because for obvious reasons the Qur'an was revealed in the dialect of Quraish of Mecca). Four standard copies were placed at Medina, Kufa, Basra and Damascus. Variant readings were destroyed. This move ensured the singularity and authority of the Qur'an and removed the possibility of critical or historical analysis of scriptural texts. Muslim theologians always assume the authenticity of the text as we have it now, and have never questioned the divine origin and inspiration and authority of the Qur'an.

5

Abrogation in the Qur'an

> Never did We send an apostle or a prophet
> Before thee, but, when he framed a desire, Satan
> Threw some (vanity) into his desire: but God
> Will cancel anything (vain) that Satan throws in,
> And God will confirm (and establish) His Signs:
> For God is full of knowledge and wisdom. (Sura 22:52)

Muslim exegetes take this word 'cancel' or 'abrogate' (in Arabic NASIKH) from the root, N S KH and use it to describe the concept of abrogation. Of this verse, Yusuf Ali notes:

Prophets and apostles are but human. Their actions are righteous and their motives pure. But in judging things from a human point of view, the suggestion may come to their mind (from Satan) that it would be good to have power or wealth or influence for furthering God's cause, or that it may be good to conciliate some faction which may be irreconcilable. In fact, in God's Plan, it may be the opposite. God, in His mercy and inspiration, will cancel any false or vain suggestions of this kind, and confirm and strengthen His own Commands and make known His Will in His Signs or revelations.

In the discussion of NASIKH, Tabari mentions the Hadith about Sura 53, generally known as an example of 'Satanic verses'. The Hadith records earlier words which God has cancelled and replaced with a better word.

Did you consider Al Lat and Al'Uzza
and Al Manat, the Third, the other?
Those are the swans exalted (or: cranes flying higher and hover
between heaven and earth like angels; or: These are exalted Females)
Their intercession is expected
Their likes are not neglected

Which now reads with the correction from God:

Did you consider Al Lat and Al'Uzza and Al Manat, the third the other? That would be unfair sharing. They are but names you and your fathers named: God revealed no authority to them. (See also Chapter 14, section 1, p. 267–268).

Abrogation may cancel the words and the ruling as in the above example. It may be that one verse cancels another, but the former verse still remains in the Qur'an. Examples: 16:6 would imply that it is permissible to drink wine, but 2:219 cancels this, saying no wine is permitted. In Sura 2:142 Jerusalem is the direction of Prayer; this changes to Mecca in 2:183–185, and the Ashura fast changes to the fast of Ramadan.

When We substitute one revelation for another—and God knows best What He reveals (in stages). (16:101)
God doth blot out or confirm what He pleaseth: with Him is the Mother of the Book. (13:39)

6

What does the Qur'an mean to a Muslim?

Colin Chapman in his book *You Go and Do the Same* presents four answers to this question: first, it is essential to realise that *the Qur'an is to the Muslim what Jesus is to the Christian.* It is a mistake to make a direct comparison between the role of Jesus in Christianity and the role of Muhammad in Islam, or between the place of the Bible in Christianity and the place of the Qur'an in Islam. Second, he points out, '*Muslims believe that the revelation of the Qur'an was itself a miracle*, since Muhammad himself was not able to read or write.' The third point he mentions is:

> *In order to appreciate what the Quran means to a Muslim we ought to hear it recited.* Since the Qur'an was revealed in Arabic, the Arabic of the Qur'an is an essential part of the message and part of the appeal of the Qur'an for the Muslim lies in the beauty of the Arabic.

His final point is that for the Muslim the Qur'an is '*a message which calls him to worship and surrender*'. This means that he is not worried by its lack of chronological order. It is not a historical account.

7

Quranic references to the Bible

It is important to see what the Qur'an actually says about the Bible. With reference to the Torah, which is the books of the Law, the Pentateuch, it states:

> We did indeed aforetime give the Book to Moses: Be not then in doubt of its reaching (thee): And we make it a guide to the Children of Israel. (Sura 32:23)

> It was We Who revealed the Law (to Moses); therein was guidance and light. (Sura 5:44)

Referring to the Injil, which is the New Testament, the Qur'an says:

> And in their footsteps We sent Jesus the son of Mary, confirming the Law that had come before him: We sent him the Gospel: Therein was guidance and light, and confirmation of the Law that had come before him: A guidance and an admonition to those who fear Allah. (Sura 5:46)

The Qur'an also states, referring to the whole Bible,

> To thee We sent the Scripture in truth, confirming the scripture that came before it, and guarding it in safety. (Sura 5:48)

There does not seem to be any doubt that the Qur'an teaches that the Bible is from God and must be believed. This presents Muslims with a dilemma which is explained in *In the Family of Abraham*:

> The chief reason why Muslims profess to believe in the corruption of the very words of the Scriptures is that they really have no choice but to do so. The Qur'an, while praising and professing to confirm the former Scriptures, contradicts them in so many important particulars that both cannot be from the same true God. Since Muslims are bound to believe in the divine origin of the Qur'an, they are placed in an awkward dilemma and one of the easiest ways out of the difficulty is to allege the literal corruption of the Bible. (p. 9).

For further discussion of the alleged corruption of the Bible see *In the Family of Abraham*, chapters one and two (Cooper 1989).

8

The crucial question

Perhaps the crucial question Christians have to ask is: 'Is the Qur'an the word of God, or isn't it?'

Some phrase the question differently, asking: Is it 'a word from God', or does it contain 'part of God's word'? Most modern scholars prefer not to answer this question. For example, Montgomery Watt in his book *Muhammad and Mecca* writes:

> In order to avoid deciding where the Qur'an is or is not, the word of God I have refrained from using the expression 'God says' and 'Muhammad says' when referring to the Qur an and have simply said, 'The Qur'an says'. Older writers, almost without exception, were more ready to assert categorically that it was not the word of God. Some were ready to label it 'the devil's supreme counterfeit.' Many would still take this view.

The orthodox Muslim has no doubt whatsoever. 'Every pious Muslim holds that the Qur'an is, in the simplest and fullest possible sense, the word of God. There is no human element in it' (Neill, 1984, p. 69).

Several points must be made:

1. The Qur'an and the New Testament contradict each other.
2. The Qur'an's 'One God' and the New Testament's 'Triune God' are different, yet similar.
3. Quranic law cannot be reconciled with the grace of God.
4. The Qur'an is said by many Muslims to deny that Christ died on the cross and rose again on the third day—facts of crucial significance for the Christian and which are affirmed to be historical events in the New Testament.

The answer we give to the question, 'Is the Qur'an the word of God or not?' will undoubtedly be influenced by our attitude to the Bible. For those who hold the Bible to be the inspired, infallible word of God the answer is clear. The Qur'an cannot be that too. It can only be, at best, the record of a sincere but misguided man seeking to express his convictions about the relation of man (the slave) to God (the master).

Some Christians, while holding firmly to the belief that the Bible is the divinely inspired and infallible word of God, would be prepared to concede that parts of the Qur'an, where it agrees with the Bible, or where it points to a Biblical truth, are true and may therefore be used as a starting point in reaching out to Muslims. So we accept that the Qur'an is true in part, without necessarily according to it divine inspiration. If one goes further and accepts the present-day pluralist view that there are many revelations of the godhead, each one designed for a particular time and culture, then both the Qur'an and the Bible are but two of many religious books, seemingly different, but basically all pointing to an ultimate in which all will eventually be found to unite.

Look back at Chapter 1 section 2, 'What the Bible says about other faiths', to remind yourself about the pluralist view.

The concept of revelation in the New Testament is quite different to that in the Qur'an. It should never be forgotten that whereas the Qur'an claims to be the revelation of the law and will of God, the New Testament claims to be the historic, divinely inspired and accurate record of the life and teachings of Jesus Christ. It also claims that he himself is *the* word of God: 'The Word became flesh and lived for a while among us' (Jn 1:14); 'For God was pleased to have all his fullness dwell in him [Jesus]' (Col 1:19).

Christians believe that the writers of the Bible were inspired by God to write the truth in their own language, rather than to receive and pass on God's actual words. 'All scripture is God-breathed [inspired by God RSV] . . . (2 Tim 3:16). John Stott, commenting on this phrase, writes:

> The meaning, then, is not that God breathed into the writer, nor that he somehow breathed into writings to give them their special character, but that what was written by men was breathed out by God. He spoke through them. They were his spokesmen. (Stott, 1972, p. 183).

Activity 4:6

Consider this question: How far is it correct to talk about 'a battle of the books'? This phrase is used by Bishop Jens Christenson in his lectures on *The Practical Approach to Muslims*. He says:

> There is a sense in which Christianity's contact with Islam is definitely a battle of the books, yet in the final analysis it is utterly wrong to speak of a battle of books as though the New Testament in Christianity had the same position as the Qur'an in Islam (p. 316).

Look back over the last two sections to make sure you are clear about this.

Books referred to in the chapter

Chapman, Colin, *You Go and Do the Same* (CMS/BMMF/IFES: London, 1983), pp. 31–32.

Christensen, Jens, *The Practical Approach to Muslims* (AWM: Marseilles, 1977), p. 316.

Cooper, Anne (comp), *In the Family of Abraham* (People International: Tunbridge Wells, 1989).

Neill, Stephen, *Crises of Belief* (Hodder & Stoughton: London, 1984), p. 69.

Stott, John R.W., *Understandig the Bible* (Scripture Union: London, 1972), p. 183.

Watt, W. Montgomery, *Mohammed and Mecca* (Oxford University Press: Oxford, 1953).

For further reading

Al-Azuzy, Muhammad, *Topical Concordance to Qur'an* (BCV Press: Lilydale, Australia, 2nd edn trs. Aubrey Whitehouse).

Ali, Abdullah Yusuf, *The Holy Qur'an: Text, Translation and Commentary* (Islamic Foundation: Leicester, 1975).

Gilchrist, John, *Jam'al-Qur'an: the Codification of the Qur'an Text* (Jesus to the Muslims: Benoni, S. Africa, 1989).

Parshall, Phil, *The Cross and the Crescent* (1989: 1st British edn, Scripture Press: Amersham, 1990).

Sell, Edward, *The Historical Development of the Qur'an* (1st pub. 1893) (People International: Tunbridge Wells, 1990).

Shorrosh, Anis A., *Islam Revealed: A Christian Arab's View of Islam* (Nelson: Nashville, Tennessee, 1988).

Tisdall, W. St. Clair, *The Sources of Islam* (rev edn, T & T Clark: Edinburgh).

5

Prophethood: Muhammad Prophet of Islam

Study guide

There are two key elements in Islam. The Qur'an (as we saw in the last chapter) and the life of the prophet Muhammad. There would be no Qur'an without the prophet Muhammad. It is his life which opens the Qur'an and his death which brings the revelations to an end. His life is also a key to the beliefs and practices, for the Sunna and Hadith are based on his example. This chapter asks the questions: what sort of person was Muhammad, how do Muslims view him, and what should our Christian attitude to him be?

When you have completed this chapter we hope you will:

1 *Have looked briefly at the life and times of Muhammad;*
2 *Understand something of his role in Islam and the attitudes of Muslims towards him; and*
3 *Have begun to think about possible Christian attitudes to Muhammad as prophet and as a leader.*

1

Who was this man?

Who was this man whose name is linked with that of God in the saying of the Muslim Creed—THERE IS NO GOD BUT GOD AND MUHAMMAD THE APOSTLE OF GOD—and also in Surah 3:132, 'Obey God and the Apostle'? (Sometimes *rasul*, apostle, is also translated 'messenger' for the Arabic word means 'the sent one'.) Some one in five of the world's population revere and honour him. He is thought by Muslims to be the last and the final prophet. He came from a humble and deprived background, but became a strong and successful leader.

This is how one Muslim describes him: 'In brief, the towering and radiant personality of this man, in the midst of such a benighted and dark environment, may be likened to a beacon-light illuminating a pitch-dark night or a diamond shining in a heap of dead stones' (Mawdudi, 1991, p. 46). 'His is the only example where all the excellencies have been blended into one personality' (p. 54). Muslims have a very high view of Muhammad. Suzanne Haneef writes:

> And while Muhammad (peace be on him) was an individual of im-mense spirituality and nearness to God, at the same time he also lived an extremely full, active and complete life, exemplifying many varied and complex roles. He was a devoted husband, father and grand-father, a kind and responsible kinsman, a faithful, affectionate friend, a leader alike in worship and battle, a ruler and statesman par excel-lence. For the Muslims of his time as well as for the Muslims of today and tomorrow, he was and is and will always be the model: the tea-cher, the guide, the leader, and above all the conveyor of the Divine guidance, the connecting link with God, and the person whom they love, revere and emulate above all other men. (Haneef, 1979, p. 25)

They hold him to be *al Insan al Kamil*, the perfect man.

Activity 5:1

Discover the other names given to Muhammad in the Qur'an. The name Muhammad is rarely mentioned there. He is usually referred to as a prophet, (*nabi*, in Arabic) but the most common name given to him in the Qur'an is apostle or messenger (*rasul*, in Arabic).

1	3:144	Muhammad is no more than an Apostle: many were the Apostles that passed away before him.
2	33:2–3	O Prophet! Fear GOD, and hearken not to the Unbelievers and the Hypocrites; verily God is full of knowledge and wisdom But follow that which comes to these by inspiration from thy Lord. . . .

(Continued over)

(Continued)

3	33:40	Muhammad is not the father of any of your men, but the Apostle of God, and the Seal of the Prophets . . .
4	74:2	O thou wrapped up [in a mantle] Arise and deliver thy warning!

He is described as a *nadhir*, or warner, and a *monvir*, or announcer.

Notes: After his name may be written:
   Muhammad (peace be upon him) or Muhammad PBUH
   Muhammad '*allah irrahummuh*' or Muhammad RA
The meaning of his name: The name Muhammad comes from the Arabic word of three letters, H M D, *Hamada*, 'to praise'.

2

The life and times of Muhammad

As Colin Chapman points out in Chapter 5 of *You Go and Do the Same*, it is important to understand something of the background from which Muhammad came. In Arabia before his birth, a number of different factors influenced the life of the area.

Geographical
See the map opposite.
   The Arabian peninsula is 1,000,000 square miles in area. Note especially the coastal area, Hijaz; Mecca, the city of his birth, and Medina, 150 miles to the north. (Originally 'the city of the prophet', *al Medina Al Nabi*, shortened later to Medina.)

Political
The Arabian peninsula was not one unit, but was peopled by a number of separate tribes, some nomadic or semi-nomadic,

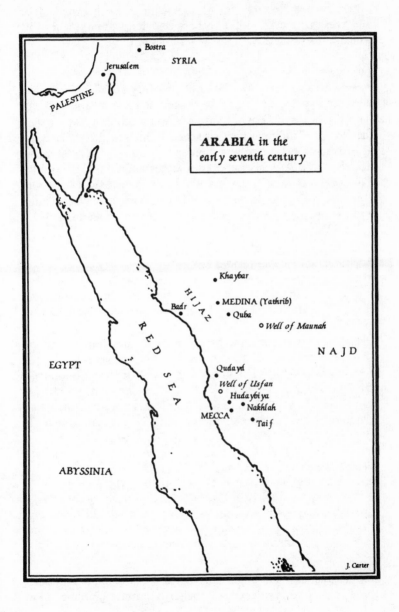

ARABIA in the
early seventh century

others settled in small towns. Some of the tribes had made alliances with each other, others had long-standing hostility which led to recurring revenge and blood feuds.

Foreign powers

Arabia was affected by the contemporary struggle for power between two great powers: the Byzantine Empire, composed of Asia Minor, Syria, Egypt, Abyssinia and south-east Europe, and the Persian Empire, which stretched from Iraq to Afghanistan. The Byzantine Empire was 'fiercely "Orthodox" (Christian) in doctrine, and strongly opposed to other "heretical" doctrines.' The political and religious struggles had exhausted both empires, their people and resources, leaving a power vacuum and the people ready to accept new rulers (cf. Chapman, 1983, p. 22–24).

Economic and social factors

Mecca was an important trading centre for the caravans that traded along the trade routes in the area. Visiting pilgrims who came yearly during the sacred months to attend ceremonies also brought financial gain to the city.

The focus of life was the family, the extended family, and the clan. It was not on the individual but the group. Family members strove in their behaviour always to bring honour to the family name and to be loyal. The people were known for their generosity and hospitality. Also it was not time which had a high priority, but people. The bedouin life was considered the ideal rather than life in the city. Children were often sent to spend a few of their early years in the desert. Yet life was not free of some social evils, such as the exploitation of women and the practice of the burial of female children (infanticide).

The Arabic language was also an integral part of the people. Poets and storytellers gave hours of pleasure, and a rich tradition exists in this art.

Religious factors

Mecca was also an important centre for worship. 'Although there is some evidence of belief in one supreme God

(Allah)', there were many lesser deities; including three goddesses Al Lat, Al Uzza and Al Manat. There were other idol cults and sacrifices and many shrines, for example the major shrine, The Ka'ba, that the pilgrims visited annually. Many had a strong belief that fate controlled their present life situation, but had very little belief in an after-life (cf. Chapman, 1983, p. 24).

Other religions There were some Jewish communities in the area; also a people called the Hanif, who were monotheistic in worship. Some of the nomadic tribes, particularly in the Yemen, had become Christian as early as the fourth century. There were also Syrian monks, living hermit-like existences in desert areas. Most of the Christians, however, were expatriates, such as the dark-skinned Ethiopians.

Colin Chapman further points out three important points about the Christianity which Muhammad saw.

It was basically a foreign religion. (Practised by foreigners not integrated into the Arab community, in a foreign language; and the Bible was not in Arabic.)

The Christian church at that time was deeply divided over doctrinal disputes about the person of Christ and the Trinity.

Christianity was associated with the political power and colonial expansionism of the Byzantine Emperors (Chapman, ibid).

LIFE OF MUHAMMAD
Dates to Remember

IN MECCA

Birth	12 Rabi'ul Awwal, AD 570
Marriage	AD 595
First Visions, Revelation	AD 610
'Little Hijra'	AD 615
Sorrows—death of wife, uncle, Al Mir'aj . . . the ascent	AD 619

IN MEDINA

HIJRA (Emigration)	AD 622 / Year 1 AH
Battles: 'Badr	AD 624
uhud	AD 625
khandaq-ahzab, 'Ditches'	AD 625
Treaty of Hudiabyah	AD 628
Conquest of Mecca	AD 629
Death	12 Rabi'ul Awwal, AD 632

FAMILY TREE:

Quraysh Tribe, in the fifth and sixth century.

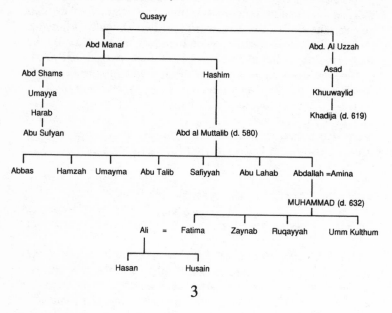

3

Birth and early years

Muhammad's father died before he was born. His name was Abdullah son of Abd al Muttalib, and he was a member of the Hashim clan of the powerful Quraysh tribe. Muhammad's mother, Amina, also died young, when he was six years old. Muslims often stress the fact that he was an orphan and that he raised himself up from nothing, by his own efforts. After his mother died, Muhammad went to live with his grandfather and a strong bond of love developed between grandfather and grandson. His grandfather was the guardian of the Ka'ba, the cube-like building which was an important shrine of idolatry in Mecca. Sadly, two years later the grandfather died. From then onwards Muhammad lived in the house of his uncle, Abu Talib, and was looked after by him. Abu Talib belonged to the poorer branch of the family. Muhammad became accustomed to living very simply and as soon as he was old enough he began to work for his living. This would account for the Muslim belief that he did not receive any education. He did, however, receive training in weapons of war, which was to stand him in good stead in later years.

According to traditions, he had travelled to Syria on trips with his uncle. It is said that he met Bahira, a Syrian Christian monk, who noticed that he had the mark of someone special. When Muhammad grew into manhood, he became a trader. There was insufficient money for him to develop his own trade, nor was it possible to arrange a marriage for him. He went to work for a rich widow, called Khadijah, and she came to trust and to rely on him. Although she was a number of years older than he was, Muhammad married her when he was twenty-five years old. The marriage was a happy one. They had six children; two boys who did not live to reach adulthood, and four girls. The youngest girl, Fatima, later married Ali, who became the fourth Caliph. Muhammad was very fond of her and she became his close companion in later years. During the twenty-five years Muhammad was married to Khadijah, he took no other wife.

<h1 style="text-align:center">4</h1>

Call to prophethood

It was while he was married to Khadijah, at the age of forty, that Muhammad received his first revelation and message from God. It is said that he was greatly disturbed by it, not knowing whether it was from God or from the devil. The revelation took place in a cave in Mount Hira, and the message was that recorded in Surah 96. ('Recite in the name of thy Lord . . .' see Chapter 4, pp 77–78). Muhammad did not receive another message until some time had elapsed, but after this they were sent down regularly. He began to realise that they were transmitted through the angel Gabriel. As the messages were received by Muhammad he recited them to his growing number of followers. As we have seen in Chapter 4, they were not written down until a number of years later.

It seems clear that Muhammad was already established as an upright, responsible person, able to give others advice and support, before his life was changed by the revelation of God calling him to be his messenger. Gradually those closest to him began to believe in his prophetic role and his messages. First Khadijah, then his cousins Ali and Zaid, followed by his great friend Abu Bakr, became the first Muslims. As the group grew larger, they began to experience opposition from disbelieving members of the Quraysh. Some of the followers migrated to Abyssinia. The enemies asked his uncle to prohibit him from reviling their gods and preaching that there was only one god Allah and that idols were not gods. There was a boycott of the Hashim clan.

5

The Hijra (Emigration)

This period of growth continued. Muhammad and his band of fellow-believers sought to obey the instructions in the messages he received. Eventually, in AD 622 the rejection of Muhammad and his message by the leaders of the Quraysh led him to look for some other place where the new religion could be established. The people of Yathrib had expressed interest and openness to Muhammad and his followers, so they secretly left Mecca and established themselves in Yathrib, renamed Medina. This move was of great significance in the development of Islam. Muslims use the date of the migration, the Hijra, as the start of the Muslim era, putting the letters A H after the numbers in expressing their dates.

Those who welcomed Muhammad and his followers in Medina entered into a covenant to protect them; they also became believers. The Qur'an speaks of the affection that God produced in their hearts for one another (8:63). They are known as *ansar* (helpers) to distinguish them from the *muhajirun* (migrants) who came from Mecca.

6

Establishing life in Medina

The people were united into one single community, a brotherhood, called the Umma. The unity was no longer based on tribe, clan or blood relationships but on their status as believers, united by faith in the one God and Muhammad his apostle. The highest loyalty is to the Umma and not the clan. The Umma was to show solidarity against crime and unbelievers. The Quraysh were unbelievers and enemies, though clans did remain responsible for blood money and ransom of their members. Muhammad's own role changed from being primarily a preacher to a leader or statesman of Medina. He was a leader of the religious affairs as the forms and practices of the believers were established, and a leader of political affairs as rules of life, marriage, inheritance, commerce, war and foreign relations were fixed. Muhammad continued to receive revelations which guided him in forming this new way of life.

Jewish tribes also had a certain amount of power and importance in Medina. They too were bound by the treaty agreement to certain obligations as allies with the others in Medina. Some of the practices of Islam were in accord with Jewish practices: praying facing Jerusalem, the fast of Ashura like the Jewish Day of Atonement, and Muhammad's role as a prophet was expressed as being in the line of the Jewish prophets who had gone before, such as Moses. But he was met with hostilities from the Jews.

7

Battles

During these early years of establishing Islam, hostility from the Meccans continued. The course of events was changed by three important battles.

The Battle of Badr. A large caravan from Mecca was moving towards Medina and threatening the city. Although smaller in number, the Muslims attacked and defeated the Meccans. This gave the Muslims much confidence not only in their own military ability, but also in the belief that God was on their side (8:17, 42).

The Battle of Uhud. The Meccans, looking for revenge for their defeat at Badr, attacked the Muslims. At first it looked as if the unbelievers would suffer another defeat. The Muslims proved to be over confident, however; when they thought that the battle was almost over and the rejoicing had begun, the Meccans counter-attacked. They found the Muslims in disarray and inflicted a heavy defeat on them, resulting in heavy Muslim losses. The Muslims were further weakened when, at the height of the counter-attack, a rumour went around that Muhammad had been killed. In fact, he and his followers had escaped to a nearby hill.

The Battle of Ahzab. The Meccans formed an alliance with some of the powerful Jewish tribes of the area. They marched together towards Medina, but were foiled by a large trench which the Muslims had built to protect their city. This battle is often known as the 'Battle of the Ditches'. Eventually, after a good deal of intrigue, the Muslims were able to put their opponents' army to rout. This also brought to a climax the hostilities with the Jewish tribes, and many were slaughtered or expelled from Medina.

8

Return to Mecca

A year later, a treaty was made with the Meccans. Muhammad decided that the time had come for the Muslims to return to worship in Mecca. When they reached the city, the leader of the Quraysh submitted to Muhammad and they entered peacefully. Most of the people of Mecca submitted to God and Muhammad, becoming Muslims. The idols were destroyed and the Ka'ba was cleansed. Then everyone was called to prayer. Muhammad soon returned to Medina where he continued to live. He went on establishing the beliefs and practices of Islam.

At the same time, the Muslims continued to gain supremacy over the remaining non-Muslim tribes, until Muhammad was virtually ruler of the whole of the Arabian peninsula. He visited Mecca again before he died.

9

The crucial question

Now we need to come back to the original question we posed at the opening of this chapter: Who was this man?

Muslims firmly believe in his prophethood, and acclaim it repeatedly as they proclaim 'There is no god but God and Muhammad is the Apostle of God' several times a day. Muhammad is honoured and respected as the 'Seal of the Prophets' (33:40). His name is not spoken or written without the words 'peace be upon him' being added. He had taken the role of husband, father, preacher of belief in One God, warner of judgment, chief, warrior, statesman of the new community and friend. He had displayed the 'stamp of the greatest', and 'excellent standard of character' (68:4). Sometimes the term *insan al kamil* (the perfect man) is used of him. For the believers his life became a beautiful pattern of conduct, the *Sunna* (33:21) along with his sayings and actions, the Hadith Traditions. These were later collected and written in books (see Chapter 7, pp 130–131).

However, after his death many miraculous signs and events were attributed to Muhammad and the cult of his veneration grew. Poems were written about him, and devotional literature giving him titles like the names of God, but without the definite article which is used for those names when referring to God: for example The Truth (God), truth, (Muhammad); similarly The Righteous . . . righteous. Another title of significance is that which calls Muhammad a light, or the lamp. This is from the reference to light in Sura 24:35, 33:45–47. Muhammad is also an intercessor (20:109, 34:23, 43, 86) able to help the believers (Yusuf Ali in his notes gives this role to Muhammad).

How can Christians respond? Kenneth Cragg, in *Muhammad and the Christian*, sets out to clarify whether Christians are right in refusing to give Muhammad the same respect as they give to Jesus. On the question of Quranic WAHY, he looks at Sura 96: 'Recite . . . Recite: and thy Lord is the Most Generous.' (96:2). He comments:

> WAHY here is a commanding awareness of the reality of God, made vocal in language of which God himself is the source— language to be spoken, commandingly, to the world. Nothing is here for private congratulation. All is for urgent public witness. The words are not for perusal but for utterance. (Cragg, 1985, p. 89).

The content and argument of Cragg's book is complex and

detailed. We cannot attempt to summarize it here. It is included in the book list at the end of this chapter.

In his concluding chapter Cragg writes:

> Hopefully we are now ready for the question, after careful review of all aspects of Muhammad's Islamic actuality in Quranic WAHY, in Hijra and Statehood, in tradition and devotion, in ethical and spiritual definition of Muslim society and culture. Christian response to the main theme of his prophethood has surely to be a positive acknowledgement of its significance . . . But that lively sense of its relevance is left taking strenuous issue with the guiding principles of action by which the message was reinforced. (pp 141–142)

Bell tries 'to get behind the usual mechanical interpretation' of the receiving of the Qur'an and pictures Muhammad in the throes of composition. He writes:

> In some way, then, Muhammad's claim to inspiration might be understood. It has analogies to the experience which poets refer to as the coming of the muse, or more closely to what religious people describe as the coming of guidance after mediation and waiting upon God. 'Guidance' is in fact one of the Qur'an's favourite words for the message. (Bell and Watt, 1970, pp 22–23).

Dr Nazir-Ali asks the question: 'What were the origins of Muhammad's religious consciousness?' He suggests: his early meditations in a cave in Mount Hira, probably in imitation of Christian hermits, and his disgust at the idolatry of popular religion. He writes: 'He turned, therefore, in meditation to Allah, the supreme but ignored deity of the Arabs. Eventually he became aware of a "presence" and experienced a "revelation".' (Nazir-Ali, 1983, p. 28).

Activity 5:2

It would be helpful to spend some time studying:
  What is a prophet?
  What are the marks of a true prophet?
  What are the dangers of false prophets?

Notes

Muslims claim that Muhammad is described in the Torah and Injil (New Testament) (7;157). Several passages in the Scriptures are said to refer to Muhammad. For example, Deuteronomy 18:14–20, 'The Lord your God will raise up for you a prophet like me from among your brothers. You must listen to him' (v. 15); 'I will raise up for them a prophet like you from among their brothers; I will put my words in his mouth, and he will tell them everything I command him.' (v. 18). Points to consider: 'from among their brothers'—could this be from Ishmael's family? 'Like me (i.e. Moses)'—Muslims compare Moses' law giving and judgment on unbelievers to be like Muhammad's life . . . but read John 1:45 and Acts 3:22–26, 7:27.

A second topic which the reader will find helpful to study is the verses in the Bible which Muslims believe to refer to Muhammad. The Qur'an says Jesus promised to send Ahmad (61:6) and they think that the verses about the promise of the Paraclete prove this. 'The word "Counsellor", in Greek *parakletos*, found in the gospel according to John 14–16 is Arabicised into *Faraqlit*, and Muslims believe that it refers to Muhammad. Much ignorance prevails among Muslims about the meaning and history of the word *faraqlit* (paraclete). The author of the *Hayatu'l-Qulub*, for instance, asserts that it is found in the Psalms. The most commonly accepted opinion is that it denotes Ahmad, 'the most praiseworthy', a derivative from the same root from which Muhammad—'highly praised'— comes. Muslims do not as a rule affirm that the word *Ahmad* itself occurs in the Injil, but *Faraqlit*, with the meaning Ahmad. Check the following: John 14:16, 26, 15:26, 16:7; and the Qur'an 61:6. For further study see *In the Family of Abraham*, compiled by Anne Cooper, pages 41–43.

Books referred to in the chapter

Bell, Richard and W. Montgomery Watt, *Introduction to the Qur'an* (Edinburgh University Press: Edinburgh, 1970), pp. 22–23.

Chapman, Colin, *You Go and Do the Same* (CMS/BMMF/IFES: London, 1983), pp. 22–25.

Cragg, Kenneth, *Muhammad and the Christian* (Darton, Longman & Todd: London, 1984), pp. 89, 140–141.

Haneef, Suzanne, *What Everybody Should Know About Islam and Muslims* (Kazi Publications: Lahore, 1979), p. 25.

Maududi, Sayyid Abdul A'la, *Towards Understanding Islam* (Islamic Foundation: Leicester, 1980), pp. 46, 54.

Nazir-Ali, Michael, *Islam: A Christian Perspective* (Paternoster: Exeter, 1983), p. 28.

For further reading

Cooper, Anne (comp), *In the Family of Abraham* (People International: Tunbridge Wells, 1989).

Cragg, Kenneth, *Muhammad and the Christian* (Darton, Longman & Todd: London, 1984).

Esposito, John L., *Islam the Straight Path* (Oxford University Press: Oxford, 1988) [rev edn 1991].

Lings, Martin, *Muhammad* (Islamic Texts Society/Allen & Unwin: London, 1983) [2nd rev edn ITS: Cambridge, 1992].

Maududi, Sayyid Abdul A'la, *Towards Understanding Islam* (Islamic Foundation: Leicester, 1980).

Ruthven, Malise, *Islam in the World* (Pelican: Harmondsworth, rev edn 1991).

Watt, W. Montgomery, *Muhammad, Prophet and Statesman*, (Oxford University Press: Oxford, 1961) [new edn 1974].

6

The Practices of Islam

Study guide

*'Behold two (guardian angels) appointed to learn (his doings).
Learn (and note them). One sitting on the right and one on the
left. Not a word does he utter but there is a sentinel by him, ready
(to note it)' (50:17, 18). 'Orthopraxy' is an essential part of
Islam. In Chapter 4 we spoke of Islam as having two major
components:* Iman, *beliefs and* Din, *duties. Chapter 4 dealt
with belief, particularly the belief in One God. This chapter will
consider the other component of Islam,* Din—*duties. These
duties/obligations form the foundation and structure of the
Islamic way of life, giving form to daily life and the yearly
pattern of rituals. The reader will find it helpful to spend some
time thinking about a Christian perspective on faith and works.
What are the Christian duties? How are we expected to live?
Is there a pattern of life? Are there rituals? How does my life
differ from that of a non-Christian? How does it reveal that I
am a Christian?*

When you have completed this chapter we hope you will:

1 Have a working knowledge of the Muslim practices; and
*2 Understand what they mean in the lives of practising
Muslims.*

Introduction

The duties of Islam (often referred to as Five Pillars) are:

1 The Declaration of Faith—*(Shahada)*
2 Five Compulsory daily Prayers (*Salat*)

3 Welfare Contributions/Alms-giving (*Zakat*)
4 Fasting during Ramadan (*Sawm*)
5 Pilgrimage (*Hajj*)

In addition some Muslims accept Holy War (Jihad) as a sixth obligatory duty.

Declaration of Faith (Shahada)

The *Shahada*, the declaration or witness to the faith of Islam is two sentences:

> There is no god but God (*La ilah illa llah*)
> and Muhammad is God's messenger (*Wa Muhammad rasul u'llah*).

These two sentences are not in the Qur'an in the form given above, but there is a clear command to believe in God and the Messenger (Surah 2:255, 33:35, 48:29, 64:8).

These are the first words said in the right ear of the baby and then the left at birth, the last words on the lips of the dying and whispered in their ears. The *shahada* is also part of the daily prayer words. A convert to Islam would be required to repeat this loudly, correctly and in sincere belief.

Five Compulsory Prayers (Salat)

> And establish regular prayers at the two ends of the day and at the approaches of the night: for those things that are good remove those that are evil: Be that the word of remembrance to those who remember [their Lord]. (11:114)

These prayers are acts of worship. They are not left up to man to decide, but the ritual is defined, the time, the place, the form, the physical action and the words. There is another Arabic word (*du'a*) to refer to private prayer, the informal prayers of request from the individual. Specific prayers are also prescribed for Fridays, the day of gathering at the mosque, for funerals, for the festivals (*Eid*), or special occasions such as the time of eclipse or for rain.

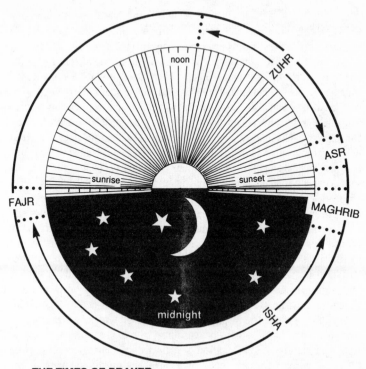

THE TIMES OF PRAYER

The Prayers or acts of worship are in Arabic. Thus those Muslims from other language groups need to learn some Arabic to practise their faith.

The time of prayer

The times are regulated by the position of the sun.

1 Dawn: *Fajr*
2 Just after midday: *Dhuhr/Zuhr*
3 Late afternoon: *Asr*
4 Immediately after sunset: *Maghrib*
5 After sunset, and before midnight: *Isha*

(See Illustration).

The place of prayer

Prayers can be said at home, in public, or in the mosque. In Muslim countries many people pray in the public street or wherever they are when the time of prayer comes. Generally, for women, home will be the place. The place must be considered physically and ceremonial clean, and not an unclean place such as a lavatory. For this reason in factories, shops, schools and office buildings a special room will be provided, kept clean and ready for prayer. A clean sheepskin or specially designed prayer mat will be placed on the floor. The correct direction is also important; it must be towards the '*qibla*', facing Mecca (2:143–145). Prayers said at the Mosque are led by the imam (a religious leader). On Fridays, the believers gather to pray together (62:9–10). There are few other regulations for prayer. Cleanliness is required, not only of the place but of the person. Prayer is always preceded by washing, and this must be done correctly. When water is not available it can be done with sand. It is expected that the Muslim will also be wearing clean clothes, not soiled or ritually unclean. Women are not to pray when they are ritually unclean; for example during menstruation, or just after the birth of a child. (The chart shows the prescribed manner of washing). Secondly, prayer is in a fixed pattern of standing, bowing, kneeling, prostration and sitting. This is called a round of action or a *raka*. The different prayer times consist of a different number of *rakas*, for example at morning prayer two *rakas*, at evening prayer four.

Call to prayer

This was introduced in Medina. Bilal, a freed slave, was the first caller or *Mu'addin (Mu'azzin)* who called the people to prayer.

The Call to Prayer

God is the greatest (*4 times*)	*Allahu akbar*
I testify there is no other god but God (*twice*)	*Ashadu an la ilaha illa llah*
I testify that Muhammad is God's Messenger (*twice*)	*Ashadu anna Muhammada rasul ullah*
Come to prayer (*twice*)	*Haya 'alas salat*
Come to success (*twice*)	*Haya 'alal falah*
God is the greatest (*twice*)	*Allahu akbar*
There is no god but God (*once*)	*La ilaha illa llah*

WASHING BEFORE PRAYER

1, 2, 3

4, 5 and 6

7

8

9

10

10

POSITIONS FOR PRAYER

At the dawn prayer, one other line is added: 'Prayer is better than sleep.' (*As salat khair min in nawm.*)

Prayer

1. Standing, facing Mecca.
   Say the Intention (*Niyya*):

'I intend to say 2/3/4 *rakas* of a *salat* at { dawn / midday / afternoon / maghrib / isha } for God facing Mecca.'

2. Hands up to your ears (men) or shoulders (women)

Allahu Akbar	God is Great

(hands on chest or just below navel).

FATIHA (Sura 1).

Bismillah ir- rahman ir-rahim	In the name of God, the Most Gracious, Most Merciful
Al hamdu lil lahi rabb il'alamin	Praise be to God Cherisher and Sustainer of the Worlds: Most Gracious.
Arrahman ir rahim	Most Gracious, Most Merciful
Maliki Yawmiddin	Master of the Day of judgement,
Iyyaka na'budu wa iyyaka nasta'in	of thee do we worship and thine aid we seek,
Ihdinas siratal mustaqim	Show us the straight way,
Siratal ladhina an 'amta 'alaihim	The way of those on whom thou hast bestowed thy Grace,
ghair il maghdubi 'alaihim wa lad	those whose (portion) is not wrath
dallin [Amin]	and who go not astray.

Sura 112.

Bismillah ir rahman ir rahim	In the name of God most Gracious, most Merciful
Qul hu wa llahu ahad	Say: He is God, the one and only.

Allahus samad	God, the Eternal, Absolute:
Lam yalid wa lam yulad	he beggeth not nor is he begotten
wa lam ya kul lahu kufuwan ahad.	And there is none like unto him.

3. Now bow, saying

Allahu Akbar	God is Great
Subhana rabbiyal Adim [Azim]	Glory to my mighty Lord (*3 times*)

4. Stand:

Sami Allahu liman Hamidah	God hears those who praise him.
Rabbana lak al hamd	Our Lord praise be to you.

5. Prostrate SAJDAH

Allahu Akbar	God is Great.
Subhana Rabbiyal A'la	Praise, (Glory) bè to the Lord in the highest (*3 times*)

6. Rise to sitting position

Allahu akbar	God is Great

7. Prostrate, second time SAJDAH

Allahu akbar	God is Great
Subhana Rabbuyal A'la	Praise (Glory) be to the Lord in the highest (*3 times*)

8. Rise, stand

Allahu Akbar	God is Great

(begins another round (*raka*), silently recites the Fatiha or another short sura.)

9. Bows, hands on knees

Allahu Akbar	God is Great
Subhana Rabbiyal Adim	Praise, (Glory) to the Lord almighty (*3 times*)

10. Stands

Sami Allahu liman hamidah	God hears those who praise him
Rabbana lak la hamd	Lord to you belongs praise

11. Prostrate

Allahu akbar	God is Great
Subhana Rabbiyal a'la	Praise (Glory) to God in the highest (*3 times*)

12. Sit	
Allahu akbar	God is Great
13. Prostrate	
Subban rabbiyal a'la	Praise (Glory) to God in the highest (*3 times*)
14. Sit	
Ata tahiyyatu lillahi	All prayer is for God
Was salawatu wat tayyibatu	and worship and goodness
As salamu 'Alika Ayyuha nnabiyya	Peace be on you O Prophet
Wa rahmatullahi wa barakatuhu	and the mercy of God and his blessing
assalam 'alana	Peace be upon us
wa 'ala 'ibadillahis salihin	and on the righteous servants of God
Ash hadu an lailaha illal Lahu	I bear witness that there is no god but God
wa Ash hadu anna Muhammadan	and bear witness that Muhammad is his
'Abduhu wa Rasuluhu	Servant and Messenger.

(Then further blessings for the prophet).

NOW—*Du'a* (supplication) prayers can be said, for forgiveness or for peace.

15. *Assalamu 'alikum wa rahimatullah* on the right, and on the left.	Peace and Mercy of God be on you.

Rise.

Welfare Contributions

Zakat is the third pillar of Islam. It is not almsgiving or charity, because it is a compulsory payment. On the other hand it is not a general tax, because it is to be spent under fixed headings. Muhammad emphasised *zakat* as a religious duty. He was an orphan himself, and so was concerned for the destitute, poor and needy. The money may also be used for travellers, people wounded in a Holy War (Jihad) or their families, and used to build hospitals.

The Qur'an says, 'Those who believe, and do deeds of righteousness, and establish regular prayers and regular charity, (Zakat) will have their reward with the Lord' (2:177). The amount is fixed at a rate of 2.5% on savings, cash gold, silver, and various ratios for animals and produce. For example,

Cows	1 cow for every 30 cows	
Sheep or goats.		
	1 sheep for every 20 sheep	
	2 sheep for every 120 sheep	
	3 sheep for every 300 sheep	
Camels		
	5–24	1 sheep or goat for each 5 camels
	25–35	1, 1 yr old she-camel
	36–45	1, 2 yr old she-camel
	46–60	1, 3 yr old she-camel.

After Ramadan, at the feast of the breaking of the fast *Eid ul Fitr* there is *Zakat ul Fitr*. This is often given to the poor, and would enable them to buy food for the family and clothes for the children to celebrate the *Eid*. The Qur'an also mentions a voluntary type of giving which is called *sadaqa* (charity).

Fasting during Ramadan (sawm)

O ye who believe! Fasting is prescribed to you as it was prescribed to Those before you, that ye may (learn) self-restraint. (2:183)

(Fasting) for a fixed number of days:
But if any of you is ill or on a journey,
(should be made up) from days later.
For those who can do it (with hardship),
is a ransom, the feeding of one
That is indigent . . .
And it is better for you that ye fast,
If ye only knew. (2:184)

Ramadhan is the (month) in which was sent down
The Qur'an, as a guide to mankind, also clear (signs) . . .

God intends every facility for you; he does not want
To put you to difficulties (he wants you to complete
The prescribed period and to glorify him). (2:185)

And eat and drink, until the white thread
Of dawn appears to you distinct from its black thread;
Then complete your fast till the night appears:
But do not associate with your wives
While ye are in retreat . . . (2:187).

The prescribed month is Ramadan, the ninth month in the Islamic calendar. Ramadan moves slowly around our calendar, beginning eleven days earlier each year and needing about 33 years to complete the cycle according to the lunar calculated months. Previously, it would begin as soon as the crescent of the new moon, announcing the ninth month, was seen by the human eye, and would continue for 29 to 30 days, until the appearance of the next crescent. Today calculations are made in advance and calendars printed. These calendars give the months and the prayer hours with the approximate sun positions estimated and according to geographical locations. The Muslim will then know when to pray or fast in London, or Mecca.

LONDON		MONTH OF RAMADAN				
Dates:	Dawn	Sunrise	Midday	Afternoon	Sunset	Evening
1–3	2:56	4:48	1:04	5:19	9:13	10:18
4–6	2:51					

Manner of fasting

The fast is from sunrise to sunset, or as the Qur'an says: eat and drink until the white thread of dawn appears to you distinct from its black thread (2:187). All adults are to fast from food and drink (this also means not swallowing saliva; no chewing gum, no medications) and from conjugal relations, and women are not to use make-up and perfume.

Muslims begin to fast as they reach the age of puberty. Children after the age of nine and ten begin to fast for a few days, a week, two weeks; by full puberty they are fasting as their parents do. Travellers and sick persons as well as menstruating women can defer fasting (*sawm*) during Ramadan and make up for it later. Young children and old people, insane persons, pregnant and nursing mothers, people with diabetes or those for whom medication is essential are exempted from observing *sawm*.

Ramadan is a busy month for the women, with all the cooking and the special food. The families often visit and invite guests to meals. But it is a sacred month so the evening will include special prayers and reading the Qur'an. It is the month the Qur'an was first revealed. This special night, called the 'Night of Power' (*Lalats Qadr*) is celebrated at the Mosque (Sura 97). Many keep the night of the 27th as that night, but others think it was the 23rd or 25th of the month. Muslims will gather to read through the whole Qur'an during this special evening. The feast of Breaking the Fast, *Eid ul Fitr*, is begun the first day of the tenth month, *Shawwal*. Often it is called the 'little feast' to distinguish it from the 'big feast' which is in the 12th month, and includes the sheep sacrifice. The little feast marks the end of the fast, celebrating with lots to eat, giving the *eid zakat* to the poor, family visits and especially dressing the children in new clothes and giving them presents. The town will be decorated too. A festive mood penetrates everywhere for several days; schools and workplaces close.

The purposes and values of fasting

Mawdudi writes:

> Rigour and discipline during this month bring us face to face with the realities of life and help us make our life, during the rest of the year, a life of true subservience to his Will . . . Fasting has an immense impact on society, for all the Muslims irrespective of their status must fast during the same month. This emphasises the essential equality of man and thus goes a long way towards creating in them sentiments of love and brotherhood. (Mawdudi, 1981, p. 91)

Activity 6:1

Ask your Muslim friend about fasting. As you are friends you may be able to ask about his or her personal experience. As you talk, think about what the Bible says about fasting (Is 58, Mt 6:16–18, Lk 5:33–35, Acts 13:2–3).

Pilgrimage (Hajj) to Mecca

Now we come to the fifth pillar, described in Sura 22:26–38

> Behold! We gave the site, to Abraham, of the (Sacred) House,
> (Saying): 'Associate not anything (in worship) with Me:
> And sanctify My House for those who compass it round,
> Or stand up, or bow, or prostrate themselves (therein in prayer).
> And proclaim the Pilgrimage among me: they will come
> To thee on foot and (mounted) on every kind of camel,
> . . . circumambulate the Ancient House
> Appoint rites (of sacrifice).' (Sura 22:26–38)

Muslims believe that the first al-Ka'ba was built by Adam. The Qur'an and traditions say it was rebuilt by Abraham and known as his house. The Ka'ba had become a centre for worship among the Arabs before the time of Muhammad. Muhammad's grandfather had excavated the closed well of Zamzam (the well is said to be the one which appeared to Hagar when she was looking for water to quench Ishmael's thirst, after she had been sent away by Abraham, Gen 21:19) and had become a custodian of the Ka'ba. Inside the building is a large room which had been full of statues of idols. When Muhammad and his followers entered Mecca in AD 630, the pinnacle of Islam's triumph, they destroyed the idols. Muslims all over the world pray in the direction of this building.

'The Black Stone' is a meteorite stone located in the north-eastern corner of the Ka'ba. It is believed to have been white at the time of Adam, but man's iniquities are supposed to have given it its present colour.

The manner of the pilgrimage hajj

The Hajj is during the first twelve days of the twelfth month of the year, *Dhu L'Hejja*. The pilgrim must prepare, be purified, washed, cut his or her nails and wear a special white garment and sandals. Women are to be accompanied.

Part One Umra (two ceremonies).

1 Going around the Ka'ba seven times and kissing the Black Stone. This is called *Tawaf*.
2 The second ceremony is *Sa'y*—running seven times between As-Safa and al Marwa (two small hills).

Part Two This begins on the 7th day till the 12th day.

7th day	There is a sermon and prayers at the mosque.
8th day	The pilgrims begin the journey which is from Mecca to 'Arafa, about 12 miles. They stop at Mina at midday then go on to 'Arafa.
9th day	At midday standing in the plain, the pilgrims cry out 'O God, here I am, *Labbika allahumma labbaik, labbaika.*' After sunset, the pilgrims go to another valley between Arafa and Mina to spend the night in vigil.
10th day	They travel back to Mina running, and collect seventy small stones. At Mina there are three pillars. Pilgrims throw stones at 'the steep one', which is called stoning Satan.
	Then there is the Sacrifice and the *Eid ul Adha* begins. All Muslims celebrate this, sacrificing animals simultaneously and sharing the meat with friends and relatives. These are public holidays in Muslim countries.
10–12th days	Pilgrims return to Mecca and go round the Ka'ba again and go on to Mina to spend the remaining days and finish throwing the stones at the pillars. Most will go to Medina and visit the grave of Muhammad.

New name: Hajj

A man who has performed the Hajj will now be known as Hajj, or Hajji; a woman, as Hajja. Omar is now Hajj Omar. Others in the community will grant them more honour and respect than previously. Often the hajj will dye his beard yellow or orange, and may wear a small white skull cap. In North Africa many wear an outer white robe. These marks then become a visible sign of spirituality.

The traditions of Muhammad say that every step taken by the pilgrim in the direction of the Ka'ba blots out a sin; and the person who dies on his pilgrimage is enrolled among the martyrs.

Holy war (jihad)

Jihad does not belong to the five practical pillars of Islam, but is repeatedly emphasised in the Qur'an and the Traditions. This has been interpreted and understood in various ways since the time of Muhammad. It is an Arabic word which means: to struggle to the utmost of one's capacity. It has various interpretations: A 'holy war' and defence of Islam; raiding and conquest during the early spread of Islam; a modern call to propagate Islam; and personal self-discipline.

Jihad has been fought with swords and modern weapons, with speech, and pen and paper, with a call to moral, intellectual and spiritual renewal. Jihad is continually being fought within the believer and, at times, between believers and non-believers. Jihad has many sides. Some writers have played down the war aspect and underlined the ethical and moral aspects instead. Most writers mention the word as propagation of and call to Islam.

Books referred to in the chapter

Maududi, Sayyid Abdul A'la, *Towards Understanding Islam* (Islamic Foundation: Leicester, 1980), p. 91.

For further reading

Esposito, John L., *Islam the Straight Path* (Oxford University Press: Oxford, 1988) [rev edn 1991].
Haneef, Suzanne, *What Everybody Should Know About Islam and Muslims* (Kazi Publications: Lahore, 1979).
Sarwar, Ghulam, *Islam: Beliefs and Teachings* (Muslim Educational Trust: London, 3rd edn 1984).

7
Islamic Law

Study guide

With the rise of Islamic fundamentalism the Shari'a or Islamic law has become of greater importance. Several Islamic states have adopted it as the law of the land and others are in the process of doing so. This chapter follows the development of the law from its source in the Qur'an and the Hadith, through the setting up of the legal structure, to its present-day application in the lives of Muslims. Ron George wrote the original chapter, which has required little revision.

When you have completed the chapter we hope you will:

1 *Know the sources of the law and something of the structures which have been developed;*
2 *Begin to see how the Traditions rule the everyday lives of Muslims; and*
3 *Be able to compare Christian and Islamic views of Divine Law.*

The Muslim ideal

The Almighty God has revealed to the Prophet Muhammad (PBUH) a Divine Law, and a permanent scheme of values. These two are the ideal on which Muslim conduct must be based . . .

Shari'a is etymologically derived from an Arabic root 'the trodden path'. It is the 'path' which leads man into submission. Shari'a is the Divine Law revealed by God to the Prophet Muhammad (PBUH) for the guidance of the Muslim community. It is the detailed code of conduct for Muslims to follow, both in their private and public lives. It is a well organized system of universal law for right conduct. It is this Divine Law which binds all Muslims into a single Umma, even those living beyond the borders of the Muslim nation, this is the Shari'a. It is mainly through this universal law that Islam has been able to evolve a civilization, a complete culture, and a comprehensive world order. (Kataregga, 1980, p. 67).

The Shari'a (Islamic law) is much more than a legal system or a code of practice. It originates from none other than God himself. It is based directly on the commandments concerning religious duties found in the Qur'an, which we studied in the last chapter. In addition, the detailed laws concerning the conduct of day to day living are based on the example of the Prophet Muhammad, as revealed to him and practised by him. The sayings and actions of the Prophet were later recorded in the books of the Hadith (Traditions). As D.G. Hogarth comments,

> Serious or trivial, his daily behaviour has instituted a Canon which millions observe to this day with conscious mimicry. No one regarded by any section of the human race as Perfect Man has been imitated so minutely (quoted by Anderson, 1990, p. 10).

Sources of authority for Islamic law

The Qur'an

As we have seen, the Qur'an is the primary authority; in fact some Muslims believe that it is the only authority. They see the Hadith as the verbal expression of the truths of the Qur'an, perhaps in the way some Christians might see the Communion Service in relation to the truths of the gospel.

The Qur'an is not a book of law; of the 6,219 verses only 600 deal with law. These are in the later Medinan suras. It contains only six offences punishable by law. These punishable offences are called *hadd* crimes. They are: illegal sexual intercourse, a false accusation of lack of chastity, theft, drinking of wine, highway robbery, and apostasy.

The Qur'an does not deal with the problems of the law in detail. There are few definitions of terms or of penalties for breaking the law; for example, usury (*riba*) is prohibited in Sura 2:275, but there is no definition of what *riba* is, nor of the consequences of practising it. The Quranic revelation is not a comprehensive legal code and a number of the pronouncements relate to Muhammad personally. For example, the effect of *qadhf* or slander (Sura 24:4) is concerned with the defamation of women. This law was the result of an incident involving Muhammad's wife, Aisha, who had lost her shells and was found wandering around the camp. A soldier took her to Medina, and she was accused of unchastity. Aisha's innocence was revealed in Sura 24:1. It was in judging this incident that the necessity of having four witnesses to the act and the punishment of 80 lashes for the offender were established. In the case of Muhammad wanting to marry his adopted son's wife Zainab, Sura 33:37 proclaimed that God had allowed this. Following this incident, adoption was prohibited in Islam.

The Hadith

These sayings and actions of the Prophet Muhammad date from the Medinan period of his ministry. They were handed down by word of mouth through his Companions and early followers. They were recorded in the collections of books known as the Hadith, some 200 years after his death. There are six main collections. Muhammad al Bukhari (died AD 870) and Muslim (died AD 874) were the main collectors.

There were hundreds of thousands of sayings which were said to have been handed down. Bukhari and the other collectors sifted these through with the utmost care, rejecting many which could not be authenticated to their satisfaction.

Each hadith consisted of two parts: the *isnad*, which was the chain of people who were supposed to have passed the tradition down from the time of Muhammad to when it was actually written down; and the text itself, the *matn*. The collectors investigated the *isnad* of each tradition, and those found satisfactory were included in the Hadith.

Sir Norman Anderson comments: 'Unfortunately, however, they confined their criticism to scrutinizing the trustworthiness of the names in the *isnad* rather than the plausability of the actual Tradition' (Anderson, 1990, p. 11).

Bukhari arranged some 7,300 of these traditions in 97 'books'. They were arranged according to their subjects.

The Hadith covers both religious practices and details of everyday life. Here are just two subjects, chosen because they are issues in present-day society:

Jihad, which is described by Maulana Muhammad Ali in *A Manual of Hadith* as follows:

> Jihad means *the exerting of one's power in repelling the enemy or in contending with an object of disapprobation*. It carries a twofold significance in Islam, being applied to both the purely missionary activities of a Muslim and his defence of the Faith, when necessary, in a physical sense. (Ali, 1978, p. 252).

Here is one of the traditions which Maulana Muhammad Ali quotes:

> A man came to the Messenger of Allah, and said, 'Guide me to a deed which is equal to jihad.' He said, 'I do not find it.' [Then] he said: 'Is it in thy power that when the one engaged in jihad goes forth, thou shouldst enter thy mosque and stand in prayer and have no rest, and that thou shouldst fast and break it not?' He said, 'Who can do it?' (Bukhari 56:1)

A second example concerns the role and status of women. Guillaume quotes 'The World, all of its property (could mean enjoyable or valuable) and the best property in the World is a virtuous woman' (reported by Abd Allah b. Umar) and: 'A woman may be married for four things: her money, her birth, her beauty, and her religion. Get thou a religious woman (otherwise) may thy hands be rubbed in dirt!' (reported by Abu Huraira) (Guillaume, 1966, p. 124).

C.E. Bosworth writes in the preface to *A Manual of Hadith*:

> . . . For the Muslim believer, Hadith is of supreme importance in his faith, because it gives first-hand guidance, once the chain of transmitters and guarantors of the tradition in question is accepted as authentic, on how the Prophet and the early Muslims acted and felt in the contexts of a multiplicity of situations in everyday life. (p. v)

It soon became apparent that different, sometimes subjective, conclusions could be reached in interpreting certain Traditions, so two other sources of authority came to be accepted.

Ijma

There is a hadith which says that Muhammad claimed that his people would never agree upon error. On the basis of this hadith, the ideas of *ijma* was developed. *Ijma* means 'consensus of opinion' and, therefore, means that if the followers of Muhammad agree upon something, they themselves become a source of law-making. Originally it was the Companions of Muhammad who agreed. Now it is the Islamic teachers, not just any group of Muslims. This is true for the Sunnis. The Shias have a similar system, in the office of the *imam*. Consequently, by agreeing upon a principle or rule they became law-makers themselves.

Qias

Finally, analogical deduction was used (*qias*). If an analogy or parallel could be drawn from a verse in the Qur'an or Hadith, then this was a valid way of applying those traditions to many situations. These sources of law are in order of authority. *Ijma* must be on the basis of the Qur'an and Hadith, *qias* on the basis of the Qur'an, Hadith and *Ijma*.

Schools of law

Muslim jurists seeking to define a Muslim code of law developed different schools of thought. Four of these have survived to the present day and all Sunni Muslims are followers of one or other of these schools. Now the differences between them are quite small, geographic area determining allegiance. In the early formative days, however, there were fierce discussions and disagreements.

The Four Schools

HANIFI	MALIKI	SHAFI	HANBALI
Largest	Second largest	Carried by traders scattered within:	
In India Pakistan Turkey Syria Jordan Iraq Lebanon Afghanistan	In Morocco Algeria Tunisia Egypt West Africa Kuwait	Middle East Lower Egypt East Africa Malasia Indonesia	In Saudi Arabia Qatar

---

Activity 7:1

It might be interesting to ask your Muslim friends about the schools of law, which they adhere to and what the school teaches. Even if they are not Sunnis, they may well have a teacher whom they follow. You could ask about the relevance of the Shari'a in today's world as well.

Historical development

It was only after the Arab conquest of Syria that a distinct Muslim code of law began to emerge. The simple tenets of belief that 'God is one', that 'the Qur'an is the word of God', and that 'Muhammad is the last and ultimate messenger of God' were unable to provide solutions to the problems of governing an empire. By AD900, at least four sources of authority that were to be important in the development of Islamic law had gradually emerged.

As the Arabs broke out of the Arabian peninsula in the seventh century, instruction had to be given as to the treatment of the conquered peoples and their lands and possessions. Umar (634–644) began to adopt certain aspects of Byzantine and Persian law in the form of administrative directives for this purpose. For example, he made use of the *diwan* system from Persia—a register of soldiers and their families which recorded their pensions. Umar expelled all non-Muslims from the Arabian peninsula and decreed that no Muslim could own land outside Arabia. Arabs could own land in Arabia if a tithe and the *zakat* tax were paid. Land was to be left in the hands of the existing population if they accepted Islam. We see that as a result of the new conquests, land law begins to develop during this period.

One example of the application of Islamic law did effect some improvement in the status of women compared with the pre-Islamic customs that were prevalent. Women were allowed to inherit possessions from their deceased husbands, the harshness of divorce was tempered, and polygamy was limited to four wives only. A woman was also to receive her dowry directly instead of it going to her father.

The institution of *idda* was developed. The divorced wife must observe three menstrual cycles after divorce before remarrying. During this time the husband could revoke his divorce, but different schools varied in what must happen to the wife during this *idda* period. The Hanafis say that she must be maintained by the husband. The Shafi School says that she does not have to be maintained.

In the pre-Islamic system the nearest male in the male line took everything after death. The Qur'an reformed this (2:180), making bequests in favour of kinsfolk obligatory. In Sura 4:7–12 a second step is taken where each relative is given a specific share of the deceased's estate. A husband takes half of his wife's; a wife takes one-quarter of her husband's.

As the law began to develop it was divided into five categories:

1 *Wajib*:   compulsory and binding on all Muslims.
2 *Mandub*:   recommended and meritable.
3 *Mubah*:   indifferent and open to choice by the individual.
4 *Makruh*:   disapproved of, hateful, but still permitted.
5 *Haram*:   forbidden acts.

The tendency was to define actions according to these categories, rather than to develop general legal principles by which a judge could officiate.

Qadis

After the first century of Islam, *qadis* or judges were appointed by governors of the Abbasid central government. They took over appointments and acted on the advice of the chief *qadi*. These *qadis* had to fulfil a number of criteria.

1 Have a good character (*adl*).
2 Be a member of the *ulema*, learned in the sacred law of Islam.
3 Be of full sight and facilities, not blind in one eye.
4 Not be a *dhimmi*, that is, a person of another religion, eg Jewish or Christian.
5 Not be a woman.
6 Hold his court in the mosque.

When judging a case, valid witnesses to any transaction in Islamic law had to be present, and written evidence was not acceptable. Two eyewitnesses had to be available for any transaction. But a woman's testimony was only worth half that of a man.

Legal procedures

To initiate a case before a *qadi* the claimant had to go to the *qadi* and take the offender with him. Later on, summonses were introduced. The burden of proof lay with the plaintiff and witnesses were required by the claimant. One hadith states that the plaintiff proves his case by two witnesses, but the defendant clears himself by an oath. Witnesses were not cross-examined. Only their character could be brought into question.

When there was a conflict between a Muslim and non-Muslim, any litigation had to go to the *qadi* and Islamic law was applied. If a Muslim had committed a tort, or civil wrong, against a non-Muslim, he only had to pay half the blood money. If the conflicts were between protected peoples (such as Christians and Jews) of the same community then the dispute had to go to an ecclesiastical court. Alternatively they could ask to go before a *qadi* who would then apply Jewish or Christian law as long as there was no conflict with Islamic policy. If people from different communities had a conflict, then the issue had to come to a *qadi* who applied Islamic law.

In particular, conflicts arose when conversion was involved. If a Jewish husband had a wife who converted to Islam it caused considerable problems, because it is illegal for a Muslim woman to be married to a non-Muslim man. The husband was given three months to convert, or the marriage would be dissolved. In India, many Hindu wives used this technique to escape from marriages.

Within Islam a system of *hiyal* was developed, whereby it was possible to keep the letter of the law while breaking the spirit of it. An example is usury, or receiving interest, which is forbidden in Islam. So a system of double sales was developed. A person would sell something to another for a certain sum, then, after time had elapsed, buy it back for a larger sum, which would correspond to the original price plus interest on it. No interest is charged and the process of buying and selling is perfectly legal.

The Hanafis always accepted such devices, whereas the Shafis originally rejected them but later saw that they were useful and therefore accepted them. The Maliki School rejected *hiyal* since they were interested in the internal intention of the law, and the Hanbalis violently rejected it.

Another example is, in certain cases, the law of pre-emption. This means that a neighbour has first right to buy a piece of land from a seller. However, if a third party offers a higher price for the land, a *hiyal* can be used to go through with the transaction. A minute strip of land is gifted to the new potential purchaser who then becomes the new neighbour. Then the seller can go ahead and sell the rest of the land to this new neighbour.

Law officers

Along with this legal system there were men who were trained in various aspects of the law and who could administrate it. The office of the *qadi* was linked with the shari'a law only, but the government under the khalif was to carry out the execution of that law. The *shurta* acted as police and the *muftis* as legal consultants. In the courts there was the *khatib*, or the court clerk, and *udul* were the notaries.

The modern period

Beginning in the eighteenth century, European countries began to take over Islamic lands. The result of this expansion was that either Islamic law was influenced by European law, or it was set aside in preference of European law.

The power of European countries has diminished during the twentieth century; Islamic countries are experiencing new freedom and new opportunities, due largely to the discovery of oil. This is thought to be God's blessing on Islam and on the faithful followers of the Divine Law. There is a movement back to shari'a law and the setting up of truly Islamic states, although it is probable that the majority of Muslims are not in favour of this. There is also pressure to allow shari'a law for Muslims in non-Islamic countries as well; the setting up of a Muslim Parliament in Britain is an expression of this. Here again, it does not have the support of all Muslims in the country. The rise of Islamic fundamentalism needs more detailed consideration, and is the subject of Chapter 13.

Activity 7:2

We have been well-informed about the reintroduction of flogging and amputation of the hand for certain types of theft and there is no doubt that in countries where Shari'a has become legal, flogging does take place regularly and amputation occasionally. John Bowker asked the Muslims he interviewed their views about punishment. Here is one reply:

> The ideal—the aim—of man behaving is to make the perfect society, or the happy society—which everybody should strive to achieve; so the laws are to encourage the good and get rid of the bad. The punishment is for protection, not for revenge. The idea is to make law and order in society; this is why we use the punishments (p. 129).

As Christians, what sort of society are we aiming for: and do we agree with this way of going about it?

The everyday lives of Muslims

For many ordinary Muslims, particularly women, the Hadith has an enormous influence on the way they live their lives. There are so many detailed traditions which must be kept that from the moment of waking in the morning until going to sleep at night they are following their instructions. This is particularly difficult for Muslims living in non-Muslim countries, where even the five pillars are difficult to perform. I remember discussing prayer with a Muslim friend. She said that she could not pray because she had not been able to work out the direction of Mecca. She believed that God would not accept her prayers if she was facing the wrong way.

Ghulam Sarvar gives a selection from the Hadith in his book *Islam Beliefs and Teachings*. They are divided into four categories: duties and obligations; basic qualities; manners, and bad conduct. In Chapter 2 (p. 42–43) we saw the importance of rules concerning foods. Here as an example of Sarvar's selection, are three hadith about eating and drinking:

> The blessing of food is to wash hands at the beginning and washing after taking it (Mishkat).

> Say Allah's name (Bismillah) and eat with your right hand and eat from near you (Bukhari).

> When one drinks, he should not breathe into the vessel (glass) (Bukhari).

From even a superficial study of a few of the thousands of traditions, it can be seen that they are the foundation on which a whole Islamic culture is built. It is not just a case of 'keeping the letter of the law', it is a way of life. Different ways of performing everyday actions are either *halal* (lawful), or *haram* (unlawful). Meat, for example, must be obtained from a *halal* butcher, one who uses the correct procedure for slaughtering animals. Where Muslims are a minority group, their slaughtering rules may not conform to the laws of the country in which they reside and they may need dispensation. Where there is no *halal* butcher, Muslims may eat Jewish *kosher* meat, which has been prepared in much the same way as *halal* meat. In countries where Muslims reside permanently they have set up factories, where *halal* meat is prepared and marketed.

It is important that we understand the basic differences between Muslim and Christian views of the law. The Muslim writer Seyyed Hossein Nasr, in his book *Ideals and Realities of Islam* believes that 'the lack of understanding of the significance of the Shari'a in the Western world is due to its concrete and all-embracing nature' (p. 94). He points out that 'the Christian view concerning law which governs man socially and politically is indicated in the well-known saying of Christ, "Render therefore unto Caesar the things which are Caesar's"' (p. 94). He believes that this teaching led Christians to adopt the Roman Law 'in order to become the religion of a civilization' (p. 95). This lack of a Divine Law is what, in his opinion, has led to the secular society of today.

As Christians, we want to complete the 'well-known saying of Christ'. It was in answer to the question, 'Is it right to pay taxes to Caesar or not' (Mt 22:17). Jesus knew that this was a trick question. He took a coin and asked:

> 'Whose portrait is this? And whose inscription?' 'Caesar's,' they replied.
> Then he said to them, 'Give to Caesar what is Caesar's, and to God what is God's.' (Mt 22:20–21)

In response to Badru Kateregga's chapter on right conduct in Islam and Christianity, David Shenk responds,

> How do we become righteous?
> Islam recognizes that rules and moral teaching are helpful in many ways. But the question remains, are moral and civil regulations sufficient? (Kateregga and Shenk, 1981, p. 73)

> 'Therefore no-one will be declared righteous in his sight by observing the law; rather, through the law we become conscious of sin. But now a righteousness of God, apart from law, has been made known, to which the Law and the Prophets testify. This righteousness from God comes through faith in Jesus Christ to all who believe.' (Rom 3:20–22)

A concluding thought:

> For Christianity, the appropriate question is, 'What do Christians believe?' In contrast, for Islam (as for Judaism), the correct question is, 'What do Muslims *do*?' (Esposito, 1988, p. 68).

Notes

Did you find discussing the Shari'a with Muslims helpful in clarifying the different views Christians and Muslims have about divine law (Activity 7:1)? What sort of society do we as Christians want? Will punishment of wrong doing lead to it (Activity 7:2)? We are probably clear that we want a society where God is honoured, worshipped and obeyed, where an increasing number of people are following Jesus as Saviour and Lord and where there is justice and freedom. But how is this to be achieved? Consider how each one of us might be more committed to achieving these aims.

Books referred to in the chapter

Ali, Muhammad Maulana, *A Manual of Hadith* (Curzon Press: London, 3rd edn 1978).

Anderson, Norman, *Islam in the Modern World* (IVP Apollos: Leicester, 1990).

Esposito, John L., *Islam: the Straight Path* (Oxford University Press: Oxford, 1988).

Guillaume, Alfred, *The Traditions of Islam* (Khayata: Beirut, 1966).

Kateregga, Badru D., and David W. Shenk, *Islam and Christianity* (Uzima Press/Eerdmans: Kenya/Grand Rapids, Michigan, rev edn 1981).

For further reading

Kateregga, Badru D., and David W. Shenk, *Islam and Christianity* (Uzima Press/Eerdmans: Kenya/Grand Rapids, Michigan, rev edn 1981). Dialogue between a Muslim and a Christian. Chapter 11 deals with Islamic law, but the whole book is very helpful in comparing Christian and Muslim teaching.

Nasr, Seyyed Hossein, *Ideals and Realities of Islam* (Allen & Unwin: London, 2nd edn 1975) [3rd rev edn 1985]. Written by a Muslim, seeking to answer criticisms and present the truth of Islam to Western readers. Chapter 4 deals with Islamic law.

PART III

Cultural, Historical and Political Development

8

Islam as Culture

Study guide

An understanding of culture is becoming more and more necessary as Christians become involved in cross-cultural ministry. In Islam, culture is such an important part of religion that it is well worth coming to grips with it. This chapter, in the middle of the book, is the pivot from which we can look back and gain a greater understanding of Islamic beliefs and practices. It will also help us look ahead to the historical and political accounts with greater understanding. It helps make sense of the social relationships which we looked at in Chapter 2, also of the different expressions of Islam found in Chapters 10 and 11.

When you have completed the chapter we hope you will:

1 Understand how cultural factors influence our behaviour patterns and give us specific worldviews;

2 Begin to see to what degree Islam is linked to a specific culture pattern; and

3 Begin to assess how much of our own behaviour is culturally determined.

A black London taxi pulled up at the station, and a smartly dressed Arab businessman alighted. He quickly paid his fare and hurried into the station. The taxi driver turned to me as the nearest passing Anglo-Saxon, and declared, 'These Muslims ain't got any culture.'

I do not know all that had transpired between the two men. Possibly the taxi driver had not received the tip he thought was due to him. However, the incident illustrated the clash of cultures that has so often occurred between the Christian West and the Muslim East. Both Christianity and Islam have produced great civilisations of which their members are proud, but they have resulted in quite different ways of life. Throughout the history of these religions this has caused misunderstanding, prejudice and even conflict.

The term 'culture' is applied in various ways. At a popular level, it is used to denote a preference for Mozart rather than Madonna, or for the Queen's English rather than local slang. The anthropologist has provided us with a broader and less critical definition of culture. In this usage the word does not mean the cultivation of the arts and social graces. It refers to learned, accumulated experience.

The anthropological concept of culture has been one of the most important and influential ideas in twentieth-century thought. As such there has been a rich variety of definitions following that first given by E. B. Tylor:

> That complex whole which included knowledge, beliefs, arts, morals, laws, custom, and any other capabilities and habits acquired by man as a member of society. (Tylor, 1871)

A definition that has been widely used by Christian missionaries is the one proposed by Paul Hiebert. 'The integrated system of learned behaviour patterns, ideas and products characteristic of a society' (Hiebert, 1976, p. 25).

Culture relates to the ways that people live out their lives in the midst of their families and neighbours. It concerns the ways that people cope with everyday problems and seek meaning to life. As such, Islam must not be seen merely as a set of religious ideas and practices, but as a complete way of life. For a person professing to be a Muslim, Islam provides a total cultural system. As Michael Gilsenan writes:

> Islam is more than a set of laws, rites and beliefs presented as a religious and social totality. As a word it covers a multitude of everyday forms and practices that are interwoven in complex, sometimes almost invisible ways in daily existence. (Gilsenan, 1980, Foreword)

In this chapter we will study the anthropological concept of culture and examine how it applies to our understanding of Muslim societies.

1

Culture is learned

The first aspect of culture to be noted is that culture is learned. Consider the way that children learn to speak. They listen to adults around them and try to imitate the sounds they hear. Gradually, the sounds made by the children become more clearly defined and communication begins. The language spoken does not depend upon genetic structure, but is quickly learned during the first few months of life. Similarly, other aspects of culture are learned, to such a degree that one can say that each child is essentially born cultureless. Quickly the child begins to acquire what are the acceptable ways of the society into which he, or she, has been born.

Before children are old enough to evaluate social practices they begin to learn and behave as society dictates. Children in Britain are scolded by their mother for eating with their fingers, and for not eating 'properly' with a knife and fork. In contrast, children in Arabia are encouraged to eat with their right hands from the communal dish.

The important role of the Shari'a within Islam means that children are given much instruction as to how they should behave. The Prophet Muhammad is presented as a model of good behaviour. A Muslim guide to bringing-up children advises:

> At the time of going to sleep, teach children to try and lie on the right side. The Prophet used to put his right hand under his cheek. Teach them to say *Allahu Akbar*, 34 times, *Subhanallah*, 33 times, and *Alhamduli'llah*, 33 times before sleeping.

> Teach children to be polite to all guests and show them respect; a guest should, if possible, be offered the best food. It is desirable to entertain a guest for a period up to three days; to feed the hungry, poor and traveller is one of the most commendable deeds in Islam. (Swidiqi, 1984)

Individuals are born into families and it is within such social contexts that their culture and social role is acquired. Although one must be careful of generalisations there are some common features throughout the Middle East. Studies of child care in Islamic societies all emphasise the early separation of boys and girls. Sons are frequently favoured at the expense of daughters. The birth of a son is usually met with celebration, while that of a girl is relatively ignored. In many families, a young girl will quickly learn that her brother has first claim to food, clothing, and spending money. (See Chapter 2, section 2, p. 47)

Children learn to behave in public in ways appropriate to their gender. In villages and in working-class homes, girls are given domestic duties and even at the age of six or seven will be charged with the care of a younger brother or sister. In rural homes, adolescent girls serve at the command of younger brothers as they do for their fathers and will later do for their husbands. Boys often accompany their father to market, or have some apprenticeship at a workshop. This will take them away from home, while girls find that they are increasingly restricted to the home as they get older.

This process, called enculturation, continues throughout the life of each human being; so gradually the social patterns become habits. These patterns simply become the accepted way by which things are done—the 'right' way! It is only through contact with people of other societies that humans begin to recognise differences in ways of life. The study of culture therefore always has an aspect of the comparative.

The first reaction, inevitably, on encountering people from another culture is to dismiss their behaviour as strange, exotic or wrong. When a British driver considers driving on the Continent, we loosely remark that 'they drive on the wrong side of the road!' The use of the word 'wrong' rather than 'other' shows our particular perspective. To view other people's way of life in terms of one's own cultural perception is called by anthropoplogists 'ethnocentrism'. This is the inherent assumption that our ways are best, and it is common to all people.

Westerners are frequently surprised to discover that other societies are proud of their own way of life and do not accept the Western' way of life as obviously the best. Arabs perceive themselves as generous, humanitarian, polite and loyal. They are proud of keeping their womenfolk in the seclusion of the home, and shocked at the apparently immoral behaviour of Western women who walk the streets open to the eyes of other men.

Hiebert has written, 'Ethnocentrism is a two-way street. We judge other peoples' customs as crude, and they feel the same about ours' (Hiebert, 1976, p. 38). The solution to ethnocentrism is to try to understand the other culture in terms of its own values and assumptions. The history of anthropology has been one of unearthing various layers of prejudice and ethnocentrism.

2

Culture is behaviour

The second aspect of understanding the nature of culture is that it relates to the total pattern of behaviour. 'Culture' is the way that people behave and relate within society. The word describes how people dress, eat, sleep, bathe, conduct meetings, work, marry and perform the thousands of other activities that are part of daily life. A foreign visitor to a Muslim country often feels the impact of the expressive styles of the people. The air is filled with music, arts and crafts crowd the markets, and men carry out long articulate conversations at the coffee shops. All this is part of the culture of Muslim societies.

This complex pattern of human behaviour can often lead to misunderstandings when members of different societies meet. For example, a simple gesture or action may signal an insult. Once a Christian evangelist, while seated, crossed his legs and pointed the bottom of his shoe towards the Saudi prince. The prince was aware that this was a common way for a Westerner to sit, and had no particular meaning. However, he could not help feeling insulted. In Arab society, to show the base of one's shoe to a person is to say that the person is worth no more than the dirt on your shoes. The evangelist's words may speak of the love of Christ, but his action signals contempt.

British exporters are becoming aware of these cultural factors in their overseas trade encounters. Getting straight down to business may be well received in the West, but in many areas of the Middle East this is found to be crude and distasteful. People prefer pleasant, friendly, casual conversation, which will eventually lead on to business. Gifts may often be exchanged, but when does a gift become a bribe?

In general, Arabs tend to stand and sit closer to other people (of the same sex) than Westerners do. It is not uncommon to see two men or women holding hands as they walk down a street, which is simply a sign of friendship. Kissing on both cheeks is a common form of greeting (again, only with members of the same sex), as is embracing. It is also common to touch someone repeatedly during conversation, often to emphasise a point.

Kinship is an important aspect of any culture. Within many Muslim societies marriages are by arrangement. A preferred match is between the son and daughter of two brothers—'patrilineal parallel cousins' as such a relationship is called by anthropologists. It is frequently said that such marriages are more stable and keep the wealth within the extended family.

To the Westerner, the closeness of the family appears restrictive and overwhelming. To him, individual rights and freedom of action are important. On the other hand, Islam places great emphasis upon the family. The closeness of family ties has been described by one Jordanian family as like a heavy blanket that covers all. Frequently the young people may like to escape from under the blanket, but they know that in times of trouble the family provides a warm and safe refuge.

An important part of behaviour in all Islamic societies relates to religious ritual. I remember travelling through Northern Nigeria one Friday when the noon call to prayer reverberated from the minaret. Within just a few minutes not only the mosque, but the square in front was lined with men at prayer. The car that I had left in the square was surrounded, and I could do no more than wait and reflect at how the whole town had come to a halt for prayer.

Activity 8:1

Pause for a few minutes to look back at Chapter 2. Make a list of the links between the different customs described and their cultural foundations.

3

Culture is a system of ideas

Faced with the bewildering variety of behaviour, the outsider may wonder how members of a society know how to behave and respond. Behind the observable patterns of culture may be identified certain basic assumptions about life experiences. People in a society may not be consciously aware of the assumptions, but they provide an unwritten guide. These can be likened to the rules of a game of chess. The chess pieces can be moved in a great variety of ways with endless permutations, but all games of chess follow a common set of rules.

Taken together, the assumptions that anthropologists use to explain a people's total response is called their 'worldview'. These assumptions provide a set of basic presuppositions about the nature of the cosmos, society, and values (Burnett, 1990).

While the continual danger of over-generalisation must be recognised, several common worldview themes can be identified in most Islamic societies. These common features are often related to religious themes, as they are in all societies. However, these themes spread wider than those classed as religious theology.

First, the will of God is a common notion among Muslims. Any expression of future action or event is almost inevitably prefaced by saying 'if God wills' (*inshallah*). This idea is often dismissed as 'Islamic fatalism', suggesting a passivity and resignation towards the events of this world. However, this interpretation is almost the exact opposite to the way in which many Muslims use the term.

Eickelman showed that for Moroccans, the inequality of people in this world is so obvious as not to be a matter for speculation (Eickelman, 1989). The actual state of affairs at any moment is a manifestation of God's will, which is inevitable. An alert person is therefore more concerned with adjusting to circumstances as they arise than with thinking about how this might have been or should be. The acceptance of God's will focuses the attention upon immediate situations, not upon general speculation. A consequence of this idea is that the responsibility of persons for one another is limited.

A second common theme is honour. 'Honour', writes Pitt-Rivers, 'is the value of a person in his own eyes, but also in the eyes of his society. It is his estimate of his own worth, his claim to pride, but it is also acknowledgement of that claim, his excellence recognized by society, his right to pride' (Pitt-Rivers, 1948, pp. 77–78).

The sources of honour are many, depending on the individual and his or her specific circumstances. These include family origin, piety, generosity and the proper use of wealth. The most fundamental component of a man's honour in the Muslim world is directly related to a woman's sexual behaviour. This aspect of honour is known as *'ard* in Arabic, and *namus* in Turkish. *Ard* can be individual, related to families, or whole clans, and none is so great as a breach of sexual codes. This may bring shame upon the whole family, and in some rare occasions, has led to the killing of the woman.

A third theme is etiquette (*ta'aruf*). In English, the word 'etiquette' gives the impression of a set of conventions to maintain dignity of persons. In Iran, the notion entails a discipline of the inner self in the service of the public self. As Beeman observes, 'Every time tea is offered to a group, every time several persons wish to proceed through one door, every time friends meet on the street . . . the constant unceasing ritualization of the assessment of the climate of relative superiority and inferiority occurs and recurs . . . rights and obligations shift constantly with changes in one's social environment, make these constant social gestures important tools in everyday social relations.' Pleasantries, courtesies and flattery abound in all social encounters. These act as buffers between opposing views, and enable individuals to keep their options open to protect themselves against sudden shifts in views.

A fourth important theme is the classification of most human activities into two categories: those that are permissible or 'lawful' (*halal*), and those that are forbidden (*haram*). In a general sense this contrast can be likened to the distinction between acts that contribute to spiritual purity and those that pollute. For example, an animal slaughtered in accordance with certain prescriptions is considered *halal* and fit for eating; if not it is *haram* and should not be eaten by Muslims. It is for this reason that Muslims demand that *halal* food be served in schools for their children.

Although no Muslim can completely achieve the full demands of the code of *halal*, most Muslims display respect for it in their manner of dress, food, and general behaviour. The most important duties are those referred to as the 'Five Pillars of Islam' that were discussed in Chapter 6. Only with the implementation of the shari'a law within an Islamic community can a person achieve a deeper commitment. It is for this reason, therefore, that Muslims seek for the establishment of the Islamic State.

Worldview provides a model for action and in so doing culture is integrated. People do not just eat one way, dress in another way, and work in another without any reference to other activities. The worldview gives a oneness to culture.

4

Culture is society

Culture is, as we have seen, how people relate in social groups. Islam is a religion, but it is also a community, a civilisation and a culture. As the Quranic teaching spread throughout the world it absorbed these cultures and interacted with them in various ways. In so doing, it provided them with common attributes that united the diversity of languages and races into the complex unity of the *dar al Islam*, the people of Islam.

This aspect is most clearly seen in the Hajj, when Muslims from different parts of the globe travel to Mecca for the great festival. Even so, in recent years divisions between various groups has resulted in violence.

Theoretically, allegiance to the national state is incompatible with the supreme loyalty due to the Islamic Umma. In practice, people recognise themselves as belonging to unique groups within the population and distinguish themselves from others. This ethnic identity is common to all people and is simply the basic 'me' versus 'them' distinction. This is not a static social identity, but one that moves and changes in intensity with history.

Language can become an ethnic marker. In the Middle East three major language groupings or families can be identified: Semitic, Indo-European and Turkic. These broad classifications encompass a number of major languages and numerous dialects. Arabic and Hebrew are Semitic languages. Whereas Hebrew is only spoken in Israel, Arabic is the national language of Egypt, Jordan, Lebanon, Syria, Iraq, Saudi Arabia and the Gulf States. The Indo-European language family includes Persian, Kurdish and Luri. The major Turkish languages are standard Turkish of Turkey, Azeri of north-west Iran, Turkmen and the languages of Central Asia.

In every state there are important communities that speak other languages, as well as many who are bilingual. This gives a political dimension to language. In Turkey, for example, there are 2,500,000 Kurdish speakers as well as those speaking Armenian and Arabic. However, only standard Turkish is used in schools.

Although language and local dialects are significant with regards to ethnicity, religion is perhaps the most important source of social identity. The all-embracing character of Islam means that the major sectarian divisions have had a strong political dimension. This is especially seen with the formation of the Shia and Sunni communities. This aspect will be developed more fully in Chapter 10.

There are many small Muslim-derived communities forming minority groups. Groups like the Druze of Lebanon amount to closed communities within the larger society. The Baha'i movement commenced in 1844 when a young man proclaimed himself the 'Bab' or 'Gateway to heaven'. These religious movements have been excluded from the *dar al Islam*, and have suffered much persecution.

The Pattaya Conference Report concluded:

We must recognize the enormous differences between the cultures of different Muslim communities. There is no such thing as a uniform 'Islamic Culture' which is found in every Islamic community. What is appropriate in one situation may be quite inappropriate in another. (Lausanne Occasional Paper, 1980, p. 19)

Culture change

It is too easy for the outsider to look at others' cultures as static ways of life. All societies change, although some do so more rapidly than others.

The term *bedouin*, or more correctly *bedu*, is the Arabic word applied to the nomadic tribes of the desert. The Bedouins traditionally raised camels with some sheep, and a few prized horses. They resided all year round in black tents woven from goat hair, and followed patterns of migration into the desert. Today, much of this has changed. Herders use trucks to reach distant grazing areas.

Most people of the Middle East live in villages. These depend on good land and a supply of water for their existence. In Egypt, mechanisation has brought economic progress. Television antennae sprout from village homes, and cars and tractors have largely replaced animal transport. In Turkey and Iran, for example, many villages have been abandoned by the younger men who seek a new livelihood in the cities.

According to Samuel Wilson: 'At least 30 per cent of the nearly one billion Muslims in the world live in more than 300 cities larger than 10,000' (Wilson, 1989, p. 51–59). The Arab population of the Middle East had an urban population of 5% in 1800, 15% in 1900, and 50% in 1990. Cities in Kuwait and Qatar have been created with the vast revenues of oil, and they show little continuity with the past.

Cities cannot be understood in terms of generalities. Abu-Lughod writes that Cairo, like any city, is more than a complex of streets, it is a mosaic of social worlds (1971). She identifies 'large segments of Cairo where residents share common social characteristics and follow particular lifestyles that mark them off from residents of neighbouring communities with whom they seldom interact' (Abu-Lughod, 1971, p. 183). Using the census data, she delineates thirteen sections that are distinct in terms of dress, literacy, occupation, patterns of marriage and residence.

Christian conversion

We saw earlier that worldview gives a oneness to culture. It is therefore not possible to 'pull out' the religion of a people and 'plug in' Christianity, without having an effect on the rest of culture. Religious conversion will always have a radical effect on a person's way of life. Likewise the Muslim whose heart is touched with the gospel is changed at the most fundamental area of his existence—changed from the inside out.

Although religious conversion results in a change of a person's way of life, it does not imply cultural conversion. An Arab does not have to take on the lifestyle of a middle-class Anglo-Saxon Protestant once he or she becomes a Christian. To make such an assumption is to fall into the same error as the Judaisers who argued against the apostle Paul (Acts 15). These Jewish Christians saw the immorality and idolatry within Greek society and could see no alternative but for Gentile converts to accept the whole of Jewish culture with its elaborate law.

If Arabs become Christian, should they stop speaking Arabic and speak only English? Should they stop eating with their hands, and use a knife and fork? These questions appear almost ridiculous, but the issues become more problematic. Do the converts have to learn Western hymn tunes in order to make music to the Lord? Should they stop arranging marriages to cousins and follow the Western dating pattern? This form of dating is perceived as highly immoral not only by Muslims but also Arab Christians.

All too often, the Christian gospel has been presented to the Muslim world in the garb of Western culture. The Christian who desires to witness needs to examine his, or her, own culture and ask whether it reflects the love of God. Essentially we need to consider, can we come to terms with our own ethnocentrism?

The West has frequently regarded Islam as sensuous and violent. It is the 'other' that needs to be controlled, sometimes with force. On the other hand Islam has often seen the West as dominant, aggressively seeking to overwhelm the purity of Islam with Christian mission and colonialism. Muslims are proud of their histories and the great Islamic civilisations that have existed around the globe. They condemn the immorality so obvious in the West that is perceived as Christian.

The West has many stereotyped images of what a 'Muslim' is like. To relate meaningfully to a Muslim the Christian must put aside the stereotypes, and seek to understand the people; the society; and the culture.

Activity 8:2

Study the first diagram below. Make similar diagrams showing your own culture and that of your Muslim friends. Now look at the other two diagrams.

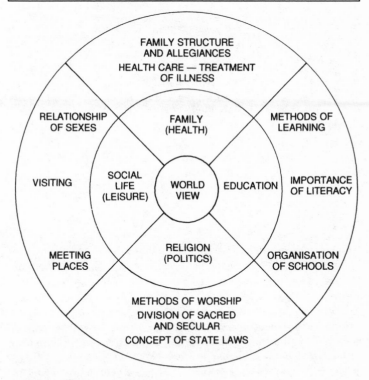

OUTERMOST CIRCLE - CUSTOMS
MIDDLE CIRCLE - AREAS OF LIFE
CENTRAL CIRCLE - WORLDVIEW

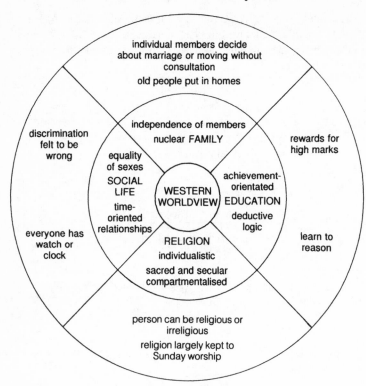

Notes

You may have detected that Christians and Muslims view culture differently. It would be difficult to describe a 'Christian' culture, although it is sometimes mistakenly identified with Western culture. When Muslims become Christians they expect to learn specifically Christian ways of doing things; how to behave when meeting other Christians, how to greet others, how to say 'goodbye', how to make conversation. They will also expect to learn how to worship, where to sit in church, how to dress, what to bring with them. In other words, they expect to learn what is *halal* and what is *haram*. As we saw in Chapter 7, the Christian faith is primarily concerned with beliefs, not actions. People from many different cultural backgrounds have put their faith in the Lord Jesus. They are encouraged to

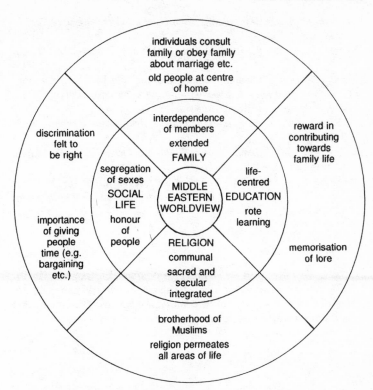

express themselves in their natural way, provided their customs do not contradict the teaching of Scripture. At the same time, Christians need to understand the importance Muslims attach to cultural factors and try to learn about them. Only in this way will meaningful relationships develop. We hope that this chapter will have helped you do this.

Books referred to in the chapter

Abu-Lughod, J., *Cairo: 1001 Years of the City Victorious* (Princeton University Press: Princeton, 1971).

Burnett, David, *Clash of Worlds* (Monarch: Eastbourne, 1990).

Eickelman, D. F., *The Middle East: An Anthropological Approach* (Prentice-Hall: Englewood, New Jersey, 1989).

Gilsenan, Michael, *Recognizing Islam* (Croom Helm: London, 1980), Foreword.

Hiebert, P., *Cultural Anthropology* (Lippincott: Philadelphia, 1976); p. 25.

[Pattaya Report] Lausanne Committee for World Evangelization, *Christian Witness to Muslims* (Lausanne Occasional Paper No 13, LCWE: Wheaton, Illinois, 1980).

Pitt-Rivers, Julian, *Honour and Shame* (Routledge, Keegan, Paul, 1948); pp. 77–78.

Swidiqi, H. M. Khalid, *Your Children's Islam* (Islamic Circle Organisation: London, 1984).

Tyler, E. B., *Primitive Culture* (John Murray: London, 1871).

Wilson, S. 'Urban Places and Islam, Past and Present', *Urban Mission*, May 1989, pp. 51–59.

For further reading

Burnett, David, *Clash of Worlds* (Monarch: Eastbourne, 1990). Different worldviews, including Islamic worldview (Chapter 7) are described with many helpful anecdotes and diagrams. The introduction of different worldviews is one of the main themes.

9
History and Political Development of Islam

Study guide

Having studied Islam as culture in the last chapter, we move on to see how this culture has been worked out over time. The rise of Islam was rapid. It was a success story. The certainties of Islam have been maintained even in times of defeat and periods of oppression. This chapter is also about the influence different civilisations have had on each other. Islam was influenced by the great Turkish and Persian civilisations which went before the Islamic conquests, and has also left its imprint on subsequent development through its own great empires in Turkey, Persia and India. We can also see some of the cultural changes which have taken place and, indeed are still taking place in the twentieth century. This chapter and Chapter 10 were originally written by Ron George and have required little revision.

When you have completed the chapter we hope you will:

1 Have assimilated an overview of the way Islam has developed historically and politically;
2 Have begun to explore some of the creative and artistic dimensions of Islam; and
3 Have begun to see something of the influence of Islam in the historical and political spheres.

'Look up at the heavens and count the stars . . . So shall your offspring be.' (Gen 15:5)

God was with the boy as he grew up. He lived in the desert and became an archer. (Gen 21:20)

But while he was still living, he gave gifts to the sons of his concubines and sent them away from his son Isaac to the land of the east. (Gen 25:6)

Where did it all start? With God's covenant to Abraham? With his son Ishmael? With Abraham's sons by Keturah and others? We don't know. But we do know that what we now call the Arabian Peninsula is the cradle of Islam.

In the years before Muhammad's birth Arabia was peopled by semi-nomadic tribes. Caravans of traders with their camels and merchandise plied the trade routes to and from Egypt, Jerusalem, Damascus, Turkey and Persia. The shortage of water in this desert area prevented the building of large population centres, or developing an integrated civilisation; only small settlements had been developed on the trade routes. One of the largest and most important of these was Mecca, Muhammad's birthplace, situated on the crossing of main trade routes and a religious focal point attracting many pilgrims to worship at its holy place, the Ka'ba.

During the sixth century AD there was a movement towards greater integration of the many tribes, probably due to the acceptance of Arabic as a common language. The people still lacked any opportunity for the learning and advancement found in the great centres of civilisation, Jerusalem, Damascus and Constantinople. For this reason the era is known as the *Jahaliyya*, the Age of Ignorance. The Arabs also lacked one coherent religion, each tribe or sub-tribe having its own idols, worshipping them and paying little attention to Allah, the chief among many gods. Into this national, cultural and religious vacuum Muhammed was born in about AD570.

Bishop Kenneth Cragg, in his book *The Arab Christian* (1992), questions how it was possible that Judaism and Christianity had made so little impact on the Arabian Peninsular. He believes that 'Judaism and Jewishness were too exclusive to "fulfill" the Arabs' (p. 34). As for the six centuries of Christianity: 'Was the emphasis of divine compassion and costly forgiveness as the heart of the Christian Gospel seen not to accord well with the Arab sense of *muru'ah*, or "standing up for rights"?' (p. 33). Cragg considers that Christian doctrine is too subtle: 'The Qur'an moves within an Arab characteristic of mind, for which concrete imagery was preferable to abstract ideas'. Perhaps the decisive factor has to do with the Arab search for identity, for an Arab self-assertion (p. 33). As we have seen in Chapter 5, the Prophet Muhammad was able to give the Arabs a sense of identity and self-assertion, first through a Book and a Prophet and later, in the Medinan period, through a community and a culture.

Before his sudden death in AD632, Muhammad had achieved the vital return to Mecca and had established Islam not as a breakaway sect, but as the main religion of the area. He did this through both religious and political supremacy. Not only did the Muslim army return victorious to Mecca, but Arabs were pressing to join the Muslims in their pilgrimage and in their worship of Allah in the holy city, around the Ka'ba.

Nevertheless, Muhammad's death did present the Muslim community with a major crisis.

1

The succession

Who would replace Muhammad and rule the new community that transcended tribal loyalty? Secondly, would the community stand the test of a transfer of power, since most of the tribes gave their loyalty to Muhammad and not to one another? In the event, the Arab leaders fell back upon the tried and trusted traditional Arab method of electing the most honourable and aged one among them. They chose Abu Bakr, the uncle of Muhammad. Not all Muslims agreed that Muhammad would have wanted Abu Bakr to be the first Khalif (or Caliph, which means 'successor'). Some claimed he had said that Ali, his son-in-law, husband of Fatima, his daughter, should take over from him. However the Arabs did not respect Ali as a wise and mature person.

Before he died Abu Bakr, having consulted the senior Companions, selected Umar to be his successor. Umar was known as Al-Faruq, which means 'one who distinguishes between right and wrong'. He was a gifted orator and was

FAMILY TREE OF MUHAMMAD

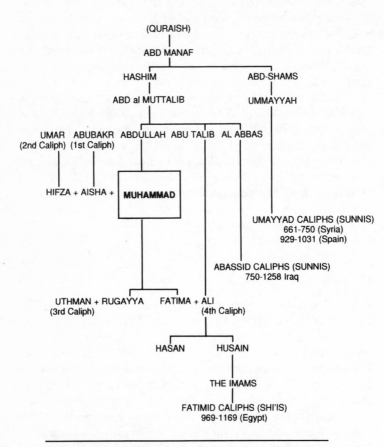

Note: The 1st and 2nd Caliphs were fathers-in-law to Muhammad, not blood-relations though sometimes called "uncles" in Arabic usage. But Ali the 4th Caliph was his first cousin as well as his son-in-law. So the Shi'is regard him as the first real *"khalifa"* (successor).

Dr Paul Shepherd. FFM

concerned for the welfare of his people. During the ten years of his leadership Egypt and large areas of the Roman and Persian Empires were conquered. He was assassinated by a disgruntled non-Muslim, having previously appointed a committee to choose his successor.

The committee chose Uthman as the third Khalif. He was a kind and generous man from a rich family. He was also pious and god-fearing. He was not, however, a strong ruler, so that discipline in his administration was lax.

He ruled from AD644–656. He was assassinated, and many suspected that the disgruntled Ali or at least his followers were responsible. Uthman's cousin demanded that justice be done and the murderer be brought to court. This cousin, Muawiya, was governor of Damascus at the time. He made no claim to rule Islam but used this quarrel in an effort to overthrow Ali. The two sides were drawn up in battle, but both parties agreed to submit the question to a panel of mature leaders who would arbitrate in the matter in order to save Muslim blood from being shed. At this, many of Ali's followers—the Kharidjites—left him, since they claimed that only God had the authority to arbitrate between the two parties, that God would be on the side of whoever was right, and that the battle should have taken place. Ali, in his determination to bring them back into the fold, ended up slaughtering most of them, but that was only to lead to his own assassination by the hand of a survivor. Today Sunni Muslims look back with nostalgia upon the period of the first four Khalifs, whom they greatly revere, considering that they were the rightly guided ones and a model for present-day Islam. In his book, *Islam beliefs and teachings* Ghulam Sarwar describes the characters of the 'rightly-guided' Khalifs: some extracts follow:

Abu Bakr   'He was the closest friend of the Prophet and he acted as the Prophet's deputy, leading prayers when the Prophet was ill' (p. 129).

              'Abu Bakr loved his faith more than anything else' (p. 130).

Umar	'Umar was a very brave and straightforward person. He was tough in his attitude and uncompromising in basic principles'.
	'Umar was a strong disciplinarian' (p. 133).
Uthman	'Uthman was a simple and very kind-hearted man. His simplicity and kindness did not allow him to take strong action against the trouble-makers and rioters. Above all, because of his simple mindedness, his administration was not as disciplined . . .'
	'Uthman was a generous man' (p. 137).
Ali	'Ali was the person who risked his life for the Prophet and slept in the Prophet's bed when the unbelievers laid seige around the Prophet's house to kill him on the night of the Prophet's migration' (p. 137).

Activity 9:1

Obey me as long as I obey Allah and his Messenger. If I disobey Allah and his Messenger, you are free to disobey me. (Part of Abu Bakr's election speech)

Sarwar comments, 'The world would be a better place to live in if we had leaders like Abu Bakr.' (Sarwar, 1980, p. 130)
Do you agree?

2

The Umayyads (AD661–750)

With Ali's death in AD661, the way was open for Muawiya to take control of the new Muslim community. He set up his capital in Damascus and modelled his rule on the Greek-Roman-Byzantine Empire, which had lost Damascus to the young vigorous Muslim armies. Thus begins the first Islamic kingdom named after Muawiya's family, the Umayyads. It was to last from AD661 to

CHRONOLOGICAL CHART OF THE MAIN ISLAMIC DYNASTIES

AD

| 600 | 700 | 800 | 900 | 1000 | 1100 | 1200 | 1300 | 1400 | 1500 | 1600 | 1700 | 1800 | 1900

● MUHAMMAD
▬ FIRST FOUR KHALIFS
Mecca

UMMAYADS
▬▬

First khalifate
in Damascus

ABBASIDS
▬▬▬▬▬▬▬▬

Capital Baghdad, then Samaria

UMMAYADS OF SPAIN
▬▬▬▬▬▬

Capital Cordoba

FATIMIDS OF EGYPT
▬▬▬

Controlled North Africa 900-972
Sicilly 909-1071

MONGOLS
▬▬▬

Capital Tabriz, then Sultaniya

OTTOMAN TURKS
▬▬▬▬▬▬▬▬

Capital from 1326 Bursa, from 1458 Istambul
Also controlled Egypt 1517-1805

UZBEKS
▬▬▬▬

In Central Asian Republics

SAFAVIDS OF PERSIA
▬▬▬▬

Tabriz, Kaswin, Isfahan

MUGHALS OF INDIA
▬▬▬▬▬

Delhi, Fatehpur Sikri, Agra

750. In turn they were overthrown by a reactionary movement from the East and replaced by a new empire called the Abbasids.

The Abbasids (from AD750 to the tenth century)

In AD750 the fourteenth Umayyad Khalif was overthrown by a new dynasty, which was to be known as the Abbasid dynasty. Professor Lewis observes that 'it was a revolution in the history of Islam, as important a turning point as the French and Russian Revolutions in the history of the West.' (Lewis, 1970, p. 80). It came at the end of a long period of dissatisfaction by elements of the population who felt that they were being treated as second-class citizens.

The new dynasty was descended from Muhammad's uncle al Abbas, and they were eventually to shift the capital from Damascus to a purpose-built city called Baghdad. The result of the geographical shift was to move the attention away from expansion in the West, particularly in Spain and Europe, to a new expansion to the East. This period has come to be known as the 'Golden Age of Islam'.

Persian influence

The old Persian Empire was to play an important part in providing a model for government, court etiquette, and the arts. Arab influences further declined and Persian culture took over.

Under Harun al-Rashid (786–809), legendary Caliph of the Thousand and One Nights, Baghdad flourished as an unrivalled centre of commerce and learning. His successor, al-Mamum (813–833), established in the capital a 'House of Wisdom', a combination of library, academy, translation bureau, and observatory. A few examples may indicate the achievements of Muslim scholars at a time when Europe was still half-barbarised. al-Khwarizmi (d. circa 850) made major advances in astronomy, wrote a pioneering treatise on algebra, and popularised the use of 'Arabic' (derived from Indian) numerals. In medicine al-Razi (895–925) was the first to make a clinical distinction between measles and smallpox, while in philosophy al-Ashare (874–935) wrestled with the problem of reconciling predestination with free will.

(School of Oriental and African Studies, p. 61)

By the tenth century the political unity of the Islamic empire had begun to fragment. It was under increasing pressure from ambitious provincial governors and, in Baghdad, rival warlords were usurping authority. In North Africa, in AD909, a khalifate was set up by the Shiite Fatimids, who claimed descent from the Prophet's daughter Fatima and founded a new capital for themselves in Cairo. In Spain, in AD925, an autonomous khalifate was established by descendants of the Umayyad line.

Turkish influence (from the tenth to the twelfth century)

The tide of conquest rolled forward again in the eleventh and twelfth centuries with armed incursions into western Africa and northern India. At the same time the Abbasid Khalifate effectively fell under the control of Turkish invaders, the Seljuks, who briefly reinvigorated it—and, in effect, provoked the Crusades. Seen against this general background, the Crusades assume the perspective of local and temporary reverses in a general trend of expansion. The chivalrous and statesmanlike Salah-al-Din (Saladin) recaptured Jerusalem from the Christians in 1187 and succeeded in briefly reuniting Egypt and Syria under firm rule. Chapter 12 discusses the Crusades in some detail. It shows that this period of history has had a profound effect on Christian-Muslim relations, even up to the present day.

Activity 9:2

Islamic achievements in the arts and sciences should be appreciated if we are to relate to Muslims. There is much of interest and beauty in the Islamic sections of museums. The various exhibits will be dated and will provide background information concerning the different Islamic empires and their cultures. We recommend a visit.

3

New influences in Islam

In 1258 the Mongol hordes of Hulagu, grandson of Ghengis Khan, struck deep into the heart of India. The last Abbasid Khalif was done to death and the glittering imperial capital of Baghdad was virtually wiped off the face of the earth. The psychological shock was tremendous, but short-lived. In 1260 the Mongols were checked in Palestine by an army of Mamluks, slave soldiers who had established praetorian rule in Egypt.

As Lewis has observed, 'most scholars would now agree that the harmful effects of the Mongol conquests were not as great, as lasting or even as extensive as was once thought'. Iraq and northern Persia were badly affected, but most other areas were either never troubled or were subject only to the most distant suzerainty. And the Mongols, once converted to Islam, became great patrons of culture.

New leadership

It can be seen with historical perspective that the Seljuks, Mamluks, Mongols and Ottomans gave Islam much-needed infusions of invigorating new leadership. The historian ibn Khaldun acknowledged their importance, and later historians have seen them as the reason for the military resurgence of the sixteenth century. They brought with them not only traditions of courage and military skill, but also techniques of statecraft and patterns of institutionalisation adapted from both Chinese and Byzantine methods. Cairo henceforth supplanted Baghdad as the hub of the Islamic world, and its University of al-Azhar became the foremost seat of Muslim learning.

There were thousands of Muslim travelling scholars, judges, merchants and pilgrims who helped to spread both the Arabic language and the religious practices of Islam, in the charitable hospices of the then Islamic world.

A story is told of a young man who left his home in Tangiers in 1325, for a pilgrimage to Mecca. He returned in 1354 twenty-nine years later, 'having visited every country under Muslim

SPREAD OF ISLAM UNDER THE UMMAYADS 622-661 AD

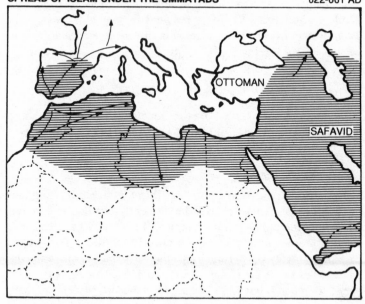

ISLAM AT THE TIME OF THE THREE GREAT EMPIRES 16th-18th CENTURIES

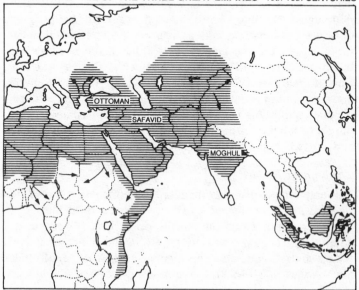

rule, from Spain to the Niger, from Crimea to Mombasa, from Delhi to Sumatra. Wherever he went he was able to earn an honourable living as a judge administering the Shari'a, the sacred law of the faith' (SOAS p. 62).

Three great Islamic empires

Spanning the sixteenth to the nineteenth centuries three important empires arose: the Ottoman in Turkey, the Safavid in Persia and the Moghal in India.

The Ottoman Empire

This empire arose from an obscure thirteenth-century kingdom in north-west Anatolia. By the fifteenth century it covered almost all the old Byzantine Empire. It reached its zenith in the reign of Suleyman the Magnificent (1520–1566). His armies conquered Egypt, Syria, Iraq, the Red Sea area and the Balkans as far as the Hungarian Plain. The Ottomans twice laid siege to Vienna, but were not able to take the city. The Treaty of Karlowitz in 1699, when for the first time the Empire was made to cede territory, was a turning point in its fortunes. Although there were serious attempts at reform, the problems of prolonged inflation, military conservatism and political corruption rendered the empire ineffectual; it did not however, finally succumb until after its defeat in the First World War, when Kemal Ataturk became leader of the Turkish Republic and set about introducing a programme of modernisation. This included abolishing the khalifate in 1924, establishing Islam as the State religion, replacing the Shari'a with a new legal code and, in 1935, having a new secular constitution.

The Safavid Empire

This empire was of shorter duration. Nevertheless, it contributed significantly to the spread of Islam. It lasted from 1503–1722. Militarily it was based on an élite of Turkish tribesmen, but administrative power was effectively in the hands of Persian judges and bureaucrats. The regime reached its zenith under Shah Abbas (1587–1629), who not only put down internal feuds and instituted much-needed reforms in the political structure of the state but also embellished the city of Isfahan with unrivalled splendour. At its heart he laid out a vast park and polo field surrounded by arcades and palaces. But its greatest glory lay in the magnificent tile-decorated mosques which are among modern Iran's most prized national treasures.

After a period of disruption, and as a result of a rebellion in the army, Reza Khan came to power in Persia. He was not a high-ranking officer, nor was he educated; but he was able to get sufficient support to set himself up as ruler.

The Moghal Empire

Babur, one of the Mongol leaders, followed up his conquests in Northern Iran and took his army eastwards, over the Khyber Pass into India. In 1526, the Moghal Empire was established by a decisive victory at Panipat near Delhi. Babur's grandson Akbar the Great (1542–1605) extended the area of conquest to take in all but the southern tip of India. Akbar's grandson, Shah Jehan, had the world-famous Taj Mahal built as a tomb for himself and his favourite wife. After he died, the power of the Moghal Empire began to fade, due to internal disintegration. First French colonists, then the British, took over the vacuum left by the weakened empire, until in 1857 the official British Raj began.

Islah—reform of Islam

Within the framework of these empires, significant internal changes took place. Historically, reform movements of a 'puritanical' variety have played an important part in the development of Islam. Not least among them is the Wahabi which arose in Arabia in the eighteenth century and currently dominates the religious practices of the Arabian peninsular. These movements invariably call for a return to the original principles and practices of Islam and protest forcibly against what they regard as idolatrous and superstitious accretions (eg veneration of saints, tombs, palm-reading, etc). They are invariably associated with political changes, providing as they do an ideological catalyst for discontent which rises up to challenge and overwhelm the existing authorities.

Not only were the reform movements which were puritanical in their outlook developing, but some more liberal Muslim thinkers were expressing the view that Islam and modernisation were not incompatible, but rather should go hand in hand towards the goal of an Islamic society equipped for the modern age.

The twentieth century

If we follow through the changes that have taken place in the three Islamic countries we have just been studying, we see something of the rapid change that has taken place all over the world. We looked at the Turkey of Kemal Ataturk, the successor to the Ottoman Empire. Many of his reforms have been overturned and there has been a resurgence of Islamic values and practices. In Persia the Shah, Reza Khan's son, was deposed in 1979 by Ayatollah Khomeni's fundamentalist Shiite revolution. In 1947, the British Raj gave way to the partitioning of India and the forming of the independent countries of India, Pakistan and (in 1971) Bangladesh.

As Bishop Stephen Neill has written in his book, *Crisis in Belief*,

> In two generations the situation of the Islamic world has entirely changed. In 1918 it was at its lowest point of humiliation—poor, exhausted, and at almost every point subject to Christian domination. In 1978 it stood before the world free, aggressive, and with a new self-confidence. (Neill, 1984, p. 61)

Most of the major Muslim countries became independent from foreign powers in the period after the Second World War: Indonesia from the Dutch; Libya from the Italians; Algeria, Morocco, and Tunisia from the French; also Syria and Lebanon in the Middle East, Pakistan, Egypt, and Sudan from the British. This has meant each has had to go through a period of finding a national identity, at the same time as learning how to govern a country, relate internationally, and set up judicial and political systems. This has been a mammoth task and has not been accomplished without heartache and even bloodshed.

The discovery of oil

Nearly half the known oil resources of the world are in the Muslim countries of North Africa and the Middle East. The ownership of this 'black gold' has catapulted these formerly backward and deprived areas into the secular, materialistic world of modern economics and commerce. Personal riches have far outstripped educational opportunities. As to the future, these are not bottomless wells; the supply will dry up one day, in fifteen years, in twenty years? What then?

A concluding thought:

The Muslim, like the Christian and the Marxist, is interested in history. History is the sphere in which the purpose of God is to be carried out. God is omnipotent and sovereign. And since the Muslim identifies his own existence with the will of God, he must expect to see in history, progressively and over ever-widening stretches of the earth, the establishment of the divine society as he has understood it. But the Muslim has been perplexed to find that from his point of view, for a century at least, history seems to have gone wrong.

The Christian can well understand this perplexity since in a measure he shares it. He too believes that the divine community must spread to every part of the earth; he too believes that it is only through the effort and witness of Christians that the community can be extended. But through all the centuries disappointed expectations have been part of the history of the Christian churches. (Neill, 1984, p. 58)

Notes

You have probably already observed the importance Islam places on its leaders. As Activity 9:1 suggests, the four 'rightly-guided' khalifs who followed Muhammad are still revered and respected. Abu Bakr does seem to have been a good man and a fine leader. Christians however, believe that God wants us not so much to look back as to live under his guidance in the presence. We need to pray that God will raise up leaders for this day and age and that we may be discerning in choosing and supporting those he chooses.

Books referred to in the chapter

Cragg, Kenneth, *The Arab Christian in the Middle East* (1st UK edn, Mowbray: London, 1991).
Lewis, Bernard, *The Arabs in History* (Hutchinson, London, 1970).
Neill, Stephen, *Crises of Belief* (Hodder & Stoughton: London, 1984).
Sarwar, Ghulam, *Islam: Beliefs and Teachings* (Muslim Educational Trust: London, 3rd edn 1984).

For further reading

Cragg, Kenneth, *The Arab Christian in the Middle East* (1st UK edn, Mowbray: London, 1991). This is a helpful and detailed history of the Middle East from pre-Islamic times until the present, indeed the last chapter looks to the future of Islam.

IO

Different Expressions of Islam

Study guide

So far in this book we have been looking at the orthodox expression of Islam, Sunni Islam, with only occasional mention of other expressions. Now is the time to look more closely at Shia Islam and the other smaller sects. You may find your Muslim friends do not want to talk about the divisions in Islam, any more than we want to major on our denominational differences! You will, however, get an idea as to what they think is important in their faith when you discuss together. When you have studied this chapter we hope you will be able to identify where their loyalties lie.

When you have completed the chapter we hope you will:

1 Be able to distinguish the main differences in the different expressions of Islam;
2 See something of the political implications of these differences in the world today; and
3 See how the oneness of Islam is maintained through the different expressions.

1

The oneness of Islam

The People of the Point—this is how Muslims have been described, indeed how they have sometimes described themselves. They look back to a particular point in time, the coming of their Prophet Muhammad; a particular point in revelation, the revealing of the Qur'an; a particular place, the Ka'ba in the holy city of Mecca. It is to Mecca that all Muslims turn, guided by the *qibla*, as they pray five times a day. It is to Mecca that the *mehrab* points in every mosque. Everything emphasises the togetherness of the Muslim community, the Umma.

It seems strange, therefore, to have a chapter in this book on the history and significance of the sects or divisions in Islam. Perhaps this is another illustration of the dilemma of human-kind mentioned in Chapter 1—made in the image of God, but separated by disobedience (although Muslims do not hold to this doctrine).

It is important at this point to make clear that all Muslims are Muslims first and adherents to a particular expression of Islam afterwards. The Muslims John Bowker interviewed played down the differences. About half of them, when asked whether they were Sunni or Shia, refused to answer in that way, saying they were simply Muslims and that was enough (Bowker, 1983, p. 54). One regarded the division as political not religious saying,

> I consider Shias a political division which came into existence in the time of the rightly guided caliphs . . . and from that developed the different philosophies of looking at Islam. Otherwise I don't consider them to be different from Sunnis. (p. 53–54)

In *Islam in the World*, Malise Ruthven compares Muslim sects and Christian denominations. This may be helpful in discussing the matter with Muslims. He writes:

> The divisions of Islam, in contrast to those of Christianity, have their origins in politics rather than dogma. This is not to say that dogmatic and theological questions do not form part of these divisions. However, the questions over which they first crystalised were political to the extent that they were primarily concerned with leadership of the community. Having a religious ideology built on the social foundations of tribalism, the Muslims expressed their aspirations first in terms of group loyalty, and only afterwards in terms of the doctrinal and theological accretions surrounding these loyalties. (Ruthven, 1984, p. 181)

There is a tradition which occurs in various forms that recognises that there are sects within Islam. Muhammad is alleged to have said, 'Did not the people of the book divide into 72 sects (*milla*) and in truth this community will one day divide into 73 sects, of which 72 will go to hell and only one to paradise.' Another form of this tradition speaks of the Jews having 71 sects, the Christians 72 and the Muslims 73.

So far in this book almost everything written has been about Sunni Islam. This is standard Islam. Now we are going to see something of the diversity, what has caused the divisions and how they have become established into different sects.

The role of Mecca

While examining the emergence of various sects in Islam, attention should be paid to the importance of Mecca in the spread of sectarian views. Whenever Muslims have gone on a pilgrimage to Mecca they come into contact with new ideas. Some returned to their own country influenced by the new ideas, and ready to propogate them amongst their own people. This has been true in the case of the Sufi brotherhoods as well as the more extreme of the fundamentalist groups.

2

Theological divisions

The status of the Qur'an

The divisions which arose within Islam were often the result of either political conflict or theological disagreement. It is assumed by most Muslims that scholars of the first and second Islamic centuries held the doctrine of the uncreated Qur'an (that is, that the Qur'an is eternal). Very few believed the Qur'an was actually a book that could be dated. It was only towards the end of the second Muslim century that the question was explicitly raised whether the Qur'an was created or uncreated, which led to the *mihna* (inquisition).

This resulted in conflict between the Islamic clergy and the khalif of the time. The assumption was that the Qur'an was the eternal book of God (an idea that developed after contact with early Christians who held that Jesus was the eternal Word of God). This was supported by the idea that the Hadith, or traditions about Muhammad, had been handed on with complete verbal accuracy from the Companions to later generations of Muslims. There is, and always has been, an immense confidence in Islam that the Qur'an and traditions are true, and that what disagrees with them is false.

The question as to whether the Qur'an was created or was the eternal Word of God posed several problems. First and foremost is the fact that if the Qur'an were the eternal Word of God, it would seem to imply that there are two eternities in heaven. God is eternal, and by associating the Word of God with God, some Muslims have argued that the sin of *shirk* is committed (that is, the sin of associating anything or person with God).

The questions of guilt or innocence

Another question which caused division within the early Muslim community was the question of guilt or innocence. In certain cases, men should not judge a question of guilt or innocence, but should leave the decision to God. This led to disputes over such matters as:

1 The choice of Uthman as leader and the demoting of Ali to fourth place in order of merit after Muhammad.
2 Not merely postponing the judgement of the grave sinner and treating him as a believer, but positively asserting that he is a believer but has erred. It was understood that all Muslims would eventually go to Paradise provided that they did not fall into the sin of *shirk* or idolatry.

The Mutazila introduced dogmatic theology into Islam. They stressed man's responsibility for his deeds, because he has been given free will. They were concerned with the question of the grave sinner, and asserted that he was neither a believer nor an unbeliever, but was in an intermediate position.

The Kharidjites wanted to establish a pure theocracy. They questioned the need for the Khaliphate, believing in the rule of Allah alone. They were far more aggressive, and positively held that a grave sinner was an unbeliever. They seemed to have placed a great majority of Muslims in this last group, since most claimed to believe that even a bad sinner could still be a Muslim.

The doctrine of Qadr

Another Islamic point of contention was the doctrine of *qadr*, the teaching that God alone has the power to create and produce things, which exists in contention with the concept of man's free will. The early controversies that divided the Muslim community into various sects in the Umayyad days were the outcome of differences concerning the true nature of faith. Was it, as the Murdjites maintained, simply 'knowledge and confession of God, together with knowledge and confession of his apostle and what he brought from God,' or was it, as the Kharidjites believed, a duty imposed by God upon his creatures so that every great sin is unbelief or polytheism?

The predestination versus free will problem was first raised by Islam as recorded in debates between Muslims and Christians in Umayyad times. It was summed up in the question, 'Can God be the cause of evil?' Christians and Muslims alike answered, 'No, the evil is from our negligence and the devil's cunning.' Further to this came the question: 'Are you then a free agent?' Most of the Kharidjites and Shiites believed in the power of God and that God fore-ordained everything that happened, both good and evil. The Umayyads claimed that their right to rule was based upon the fact that they were already ruling. If it had been God's will that they should not rule they would never have been in a position of power. Thus, theological arguments were mobilised to undergird and legitimise a 'corrupt' Umayyad dynasty.

3

Political division

Sunnism

Sunnism gradually became the orthodox, most widely accepted position held by some 90% of Islam, and all other groups came to be considered as sectarian. As various leaders and teachers arose within these groups, they set up their own schools of thought and became sub-sects. This was particularly evident with the argument over who should lead the community after Muhammad died. Some claimed that it should be left to a democratic process among the elders of Islam; others claimed that it was an inheritance left to Ali. The followers of Ali (the party of Ali, *Shiat Ali*) eventually became known as the Shiites.

Activity 10:1

As the oneness in Islam is so important, it would be good to make a list of the factors which emphasise its unity. What about the problems which have caused disunity? List those too. Do the same for Christianity, thus enabling you to compare the two religions and see what the differences are.

The emergence of Shia Islam

Shia Islam emerged from the argument as to whether Ali should have been the first Khalif or not. They also developed a different view of government. The Sunni Muslims held that the *Sunna*, or practice of the prophet, was an authoritative source of law-making.

On the other hand, the Shias held that when Ali was killed, the claim that he was the rightful successor to Muhammed was passed on to his descendants. This succession of leaders, called imams, gave spiritual leadership until, in the ninth century, the twelfth imam was said to have gone into hiding and still to be alive today. Shias claim that he is the only legitimate ruler of the Muslim world. However, as long as he remains in hiding the government falls on the shoulders of his representatives, the Islamic clergy. We have seen this happen since 1979 in Iran, where the Ayatollahs, who are Islamic clergy, have ruled the country.

Shias differ in some respects from the majority of Muslims. The traditional creed is expanded to include the term 'and Ali is the friend of God'. They reject the idea of the Muslim being able to have a concubine; but alternatively they introduced the idea of *muta* marriage, which is legal, temporary marriage while a man is on pilgrimage or on a business trip.

As we have seen, the Shias claim that Ali was the rightful successor to Muhammad. When he was killed he left a line of descendants. There have been two great schisms concerning the succession of leaders (imams). The first was after the death of Ali as Sajad, when part of the sect adhered to his son, Zaid, the founder of the Zaidiyyah sect. The second was on the death of As Sadiq, when his father nominated his second son, Musa Al Kazim, as his successor, instead of allowing the khaliphate to go to Ismail's family. This was because of Ismail's alleged alcoholism. Those who follow Ismail are called the Ismailiyyah; today they are led by the Aga Khan. The greatest number of the Shias acknowledge Musa Al Kazim (the second son of As Sadiq) and his descendants as the true line. They are thus called the Ithna Ashariyyah or the Twelvers. A dispute over the political leadership of the Shia sect resulted in a theological difference as well. A small minority regarded Ismail's drunkenness as evidence that he accepted the hidden meaning of Islam but not the legal precepts. Of the proverbial 73 sects of Islam certainly no fewer than 32 are assigned to the Shia's and possibly as many as 70. Many of the Shia's have carried their dedication to Ali so far as to raise him to the divine status; some also believe their imams to be partakers of the divine nature.

Another way in which the Shiite teaching differs from the Sunni concerns suffering. Sunnis experienced considerable success both during the latter part of the Prophet's life and in the conquests they made after his death. Their armies carried all before them and, as we saw in Chapter 9, Sunni Islam conquered much of the then known world. It is not surprising that to this day, Sunnis tend to be success-orientated; they function best when in a dominant position. This has not been the case with Shias; they are the losers, the sufferers. Ali and his two sons all suffered violent deaths. Hassan, the elder, was mysteriously killed in Mecca. Hussain, in an attempt to seize the khalifate in Damascus, was ambushed at Karbala in Southern Iraq and was killed along with his followers. This tragedy is re-enacted each year on the 10th day of the Muslim month Muharram with intense sorrow and passion. From this sad event, martyrdom—the ultimate sacrifice of innocent victims—has become the hallmark of Shia Islam. History continued to mark Shias out as the underdogs.

Even in modern Iran suffering continues, despite the fact that it is a fundamentalist Shia state. Ayatollah Khomeini took power in 1979 amidst much bloodshed and the killing of those who had supported the Shah's regime. The suffering was increased when the Iran-Iraq War started. Both sides looked upon it as a jihad, a holy war. Many young men, fired up by Khomeini's rhetoric, willingly went to fight and die as martyrs. Even when the war was over with neither side claiming victory, the Shia community in Iraq continued to suffer much.

Another characteristic of Shia Islam is its intense loyalty to its leaders. Not only do Muhammad, Ali and his sons arouse intense and passionate love; the violent scenes at the funeral of Ayatollah Khomeini indicate the adoration which he had engendered.

Seyyed Hossein Nasr, in his book *Ideals and Realities of Islam*, emphasises how both Sunni and Shia can contribute to the unity of Islam:

> They are two streams which originate from the same fountain, which is their unique source, namely the Quranic revelation and they finally pour into one sea which is the Divine Unity whose means of realization each contains within itself. To have lived either of them fully is to have lived as a Muslim and to have realized that Truth for the sake of whose revelation the Qur'an was made known to men through the Prophet of Islam. (Nasr, 1979, p. 176)

Activity 10:2

It will not be difficult to find Shia Islam mentioned in the newspapers, or on the television screen; you can also discuss it with your Muslim friends. Can you pick out some of the characteristics of Shia Islam in what you see or hear?

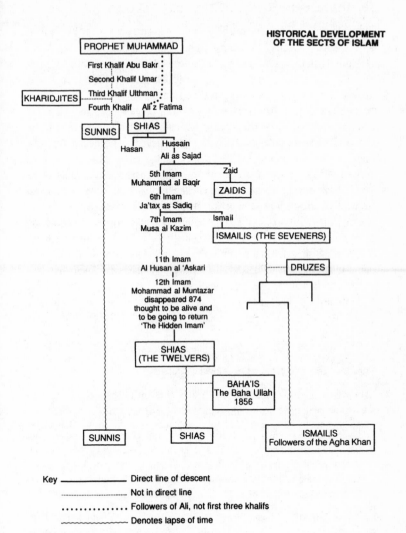

HISTORICAL DEVELOPMENT OF THE SECTS OF ISLAM

PROPHET MUHAMMAD

First Khalif Abu Bakr
Second Khalif Umar
Third Khalif Ulthman
Fourth Khalif · Ali z Fatima

KHARIDJITES

SUNNIS

SHIAS

Hasan · Hussain
Ali as Sajad

5th Imam
Muhammad al Baqir · Zaid

ZAIDIS

6th Imam
Ja'tax as Sadiq

7th Imam
Musa al Kazim · Ismail

ISMAILIS (THE SEVENERS)

11th Imam
Al Husan al 'Askari · DRUZES

12th Imam
Mohammad al Muntazar
disappeared 874
thought to be alive and
to be going to return
'The Hidden Imam'

SHIAS
(THE TWELVERS)

BAHA'IS
The Baha Ullah
1856

SUNNIS

SHIAS

ISMAILIS
Followers of the Agha Khan

Key ———————— Direct line of descent
.... Not in direct line
• • • • • • • • • • • • • Followers of Ali, not first three khalifs
〰〰〰〰〰〰 Denotes lapse of time

The Druze

The Druze are a community living mainly in the Lebanon, Israel, and around Damascus. The name is derived from Beth Darazi. It is probable that the people of this area were already racially distinct before the founding of their religion and that they were never truly converted to Islam. They have sometimes been regarded as the descendents of Persian colonists. In the seventeenth century they were thought to be survivors of the Latin Christians who escaped the massacre of Acre in 1291, but this has been disproved. The Druze claimed that they were descended from Godfrey Bouillon, one of the Crusader knights. The Druze religion is a system of doctrine which only the *Uqqal* (learned) know. Those who do not know this system are called the *juhhal* (the ignorant). The religion was founded in the time of the Fatimid Khalif Hakim (996–1021) as a splinter group from the Shiite Ismailis. They held the view that God became incarnate in man. The Khalif Hakim represented God in his unity and is worshipped and called 'Our Lord'. His eccentricity and cruelties are explained symbolically. He was the last incarnation of God and did not die but is still living, hidden in a secret place.

Sufism—the mystical expression of Islam

In answer to the question, 'What is Sufism?', Martin Lings, in his book of that name, describes it like this;

> From time to time a Revelation 'flows' like a great tidal wave from the Ocean of Infinitude to the shores of our finite world; and Sufism is the vocation and the discipline and the science of plunging into the ebb of one of these waves and being drawn back with it to its Eternal and Infinite Source. (Lings, 1981, p. 11)

Later in the book Lings answers the question 'What form does the tidal wave take?' with 'Above all the form of a book namely the Qur'an' (p. 25). He also explains, quoting Ibn Kaldun, that for the first three generations of Islam, mysticism was a general attribute. It was only after worldliness crept in and people became more and more bound up with the ties of this life that

'Those who dedicated themselves to the worship of God were distinguished from the rest by the title of Sufis' (p. 45). Sufis come from both Sunni and Shia Islam; it is their mystical approach which distinguishes them.

Between one-third and one-half of the Muslim world is involved in some kind of Sufi brotherhood. The Sufis represent a more mystical, poetical dimension of Islam, and are found in most of the schools, or sects, of Islam. It was al-Ghazali who began to combine classical learning with mystical Islam around AD1111.

The word *suf* is usually interpreted as meaning 'wool' and represents the woollen garments that the early Sufi mystic used to wear. This was a carry-over from the monkish habit of the Christian ascetics of the sixth and seventh centuries: for Islam, however, Muhammad himself is seen to be the prime example of a mystic, because of the mystical nature of the revelations and visions that came to him.

In the developing centuries of Islam, the study and practice of the law was seen to be far more respectable than the gyrations of babbling, wild-eyed, ascetic mystics. It was not until al-Ghazali became disenchanted with his academic, legalistic studies and took up the practice of meditation and the Sufi internalisation of the law that Sufism became respectable. Traditional Islamic law is an external imposition of rules and regulations. The Sufi sees beyond the external and seeks to internalise an experience with the help of either his particular teacher or with Muhammad, who will then be able to lead the initiate into communion with God. Muhammad is seen to be the pole round which the universe is ordered because he pleased God. Disciples strive towards this 'pole' or 'axis' of pleasing God.

The Sufis are divided into numerous religious orders of dervishes or faqirs. Although they differ in name and in some of their customs, such as dress, meditations, and recitations, they are all agreed in their principal tenets; particularly those which inculcate the necessity of absolute submission to a *murshid* or 'inspired guide'. It is generally admitted that, irrespective of minor sects, the Sufis are divided into those who claim to be only the *ilhamiyya* or 'inspired of God' and those who assert that they are *ittihadiyya* or 'in union with God'.

This complete union with God is the goal Sufis are hoping to attain. 'Relax the mind and learn to swim' was the advice of the Shaykh Ali al–Jamal to his pupil Shaykh ad-Darqawi, regarding the state of perplexity.

> In other words, let go of your mind so that your soul, now out of its depth, may experience the spontaneous stirrings of intuition, just as a body out of its depth in water may experience the spontaneous stirring of its limbs in the movements of swimming, provided that there is no 'straw' to clutch at. (Lings p. 67)

One of the first known teachers of Sufi ideas was al-Sufi, who was a Shia chemist in Kufa. Hasan al-Basri, who died in AD728, was also a teacher of mysticism. One of his sayings was, 'He that knoweth God loveth him, and he that knoweth the world abstaineth from it.' Lings describes this saying as 'the very quintessence of Sufism' (p. 106). As time went on, Sufi teaching aroused criticism. Hallaj made the statement, 'I am the truth.' Many people took him to mean by this statement that he was God; he was saying, however, that he had come to such a height of spiritual experience that he had found complete union with God. Nevertheless, after a trial lasting seven months, he was condemned to death in AD922. Sufis have a genealogy of spiritual teachers, a hierarchy reaching back to Muhammad. Modern Sufis each have their own individual line reaching back to the Prophet and, through him, to God himself.

During this period 900 to 975, four poets from Basrah were responsible for the collection of what is called the *rasa'il* or 'letters', numbering 51 or 52. Incorporated into this is a collection of Hindu folk laws, among which are stories and fables of a ringed dove (taken as the symbol of fellowship). Their followers came to be known as the Brethren of Purity (*Ikhwan al Safa*). The collection was divided into four parts:

1 Mathematical sciences, arithmetic, geometry, astronomy, music.
2 Physical sciences, medicine, logic, chemistry, biology.

3 Intellectual/moral sciences, soul, intellect, resurrection.
4 Metaphysical, jurisprudence, rational perception of certain subjects, astrology, magic under a religious title.

The whole of life was reduced to a single creative impulse, having as its objective the release of the soul and union with the universal. (Here we can see the influence of neo-Platonic Greek thought, as well as Zoroastrianism and Hinduism, upon Islam.)

Sources of revelation

The Sufis claim that divine reality is perceived by three organs of human perception. First, *qalb*, or 'the heart', which is the seat of the emotions; secondly, *ruh*, or 'spirit', through which knowledge is perceived; and thirdly, *sira*, or 'secret', which would be a secret developed or revealed by a teacher, who passes it on to his disciples when he feels they are ready to receive it.

The Sufi disciples are gathered together in orders known as *tarikas*. Each *tarika* develops its own ritual and style. Common to many of them is the *dhikr*, which is the constant repetition of the name or names of God. This constant repitition induces a trance-like state and is accompanied by drum beating, the playing of various musical instruments, and the rhythmic movement of the body. By contrast, another technique is meditation, where silence provides an atmosphere within which the disciple thinks about the names of God. Finally, there is the use of dreams to reveal inner truths.

One way in which Islam spread, particularly into black Africa, Central Asia, and India, was through travelling holy men or *awliya*, known as *pirs* in the Indian sub-continent. They were popular with the local people, since they brought with them special powers of healing and miracle working and were not strict in their position on Islamic law. They were the possessors of a certain type of charisma known as *baraka*. (In fact, when these men died, tombs were erected over their graves and they became places of pilgrimage. Just to touch the tomb was believed to transfer the *baraka*, or blessing of the dead, to the one coming to receive a blessing.)

The miracle worker (*karama*) was also a popular figure. He would write verses of the Qur'an on pieces of paper and then dip them in water; people would be healed by drinking the water. The miracle worker might also be someone to go to for advice concerning a marriage, planting of crops, or to seek the inducing of conception.

The organisation of Sufi orders into *tarikas* brought a standardisation within the order and the possibility of promoting its goals amongst the general population.

A number of Sufi movements were established, particularly in Turkey, India and West Africa. One such movement was the whirling dervishes, followers of the Mevlana Rumi. They spent their time meditating on the Names of God while spinning round on their feet; a technique which induced trances.

Sufism has gradually moved away from Islamic culture founded on the Hadith and the Shari'a and has been influenced by the popular, indigenous cultures. Popular Islam is the subject of the next chapter, where we shall see something of the grip that it holds over many Muslims.

The Ahmadiyya sect

This is probably the most well-known and most aggressive Muslim sect today. It came out of British India. It was founded by Mirza Ghulam Ahmad, a chief of the village of Qadian in the Punjab. Religious syncretism seems to have run in Ahmad's family, and the Ahmadiyya movement has become very adept at this process. Whilst remaining a Muslim he posed as a guru (teacher), professing to have come into the spirit and power of Jesus Christ and to be the promised Messiah. He also claimed to be in the spirit and power of Muhammad and to be the promised Ahmad ('Praised One'), as well as the spirit and power of Krishna and the promised, future incarnation expected by all Hindus. His attempt to unite the main religions of India (Islam, Hinduism, and Christianity) could be seen as a pacifist attempt to combat the rule of the British in India and to re-establish Indian glory. To have embarked upon a bloody, holy war against the ruling British would have been suicidal for him: and thus, one of the central claims of the Ahmadiyya movement has been non-violence.

In order to clear the way for his own messianic claims he held that Jesus Christ did not die on the cross, but actually went to India to preach to the descendants of the ten lost tribes in Afghanistan and Kashmir. Jesus is said to have died a natural death in Kashmir, where his tomb exists today.

Ahmad claimed that Jesus was on the cross only a few hours and that his legs were not broken. He only became unconscious through the loss of blood and finally was revived in the darkness and coolness of the tomb. Later he left the Holy Land to go to India. This is a revival of the nineteenth-century 'swoon' theory. Ahmad interpreted Jesus' claim to be the 'sign of Jonah' as confirmation that Jesus never died. Jesus said, 'For as Jonah was three days and three nights in the belly of a large fish, so the Son of Man will be three days and three nights in the heart of the earth' (Mt 12:40). But, says Ahmad, Jonah entered the belly of the fish alive and remained there alive and came out alive; so must Jesus have entered the tomb alive, remained there alive, and come out alive in order to make the analogy complete.

Finally, he points to the spiritual death of Christianity, since the fruits of Christianity in the West are obviously corrupt. The Ahmadiyya were the first Islamic group to establish a mosque in Britain (Woking, Surrey), and have embarked upon an aggressive 'evangelistic' campaign to convert Europeans to the Muslim cause.

In September 1974, following the recommendations of an International Muslim Conference held in Saudi Arabia in February of that year, the Ahmadiyyas were declared a non-Muslim sect by the government of Pakistan. The reason was that Ahmad claimed that he, not Muhammad, was the final prophet.

The Ahmadiyya have been through periods of persecution. Many lost their lives after the partition of India and others more recently since the sect was declared non-Muslim.

Modern movements

Since the end of European domination in India, Egypt and other countries of the Middle East, European culture has had less influence and a new vibrant Islamic fundamentalism has arisen. This back-to-the-roots fundamentalist movement is found among both Sunnis and Shia's. It is the subject of Chapter 14. An older puritanical expression of Islam is found among the Wahabis in Saudi Arabia; it, too, seems to be gaining strength. Both these movements appear to be a reaction against Western secular society.

Notes

How did you get on with making your lists in Activity 10:1? The tight-knit structure of Islam, with its set prayers and detailed rules, helps to keep people together. So do the focus on the holy city of Mecca and the concept of the Umma. Christians focus on Jesus Christ and the Bible, but are free to worship and live in different ways, as long as they are in line with biblical teaching. One problem for Muslims, as we saw in the last chapter, was the succession after Muhammad. Another problem is that Islam is so bound up with Arab culture that it may clash with local, indigenous cultures. We can see the results of this in the next chapter. The section on Islam in Africa in Chapter 13 illustrates this problem. Is it true, do you think, that divisions in Christianity are usually doctrinal and in Islam usually political? Have you been able to compare Sunni and Shia Islam (Activity 10:2)? Perhaps recent events in Iran help us to see the different attitudes.

Books referred to in the chapter

Bowker, John, *Worlds of Faith* (BBC Ariel: London, 1983).

Lings, Martin, *What is Sufism?* (Islamic Texts Society/Allen & Unwin: London, 2nd edn 1981).

Nasr, Seyyed Hossein, *Ideals and Realities of Islam* (Allen & Unwin: London 2nd edn 1975).

Ruthven, Malise, *Islam in the World* (Pelican: Harmondsworth, rev edn 1991).

For further reading

Lings, Martin, *What is Sufism?* (Islamic Texts Society/Allen & Unwin: London 2nd, edn 1981) [new edn ITS: Cambridge, 1993]. A concise and authoritative introduction to Sufism.

Molteno, Marion, *A Language in Common* (The Women's Press: London, 1987). The story entitled 'The Flood' gives a sensitive and sympathetic account of the Ahmediyya Movement in narrative form.

Mottahedeh, Ron, *The Mantle of the Prophet* (Penguin: Harmondsworth, 1985) [new edn 1987]. The history and politics of Iran, told through the eyes of a young Mullah in the holy city of Qom. Gives a detailed description of Shia Islam.

Ruthven, Malise, *Islam in the World* (Pelican: Harmondsworth, rev edn 1991), Chapter 5 ('Sects and Solidarity') discusses the various Muslim sects and gives an historical analysis of them.

Wootton, R. F. W., *Understanding the Sects of Islam.* (rev edn of Wootton, *Understanding Muslim Sects*) (FFM/CPO: Worthing, 1992). A useful summary.

The Popular Face of Islam

Study guide

In the last chapter we read about the travelling sufis, organised into tarikas, *who spread Islam into Black Africa, Central Asia and India (Section 6, p 187). As their teaching mingled with local indigenous cultures it produced a popular expression of Islam very different from the orthodox Sunni Islam described in Part II of this book. This chapter describes popular Islam and gives something of the feel of being under its power. It is the Islam of the masses of Muslims at the 'grass-roots' level.*

When you have completed the chapter we hope you will:

1 *Understand that large numbers of Muslims are involved in the popular expression of Islam;*
2 *See how people can be bound by taboos, magic and occult practices; and*
3 *Recognise that it is only the power of the Lord Jesus Christ which can cast out evil spirits and bring love, joy and hope to those oppressed by them.*

The great veil

In the name of God, the compassionate, the Merciful.

Praise be to God, Lord of the two worlds, and blessing and peace be upon the most noble of his messengers, our Lord Muhammad and his family and followers, every one of them.

It was reported by Solomon, son of David, peace be upon them, a son of God, that he saw an old gray-haired woman with blue eyes and eyebrows which joined in the middle, thin legs, dishevelled hair and mouth agape, from which came a breath of flame. She was breaking up the ground with her nails and felling trees with her voice. So our Lord Solomon, peace be upon him, said to her, 'Are you human or a demon? I've never seen anyone uglier than you!'

She replied, 'I'm the mother of children, mistress over the sons of Adam and the daughters of Eve. I enter a house and shriek in it with the call of the cockerel, I bark in it with the bark of a dog. I drop manure like the bull and cow. I cough like a camel. I neigh like a horse. I bray like a donkey and hiss like a snake and I mimic them all excellently. I bind up wombs and destroy children without anyone knowing it's me. I visit a woman and close her womb; I block her so that she can't become pregnant . . .

Solomon, peace be upon him, grabbed hold of her and said, 'O wicked woman, you're not leaving my grip until you give me your word and bond concerning the sons of Adam and the daughters of Eve and the swelling of their wombs and their children and their women. If you don't cooperate, I'll kill you with this sword!'

So she said to him, 'O son of God! Here is my word and agreement: it is contained in this covenant. I won't approach or harm anyone who has had it written out and who carries it with him or hangs it in his shop or business premises or who pins it on his cattle or children, sons and daughters. I won't come near him as long as the covenant is protecting him. He can travel in peace and arrive anywhere in peace. I swear to you that I will not approach anyone on whom it is carried. God is my witness and guarantor over what I declare.

So run the opening paragraphs of one of the most popular amulets of protection in the Muslim Middle East. The Prophet Solomon is especially renowned as having authority to assist human beings troubled by *jinn*. The spirit who goes by the name Mother of Children (*Umm al-Subyan*) is believed to be one of the most powerful forces for harm amongst Egyptian Muslims. She has her named equivalents in North Africa, Iran and other areas of the Islamic world. At times of vulnerability in human life, this spirit delights in interfering and causing damage. Protection from the havoc wrought by her is constantly sought by ordinary Muslims.

The Seven Covenants of Solomon, as this amulet is often entitled, projects us into a world far removed from that of formal faith. Prophets are sought out, in this definition of their significance, according to their reputation in handling demons. Verses from the Qur'an, names of God, archangels and angels of renown are enlisted to help ordinary people recover their equilibrium in a world knocked out of kilter by a huge variety of trans-empirical persons and forces. Millions of Muslims spend much of their time and money seeking to reset the balance of their personal worlds. They are far removed, in such activities, from the theological niceties of faith and submission. Instead, they are locked into the concepts and intricate activities of the world of popular Islam.

1

Sickness

Ordinary Muslims are intensely pragmatic people. When illness strikes, their goal is to find out precisely what is wrong and how best to remedy the situation. In searching out what is wrong, their focus is concentrated on the 'why' of the problem. With the real cause laid bare, a remedy can be deduced which will meet the full impact of the scenario lying behind the symptoms. In the worldview of popular Islam, that scenario includes many complex possibilities both as to cause and to potential cure.

Natural causes

Lots of sicknesses are seen as the result of purely natural causes. Purely natural solutions are therefore appropriate in those cases. The whole range of orthodox medical skill, backed up by pharmacological practice, is designed to meet such needs and is increasingly available at town and village level throughout the Muslim world. Equally, many traditional societies categorise foods and natural medicines on a 'hot' and 'cold' basis. If a person falls ill of a 'hot' condition, the remedy consists in defining an appropriately 'cold' substance to counterbalance the overheating. The process is the equivalent of some of the inherited lore of Westerners with regard to medical problems: 'Feed a cold but starve a fever' for example. Grandmothers, midwives and baths attendants are the repositories of such wisdom.

Taboo-breaking

A different kind of cause of sickness is found in the idea of taboo-breaking. Failure to observe taboos can reap serious illness for the persons concerned. A common taboo is that of naming diseases which are considered fatal. In Sudan, for example, tuberculosis is euphemistically called 'the cold disease' (*al-marad al-barad*). To name the actual disease would call it into being. In the complex *mushahara* customs of Egypt, sickness in a woman who is in a state of vulnerability around childbirth is nearly always seen as the result of taboo-breaking. The word *mushahara* is derived from the Arabic for 'moon' or 'month'. The period of *mushahara* stretches from about the seventh month of pregnancy until a week after giving birth. During this period, the woman is considered to be in a period of crisis. Evil spirits are especially feared for the damage they might cause to the woman or the child. Such spirits are easily transmitted by contact with the dead, the sick, some precious metals, some foods, even visitors who have been to a funeral. People visiting a woman around the time of childbirth carefully exorcise such spirits from themselves by looking into a well or spinning around outside the door before entering. The parturient woman herself is forbidden from seeing the sick or visiting a bereaved neighbour. Should the taboos be broken, certain procedures are put into immediate effect in order to restore equilibrium before a tragedy occurs. (cf El-Safi, 1971, p. 20–21)

Evil eye

The evil eye is recognised as a common cause of sickness, even death, despite the many precautions taken to prevent its effect. An investigator in an Iranian village uncovered a typical case of illness induced by the evil eye. A child was taken ill with throat irritations and coughing. Some herbal medicine was administered. When, on the third night, he suddenly developed a fever, it was concluded that he had been struck by the evil eye. An egg-breaking ceremony was held to discover the culprit. In this ritual, a practitioner (a local woman) held an egg lightly between the palms of her two hands, gently exerting pressure on it, while the names of people recently encountered by the child were spoken out one by one. The egg broke when a female attendant at the village bath-house was named. This lady, though she had no history of throwing the evil eye, was recalled to have admired the child. With the spell thus broken and with a special herb burning around him as a further precaution, it was expected that the boy would quickly recover. However, the child's condition did not improve and he was finally taken to a doctor for injections and cough syrup. Within two days he had recovered. When the investigator asked the child's father how it was that the doctor had cured the child if the cause had been the evil eye, he was told: 'The child of course had two conditions at the same time. He had a cold, but he had also been hit by the evil eye. The doctor cured the cold, but of course he was powerless against the bad eye and we took care of that in our own ways' (Alberts, 1963, p. 928).

Magic

Sorcery and harmful magic are seen as strong causes of illness or misfortune. They are much more serious than the evil eye, though thankfully not so common. Om Naeema's mother was the second wife to her husband. When she became pregnant, the first wife (who had produced only daughters) went to a seer to find out if Om Naeema's mother was carrying a boy or a girl. When the first wife (Fatma) discovered from the seer that she was about to be upstaged by a son-producer, she decided to resort to magic:

> Fatma then went to her maternal uncle who was a wise man and asked him to help. She wanted to place a spell on my mother which would make her seem hideous to her new husband, causing him to reject her. This she did by taking some of my mother's hair, her head scarf, a string to represent her height, a piece of her underclothing, and a five pound note in payment for the man's

services. The spell was cast, and soon the magic began to work my father over. One day he got up and announced to all that, come what may, he did not want this woman who was his new wife. People said to him, 'Think, Ahmad, this woman is pregnant with your child and may give you a little son.' But he would not listen and answered, 'Let her go to hell. I don't want her. When she stands before me, I see a monkey.' So he rejected her and sent her back to her father's house. There she gave birth to her first child, my eldest brother. People then came again to my father and said to him, 'Be reasonable, Ahmad, take back your wife. You are now father to a son.' But he persisted, answering, 'I don't want the boy or his mother.' (Atiya, 1982, p. 133)

Diagnosis of such a cause usually requires a special practitioner and will include some form of divination. A counter-measure of stronger power is the solution aimed at.

Jinn

Certain named *jinn*, such as Umm al-Subyan, are thought to cause specific diseases and even death. In Morocco the best-known inflicter of disease is the infamous A'isha Qandisha, a female spirit with very alluring qualities around whom a group of dancing devotees, the Hamadsha, has developed:

Q. was about 14 years old when he was first struck by a *jinn*. His family had recently moved to Moulay Idriss to find work and were staying with his sister. Q. laughed at a group of Sidi Ali's followers who were performing in the street. He claims that he had never heard the Hamadsha before. The moment he laughed, he was stricken with a paralysis of the lower limbs. His sister immediately understood that A'isha Qandisha had struck him, and invited in the Hamadsha to perform the hadra (trance-dance) for her brother. First a sacrifice . . . was made, and then the Hamadsha danced for Q. Q. too began to dance and to slash his head. He has been a follower of Sidi Ali ever since, and considers himself to be dependent on A'isha Qandisha. (Grapansano, 1973, p. 160)

Different kinds of *jinn* possess differing grades of power. The Qur'an authenticates their existence and many ordinary Muslims know the effect of their mischief in their daily living.

Qarina

The spirit-double of the human being (the *qarina*) is also thought to be responsible for some sicknesses. In the Philippines, offending the *inikadowa* or twin-spirit of a person is a sure cause of trouble for contemporary Muslims (cf Gowing, 1969, p. 23). Various ceremonies performed by, or in the name of, the sufferer are designed to appease the twin-spirit.

Fate

Fate is often blamed for sickness, especially where it has led to permanent disability or death. A friend who was a lawyer in Cairo ran over and killed a girl with his car. The court case extended for several months with the prosecutor wanting especially to punish the lawyer for various political reasons. Suddenly the charges were dropped and the bereaved family no longer wanted to continue with the prosecution. They had come to the conclusion that the hand of *qadr* (fate) had been behind their daughter's death. Why punish a mere human being?

God

The ultimate appeal in the matter of causality in sickness is to God. Maybe he has punished someone for some sin. Maybe he has simply willed that now is the time for that person to die.

Sickness is one of a variety of crises ordinary Muslims have to face. The formal faith of Islam might emphasise the sovereignty of God, even to a degree which encourages a deterministic or fatalistic outlook on life. In practice, however, Muslims work hard at finding ways and means to combat the crises that overtake them. Their view of reality is complex. Their world is filled with potential powers and persons, both harmful and helpful.

It is in the activities arising from their concepts of causality that we are able as observers to learn more of the intricacies of the world in which they exist.

Activity 11:1

Can you think of any taboos we have in our own societies
concerning illness?

2

The unofficial feast

There are two major Islamic festivals which come round every
lunar year, celebrated with great joy by nearly all Muslims.
They are the feast days at the end of the month of fasting and
the sacrifice days at the end of the time of pilgrimage.

There is another festival, however, not officially counte-
nanced but in practice enjoyed by many Muslims: the Birthday
of the Prophet (*Mawlid al-Nabi*). It is celebrated on the twelfth
of Rabri al-Awwal, the third month of the Islamic year. For
Muslims, the birth of the Prophet constitutes one of the most
important events in world history. In many places, the whole
of the month of Rabi' al-Awwal is given over to gatherings of
Muslims intent on 'remembering' him.

Songs of praise

Various praise-songs are sung in memory of Muhammad,
Ahmad or Mustafa as the Prophet is variously called. Al-
Busiri's 'Mantle Poem' is one of the most popular recitations in
the Arab world. In Turkey, Suleman Chelebi's '*Mevlidi Sherif*'
(Birth-Song of the Prophet) is commonly chanted.

Chelebi was a contemporary of Chaucer. He died in AD1421
and was buried at Bursa, where his tomb is still revered. At the
end of the fourteenth century, Chelebi was a royal cleric to
Sultan Beyazid. When Tamerland overthrew Beyazid, Chelebi
took refuge in the Great Mosque in Bursa. There he completed
his '*Mevlidi Sherif*' to confute a teaching that Muhammad was
no greater than other prophets.

The song-poem is hauntingly beautiful. After an introduction,

Chelebi describes the prophetic succession as it makes its way from Adam to fulfilment in Prophet Muhammad:

> When man was first by Allah's pow'r created,
> The ornament was he of all things living.
> To Adam came all angels in submission,
> A gesture oft, at God's command, repeated.
> On his brow first God set the Light of Prophets.
> Saying: This Light belongs to my Beloved.
> Long years that Light shone there, nor ever wavered,
> Until the prophet's earthly life was ended.
> Know that to Eve's brow next the Light migrated,
> Remaining there through many months and seasons.
> Then Seth received this sigil of Mustafa,
> Which glowed more bright as year to year was added.
> Thus Abraham and Ishmael received it—
> My time would fail should all the line be counted.
>
> From brow to brow, in linked chain unbroken,
> The Light at last attained its goal, Muhammad.
> The Mercy of the Worlds appeared, and straightway
> To him the Light took wing, its journey ended.
> Give ear, then to his merits, O ye pious,
> And know who is the one will justify us.
>
> If from Hell's flame you hope to find salvation,
> With love and zeal repeat the Salutation.
> *Response*
> Blessing and greeting upon thee, O Apostle of Allah!
> Blessing and greeting upon thee, O Beloved of Allah!

The birth of Prophet Muhammad is next described. Three angelic beings greet Muhammad's mother, Amina, as she is about to be delivered of a special son:

> No son like thine, such strength and grace possessing,
> Hath God to earth sent down, for its redressing.
> Great favour hast thou found, thou lovely mother,
> To bear a son surpassing every other.
> Sultan is he, all hidden truth possessing,
> Full knowledge of the Unity professing.
> For love of him, thy son, the skies are turning;
> Mankind and angels for his face are yearning.

This is the night foretold in song and story,
In which the worlds rejoice to see his glory.

On goes the paean of praise, describing the apostle's character, miracles and journey to heaven where God himself communes with Muhammad:

'I am your heart's desire,' he said, 'your solace,
Your only love, the only God you worship.
For me by night and day you sigh, unceasing,
And say: 'Why may I not behold his beauty?'
Come Friend, the love I feel for you is boundless,
To you I give all people for your bondsmen.
Whatever you desire shall now be granted;
For every ill a thousand cures stand ready.'

And what does Muhammad ask for? He asks for grace for his halting, rebellious people:

O Majesty, this is my sole petition—
My people, may they be by thee accepted.

And the response from on high?

From Truth Supreme a loving cry resounded:
'I grant them all to you, my friend, Muhammad!'

At the end of the chant comes a petition on behalf of Muslims of all ages. It constitutes a deep confession of sin. It looks for hope to God's mercy and to Prophet Muhammad's intercession for his people:

So come, let us confess our sad rebellions;
With secret moan and bitter groan repenting.
Though life should last however many seasons,
Death shall one day become our sole employment.
So let us now defeat death's pangs and sadness,
By evermore entreating: 'God forgive us!'
Our deeds have ever been of God unworthy;
We know not what may be our last condition.
Our worthless course have we not left nor altered
No preparations made for life eternal.
Our names we make to shine before the people,

But secretly our hearts we all have tarnished.
Each breath sees us commit sins by the thousand,
Yet not once in our life repent we one sin.
Yielding to self we sin and know no limit—
What shall we do, O God, how make repentance?
No one of us but knows his heart's sedition,
Yet we have come, thy mercy to petition.
We hope for grace to make a good profession,
For Mercy's touch, and Ahmad's intercession.

(Chelebi, 1943)

Equivalent song-stories of Prophet Muhammad's life, mission, character, sufferings and success are recited throughout the Muslim world during *Mawlid al-Nabi*. Processions frequently take place during the festival, with Sufi orders leading public dances in honour of the Prophet. People buy and wear new clothes and eat special sweets. Communities vie with one another to put on the most spectacular Mawlid entertainments.

Activity 11:2

This beautiful poem can only offer a life 'evermore entreating: "God forgive us!"' How would you explain God's forgiveness and what it means to you?

3

For love of the Prophet

The many-faceted phenomenon of Muhammad-veneration, by no means confined to acts of popular devotion during *Mawlid al-Nabi*, is by and large accepted by proponents of the formal faith of Islam. Reverence for relics of the Prophet, such as the footprints on the rock in the Dome at Jerusalem or his tomb in Medina or the hair from his beard in Topkapi, Istanbul, is shared by all pilgrims, whether they are professors or peasants. Addressing the Prophet with blessings and prayers constitutes an important facet of daily religious experience for most Muslims. It takes the form of pronouncing the *tasliya*: the words *Salla Allah alayhi was sallam* give the sense of 'God bless him and grant him peace.' The *tasliya* is traditionally uttered every time a Muslim enters or leaves a mosque.

Saints and shrines

On the wings of such veneration of Prophet Muhammad, the whole theme of sainthood and *pir* worship has flown into the centre of the received and accepted expression of the faith. Shrine visitation, with its focus on vow-making, occurs on a massive scale throughout the Muslim world. The possibility of poorer Muslims making a substitute pilgrimage to a local shrine, instead of the preferred pilgrimage to Mecca, has helped popularise such activity.

The orientation of Muslim pilgrims at such shrines is towards either living or deceased saints. The words used for 'saint' evoke various aspects of the kind of help expected from them: *wali* (friend, patron, saint), *murshid* (guide), *shafi* (intercessor), *shaykh* (leader), *pir* (holy man), *murabit* ('one who has joined himself' to God). The processes of interaction with saints are two-way (saint to pilgrim and pilgrim to saint) so that both parties benefit.

The Indian subcontinent is covered with shrines. Such shrines may be tombs of deceased saints, places where a living saint (*pir*) resides, or a combination of the two. Parshall describes a visit to a *pir* of the Naqshbandi order:

> There in the most remote of villages was what looked like a small town. Hundreds of lights were strung over two mammoth buildings, each the size of a football field. Huge tents had been erected; under these, one hundred thousand devotees were sitting and listening to a fiery orator holding forth regarding the virtues of the *pir*. Scores of small stores were selling everything from tea to religious charms. The government had made special arrangements to bring electricity and even a telephone exchange to the *pir*'s home. I was told a runway was soon to be constructed to enable people to fly in to see the *pir* . . . As we walked around in bare feet (no shoes were allowed on such holy ground) we were amazed to see the enormity

of the *pir*'s following. We heard the *pir* extolled as a 'flower descended from heaven.' The meeting place was described as the 'center of the universe' . . . The *pir* did not make an appearance during our time at the meeting. We understood that he would lead in prayers at 3am. He is about sixty years old and has two sons. His devotees worship him, while his critics consider him a corrupted religious leader who has turned Islam into a business venture. He initiates his disciples by pressing his finger into their chests just over the heart. At that time the devotee becomes filled with God and actually hears the voice of Allah within his body.'

(Parshall, 1983, pp. 46–47)

The veneration of Muhammad and the common appeal of ordinary Muslims the world over to local dead and living saints betrays the sense of 'need-for-help-now' which formal Islam fails to address adequately. When all is said and done, the concerns of ordinary Muslims will continue to require attention. The worldview of popular Islam, illustrated in this chapter in terms of concepts of causality, is built upon and integrates with those daily concerns. Ideal or theological Islam has few resources for handling the daily needs and nightly dreads of ordinary Muslims.

Activity 11:3

Pause and think about the power of the Lord Jesus over evil spirits. Read Dr Luke's account of one occasion when this was shown in Luke 9: 37–45.

4

The burden-bearer

Jesus Christ and his apostles lived in a world where the needy folk around them—Jews, Romans, Syro-Phoenicians—had a fear of disequilibrium similar to that of ordinary Muslims today. The realities of sickness, demon-possession, sorcery, encounters with the devil, angels and deceased ancestors, dreams and visions, exorcism, miracles of nature and so on fill the pages of the New Testament.

Getting to know the Om Naeemas of the Islamic world can help recapture for Western secularised Christians something of the fuller reality, seen as true by first century people and treated as true by Jesus and his followers.

Getting to know better the Christ of the New Testament can help Western Christians work with greater compassion and power within the construct of the world embraced by ordinary Muslims. Mission to Muslims is not necessarily so much a matter of trying to convey critical information, against most of which the Muslim is already 'inoculated'. It is a question of preaching the gospel with power, with the Holy Spirit, and with deep conviction, as well as with words (1 Thess 1:5). Issues of healing in Christ's name, deliverance from evil, public trust in a Son of Mary already admitted by Muslims to be alive and well in heaven (even if uncrucified!) can become areas of experiential growth for Western Christians, if we will take seriously both the New Testament record and our Muslim friends.

The 'heart of the matter' lies here, according to Glasser:

> Only when Muslims reach out to Jesus and find in him the solution to their immediate needs do they become aware of their greater needs—access to God, the forgiveness of sin, justifying grace and eternal life. And when they begin to seek him as Lord and Savior, their 'theological problems' begin to evaporate . . . (Glasser, 1978, pp. 137–138)

Can we learn to be faithful, sensitive introducers of the great burden-bearer to our Muslim friends?

Notes

This chapter has shown something of the hold that popular Islam has over ordinary people; it has also revealed something of the hidden occult powers it uses. Before we dismiss it as being irrelevant to the rationalistic West, remember the increasing prominence of horoscopes, superstitions and more damaging occult practices in our own cultures. Yes, we have our taboos as well (Activity 11:1). They are often connected with illness and death; things we don't talk about, words like 'cancer' we don't use.

Assurance of forgiveness is such a wonderful truth that it is difficult even for Christians to fully grasp it. We need to do more than explain how 'Jesus died that we might be forgiven'. We need to live our lives like forgiven people (Activity 11:2). We need to do something else, as we think about this chapter. We need to call on the Lord Jesus to overcome evil spirits and occult practices whether in Islam, Christianity, or any other religion (Activity 11:3).

Books referred to in the chapter

Alberts, Robert Charles, *Social Structure and Culture Change in an Iranian Village*. 2 vols. (University Microfilms: Ann Arbor, Michigan, 1963).

Atiya, Nayra, *Khuyl-Khaal: Five Egyptian Women Tell Their Stories* (American Univ in Cairo Press: Cairo, 1982).

Chelebi, Suleyman, tr. F. Lyman MacCallum, *The Mevledi Sherif* (John Murray: London, 1943).

Crapanzano, Vincent, *The Hamadsha: A Study in Moroccan Ethnopsychiatry* (Univ of California Press: Berkeley, 1973).

Gowing, Peter G., 'How Muslim are the Muslim Filipinos?' *Solidarity*, vol iv no 8, 1969.

El-Safi, Ahmed, *Native Medicine in the Sudan: Sources, Concepts and Methods* (Salamah: Prizes Series No 1. Sudan Research Unit: Khartoum, 1971).

Parshall, Phil, *Bridges to Islam* (Baker: Grand Rapids, Michigan, 1983).

Glasser, Arthur F., 'Power Encounter in Conversion from Islam' in Don M. McCurry (ed), *The Gospel and Islam: A Compendium* (MARC: Monrovia, California, 1979).

For further reading

Musk, Bill, *The Unseen Face of Islam* (MARC Monarch: Eastbourne, 1989). By the author of this chapter. It covers in detail the subjects discussed here and gives a sensitive and comprehensive overall view of popular Islam.

A Christian Response to Islam

Study guide

Having looked at the history of Islam and at its different expressions, we turn now to spend this chapter looking at the Christian response down through the years. We hope that you will find the lives of those Christians whose one aim was to win Muslims to Christ both helpful and inspiring. We hope, too, that an understanding of historical events such as the Crusades will help to explain some of the barriers and the prejudices you may have to overcome. The original chapter was written by Ronald Waine. Much of his material is used in this revision.

When you have completed this chapter we hope you will:

1 Have an overall view of Muslim-Christian relationships;
2 By looking at the lives of some Christians who have worked among Muslims, have seen why they were able to accomplish so much; and
3 Have considered the place of the Eastern Orthodox Churches for mission in the future.

Let us go first to Jerusalem.

Here is where the three monotheistic religions meet. Here is where their beliefs conflict.

Jews, praying on the Sabbath at the massive Western Wall—all that remains of their temple, first built by Solomon.

Christians, following the Via Dolorosa to the Church of the Holy Sepulchre, the path Christ took to his crucifixion.

Muslims, visiting the Dome of the Rock, the third most holy

place in Islam, bowing before the footprints of their Prophet Muhammad, from where he ascended to heaven on the Night Journey.

A city where millions have worshipped their God. But one torn apart by strife down through the ages. Again we see the dilemma of humankind. It should not surprise us that relationships between Christians and Muslims have also been marked by hostility and conflict.

At first it seems that Muhammad was hoping for some sort of alliance with the Jews and Christians of the Arabian peninsula. This soon proved to be an impossible dream and as his teaching developed, his attitude changed from one of friendly association to open disagreement. However, he did recommend to his followers that they should not dispute with the 'people of the Book':

> And dispute ye not
> With the people of the Book,
> Except with means better
> (Than mere disputation), unless
> It be with those of them
> Who inflict wrong (and injury):
> But say, 'We believe
> In the Revelation which has
> Come down to us and in that
> Which came down to you:
> Our Allah and your Allah
> Is One; and it is to Him
> We bow (in Islam).' (Qur'an 29:46)

Some Christians welcomed the Muslims as 'liberators', and the Muslim armies spread the new faith through the lands surrounding Arabia. The two faiths, either in friendship or on sufferance, managed to live side by side.

The early relationship between Islam and Christianity might perhaps have been different if:

1 *Muhammad's knowledge of Christianity had been more accurate.* He seems to have gained his knowledge from his acquaintance and association with a decadent form of Christianity.

2 *The church had been stronger and nearer in doctrine to the apostolic teaching.*

3 *Muhammad had been able to consult the Bible in his own language.* There was no translation of the Bible available in Arabic before AD737, more than 100 years after his death.

1

The spread of Islam

As early as AD633, one year after the death of Muhammad, army detachments had penetrated Syria to the North and Persia to the East. An astonishing number of towns, regions, and states were conquered in an incredibly short time. A list of the dates when the towns fell helps us appreciate the speed of the advance.

Damascus	635
Jerusalem	640
Alexandria	642
Isfahan	643
Tripoli	647
Cyprus	649

Tunisia, Algeria, and Morocco were occupied, and toward the end of the seventh century the Atlantic coast was reached.

The churches in the Middle East and Mediterranean World which had been founded by the apostles were, at first, flourishing Christian communities. They began to struggle against the power of the Byzantine and Persian Empires. Their cause was not helped by the fact that they were formed from three culturally and ethnically different groups. With the rise of the Islamic empire in the seventh century AD, the churches were treated as one Christian group, which made them seem both disunited and, as some thought, decadent. They were seen to be more preoccupied with doctrinal disputes and heresy-hunts than with the declaration of the gospel.

The Arab conquest swept aside old frontiers. From the seventh century onwards the Coptic and Syrian Churches do not seem to have played a decisive role in the history of their own territories. Theirs was a culture in isolation and decline and the interest of their story lies in the consequences of the reception given to the Muslim armies by the church leaders: thereafter it is a tale of the dour struggle for survival. In spite of the fact that millions of Christians were to live in close contact with Muslims, only small numbers were brought into the churches. There was, however, a steady stream of converts consistently brought into the Coptic and Syrian Churches through their system of catechism.

At first the Muslims did not seek to propagate their faith amongst their subjects except those of the Arab race. During the first seventy years of Muslim expansion the subjected people were left very much to their own devices. But, by AD705 the church of St John at Damascus, which until then had been shared for Muslim and Christian worship, was completely taken over by the Muslims. From then on Arabic began to replace Greek as the language of administration.

With the fall of the Umayyad Khalifate in AD750, the Abbasids intensified the hostility against Christians.

History records the forcible conversion of the 'last Christian tribe in Syria', the Banu Tanukh. They had been resisting Islam for many years and had appealed to, and received help from, the Byzantine emperor; but on the order of the Khalif al-Mahdi (AD775–785) they were compelled to become Muslims.

There was always the danger that some fanatic might invoke the Shari'a (Islamic law) as an excuse for destroying Christian churches. By AD807 the Khalif Harun-al Rashid had ordered Christians and Jews to wear distinctive dress. His grandson al-Mutawakkil revived these orders and added further decrees designed to humiliate Christians.

Meanwhile the Muslim armies had crossed the straits from Tangier and captured Spain and were only halted between Tours and Poitiers (a mere 100 miles from Paris) in one of history's decisive battles in AD732. Spain was to remain Muslim for a further 700 years, and for much of that time the land enjoyed peace and prosperity. It was only after the dreaded Inquisition that Muslims were finally expelled from Spain in 1492.

2

The first translation of the Bible into Arabic

Up to the middle of the eighth century, as we have seen, relations between Muslims and Christians were varied.

The appearance of the first translation of the Bible into Arabic seems to have stirred some Christian writers into action. Perhaps the best known was John of Damascus (c.675–c.749) whose work *Sources of Knowledge* includes an important section on Islam, which he calls the 'deceptive error of the Ishmaelites'. The title derives from Ishmael who was born to Abraham by Hagar. At this time Muslims were often called Hagarenes (after Hagar). John of Damascus notes that they call themselves 'Saracens', which he seemed to think was derived from the Greek and referred to their being 'sent away empty by Sarah'. More extensive is John's work *Dialogue Between a Christian and Saracen*. (Translations of extracts of these works in English are to be found in issues of *The Moslem World* for 1934 and 1935.)

For the next century or so Muslims and Christians remained in close contact. In some places, like Spain, the contact and relationships proved on the whole peaceful and beneficial. In others they were marked by enmity and hostility, while elsewhere the two faiths existed side by side almost indifferent to each other.

An important piece of apologetic writing came from the pen of a Nestorian Christian serving in the court of the Khalif of Baghdad at about this time. Known as *The Apology of Al Kindy*, this was translated by Sir William Muir. Up till the tenth century this style of polemic writing continued. It seemed to be a kind of a game. But it was a 'pretty barren substitute for evangelism' (Caetani, 1942, p. 29).

3

The Crusades

Until now the Muslims had been the dominant, and (except in Europe) the most successful disputers in the dialogue. But now follow 200 years of conflict between the powers of Islam and the armies of the Christian powers of Western Europe. These armies aimed to conquer the lands held by Muslims and to wipe out Islam by force. Not for the first or the last time, atrocities were committed in the name of religion.

It has to be admitted that the first intention in the minds of the Crusaders was to win, for Christ, a kingdom by the sword. There was no desire to make converts; Islam was the enemy. Laurence Browne, former Principal of the Henry Martyn School of Islamics, says in his book *Eclipse of Christianity in Asia*: 'One cannot help regarding the Crusades as the greatest tragedy in the history of Christianity, and the greatest set-back to the progress of Christ's kingdom on earth' (Browne, 1933, p. 144).

The eastern and western armies of the church had enjoyed a period of comparative equilibrium, and most Christians had been granted permission to rebuild all destroyed churches. At the same time, through long contact with groups of Muslim tribesmen, some Christians had abandoned their links with Nestorian Christianity and become zealous, if unconventional, followers of Islam. Then gradually the Muslim rulers of Southern Syria and Palestine began to surrender to the Turks, who by 1070 had captured Jerusalem.

This was the situation which led the Byzantine emperor and the Pope to call Christians to action to save the Empire and rescue the holy places from the Turks.

By 1217 a truce was declared, and in 1229 access to Jerusalem and the Christian holy places was granted. But by 1244 the Muslims were again in control. Jerusalem was to remain in Muslim hands until 1918.

Activity 12:1

This turbulent period in the history of Christian-Muslim relationships has, understandably, been interpreted differently by Christians and Muslims. You may have opportunity to discuss the Crusades with your Muslim friends. How far do you think these events in history influence present-day relationships?

4

Christian missionary activity begins

With the founding of the Franciscan and Dominican Orders in the thirteenth century a new chapter in the history of Muslim-Christian relations was opened. For the first time since the Nestorians (who under the Abbasid Khalifate had exercised some Christian witness, particularly in the court of Baghdad) we can record a deliberate attempt to abandon forceful means to re-establish Christ's kingdom, and to organise missions to win converts by peaceful means.

Francis of Assisi seems to have taken the initiative or set an example by actually visiting the Sultan of Egypt while the Fifth Crusade was still going on. His visits proved fruitless, but at least he had started something. Later the same year some of his newly formed order went to Morocco. At least five were martyred. A similar mission to Tunis proved impossible because of the opposition of the Christian merchants in the city, who thought the preaching of the gospel might interfere with business.

In 1225 groups of Franciscans and Dominicans entered Morocco but worked mainly among Christian slaves. There is no record of any missionary success as a result of this witness. Yet some attempts were made to understand the Muslim faith and the Qur'an was translated into Latin at about this time by Peter the Venerable, the Abbot of Cluny.

Raymon Lull: A case study

As Bishop Nazir-Ali writes in his book, *Frontiers in Muslim-Christian Encounter*, some individual Western Christians at this time 'tried to relate positively to Islam: Raymond Lull advocated a peaceful approach to Islam instead of the Crusades . . . ' (Nazir-Ali, 1987, p. 18).

As a scholar and philosopher he was typical of his time. But as a missionary enthusiast, whose main aim was to win Muslims for Christ, he was far ahead of his time. As a teacher and thinker he was successful and as a missionary zealot he almost always encountered misunderstanding and failure.

He was born around the year 1232, of wealthy parents in Palma, Majorca. It was not until he was 31, while busy one day composing a 'love song' to his latest mistress, that he seems to have experienced a moving vision of Christ on the cross. After a long and agonising struggle he finally yielded to Christ. With the failure of the Crusades Ramon Lull came forward to proclaim the power of loving persuasion as the only means worthy of Christ. Within weeks of his conversion a plan was taking shape in his mind. This involved three separate but related objectives:

1 To write books of apologetics that would win by 'irrefutable logic' the minds and hearts of unbelievers and infidels;
2 To work towards the founding of schools for the training of missionaries; and
3 To give his life, to martyrdom if necessary, in the service of Christ as a witness to Muslims.

When he was 60 Lull seems to have discovered new reserves of will-power. He sailed for Tunis where for a time he was able to confront groups of learned Muslims with the arguments he had been developing over the years. His approach seems to have aroused a certain amount of antagonism, as a consequence of which the local ruler and his council condemned Lull to death. The decree was changed to banishment and reluctantly he returned to Naples. In 1301 he set out to visit the Holy Land but got no further than Cyprus where he stayed a few months, returning by way of Armenia to Majorca.

Six years later in 1307 after a period of lecturing and writing in Montpellier and Paris, he once again set sail for North Africa, landing at Bugia (now Bejaia) about 100 miles east of Algiers.

Lull preached openly in the market place and attempted to expose the falsity of the Muslim creed. This so aroused the anger of the crowd that only the intervention of the *qadi* saved him from death. After a period in prison, during which he continued to dispute with some of the learned Muslims who visited him, he was deported and, having survived a shipwreck off the Italian coast, landed at Pisa.

Lull now moved his sphere of activity to Paris and there for two years set out to disprove the teaching of ibn Rushid (known better by his Latin name of Averroes). He continued to pester the Pope with the request that missionary colleges be established. His requests were accepted by the Council of Vienne, but there is some doubt as to whether the decision was ever implemented.

At some time during the end of 1315 and the spring of 1316, when he was in his eighties, he seems to have been seized by a desire for martyrdom and, leaving Tunis for Bugia, defiantly, there, in the open market place, proclaimed his message. He was stoned by an angry mob and probably died on board the ship that had attempted to rescue him.

Ramon Lull was something of a paradox; part scholar, part mystic, and eventually martyr. Certainly his was a new approach; equally certain was his lack of success. Yet to stand on the beach at Bejaia is to feel even today, over 650 years later, the challenge of this amazing man.

Activity 12:2

Are there things we can learn from Ramon Lull's life and work which might help us in our ministry to Muslims today? As you look over this short account of his life, make a list of any points which might be helpful.

Muslim ascendancy in the Middle and Near East

In spite of many reverses and changes of fortune with which the history of Mongol, Turkish, Egyptian, and the Western powers are interwoven, the Muslim armies gradually achieved the ascendancy once more. By the middle of the fourteenth century, Christian dominance had been virtually eclipsed in the lands of the Middle and Near East. The Mediterranean had virtually become a Muslim sea and Europe, cut off from its eastern markets, turned westward toward the Atlantic Ocean.

The Ottoman Empire continued to expand and reached its zenith in the middle of the sixteenth century. By this time theological interest in Europe was no longer focused on Islam but on the new doctrines being expounded in continental Europe by Luther (1483–1546), Zwingli (1484–1531) and Calvin (1509–1564), and in England by Thomas Cranmer (1486–1556) and William Tyndale (d. 1536).

For nearly two centuries there was little missionary vocation in the churches of the Reformation. The foremost leaders named above displayed neither missionary vision nor missionary spirit. For Luther, the real Antichrist was not Muhammad but the Pope. The Turks were simply vicious enemies; Luther protested at turning the war against them into a religious crusade.

The Moravians

Until the end of the eighteenth century the only Protestants to show any zeal for evangelism among the Muslims (except for a relatively obscure band of German Pietists) were the Moravians. Dr Hocker, a Moravian doctor, worked in Cairo. On the other hand, the Society of Jesus (founded by Ignatius Loyola) had entered India. From a base in Goa, a minor Portuguese outpost, they sent a small band of missionaries to the court of Akbar the Emperor with the aim of winning the people of India for Christianity.

The results of this mission were certainly not spectacular. In two decades the genuine converts from Islam could probably be counted in dozens. This is, however, as Marcia Sayre points out, a better record than much Muslim evangelism and ought not to be disparaged.

4

European colonialism

The colonial era which stretched from the end of the fifteenth to the mid-twentieth centuries probably made a much greater impact on Muslim-Christian relations than even the Crusades had done. Except for Turkey, Iran and Afghanistan, nearly all Muslim countries became colonies or protectorates of European 'Christian' powers. When the Moghal Empire declined, the British, at first through the East India Company, then through the Crown and the state, ruled the vast country of India. The Dutch colonised Indonesia, and the Muslim countries of North and West Africa and the near East were divided between France, Britain and Italy.

Islam had spread and conquered along trade routes, holding power not only through conquest but also through control of trade. In the eighteenth and nineteenth centuries European powers spread their influence through their developing maritime power. This enabled them to set up trading posts and to appropriate riches from an increasing number of areas of the world, among which were countries formerly under Muslim rule. During and after the Industrial Revolution the needs of capitalist countries for increasing resources, both to feed their work-forces and to be used in their industries, necessitated further acquisition of territory and obtaining economic and political control.

The effects of colonialism were profound. The whole manner of life of those colonised was changed. Colonies were split into two classes, the colonisers and the natives, so that the natives themselves came to believe that they were inferior. Work-patterns were changed, with labour demands causing people to leave subsistence farming to work in mines and on plantations set up by the colonial power. The extremes of exploitation were sadly not abolished with slavery, but lived on in other types of forced labour and land dispossession.

In some ways this was an era of great missionary opportunity. The 'Christian' colonial powers not only exploited, but felt a genuine responsibility to share their civilisation and their material progress with, the people of the colonies they had acquired. The heritage they believed they should pass on was a Christian one, so missionaries were for the most part encouraged and respected. They were even able to influence the colonial administrators from time to time, and to pass on insights they had gained through their pioneer work and their closeness to the indigenous people.

In spite of their diminishing power in the world, most Muslims remained firm in their Islamic faith. Christians found them resistant to the gospel and, in the main, the only real contact between the two religions was polemical, in the setting up of public debates between Christian and Muslim scholars.

5

Christian outreach, eighteenth–twentieth centuries

As we have seen, from the time of Ramon Lull to that of Henry Martyn at the beginning of the nineteenth century, the only serious attempts to reach Muslims were those of the Moravians in Egypt and the Jesuits in India.

In 1734 a translation of the Qur'an by a Dr Sale appeared in English. This work revived an interest in the Muslim world. In 1786 William Carey addressed a conference of Baptist ministers on the subject of mission: 'The Commandment given to the Apostles to teach all nations in all the world must be recognised as binding on us also, since the great promise still follows it.'

Thus begins a new era in missions. This coupled with a new awareness of the Muslim World resulted in a new approach to Muslims.

Henry Martyn

In 1781, Henry Martyn was born. Arriving in Calcutta in 1806 he wrote in his diary, 'Now let me burn out for God.' He did just that. Educated at Truro Grammar School and St John's College, Cambridge, he was a brilliant student who intended to read law but, after the death of his father and his conversion to Christ, felt that God was calling him to the ministry of the church. Following a curacy served under Charles Simeon in Cambridge, he turned his back on the prospect of marriage to his beloved Lydia; and upon appointment as Chaplain of the East India Company, he set sail for India in July 1805.

He was a keen linguist. Even before he set sail he had a desire to translate the Scriptures into the languages of India. In June

1807 he wrote of being 'constantly engaged in works of translation and languages', and by the spring of 1808 was well into his greatest achievement—the translation of the New Testament into Urdu. Subsequent translations into Persian and Arabic owe much to his scholarship. He did not live to see any of his translations in print, for he died at Tokat in Turkey in 1812.

Vivienne Stacey states in a short biography of Henry Martyn that he 'still challenges Christian students and young people of each generation with their responsibility of sharing the good news about Jesus Christ' (Stacey, 1980, p. 75). His life and work made a major contribution to the task of presenting the gospel to Muslim peoples, by making it possible for many to read the New Testament in their own tongue.

Abdul Masih

The only known Muslim convert from the ministry of Henry Martyn was Abdul Masih. We are indebted to Vivienne Stacey for the following summary of his life.

Abdul Masih was one of those listening from afar to Martyn's outdoor preaching to beggars, which took place every Thursday. He was a man of importance in the court of the King of Oudh. His original name was Sheikh Salih. He was converted after Martyn left India. The main influences in his conversion appear to have been Martyn's life and the reading of the New Testament, when he was entrusted with its binding by Martyn. He was baptised at Calcutta by the Revd D. Brown on Whit Sunday 1811. He was the first agent of the Church Missionary Society, being engaged as Catechist in 1812. The Revd Daniel Corrie located him to Agra in 1813 and worked with him there for two years. In 1820 he received Lutheran orders. The ordination helped his standing among former Muslim friends. They said, 'The English do indeed regard him a brother.' In 1825 he received Anglican orders, being made Deacon by Heber, Bishop of Calcutta. He was the first Muslim convert to be ordained in India. He died at Lucknow in 1827.

Abdul Masih became an outstanding evangelist in his own right. On the river-boat from Calcutta to Agra he held services and preached to the boatmen, Christian children and servants.

He refused to visit the tomb of a Muslim saint, explaining that he had been a Muslim and had now come to visit the living. He gave them the Gospel of Matthew as a valuable present. He did not eat with his brother and nephew until they understood the reasons for his conversion. Abdul Masih's brother believed, but delayed baptism so that he could explain his faith to his friends first. Through Abdul Masih's preaching and teaching over 40 Muslims joined the congregation at Agra. He composed hymns and set them to indigenous tunes, and also put Christ's conversation with Nicodemus into verse for use in evangelism. His general evangelistic method was to explain the Books of Moses and the Gospels. Whenever Muslim customs seemed to derive from the Bible, he indicated this. He never discussed their prophets but asked if they could show anyone to compare with Jesus. He usually expounded a chapter rather than a verse. The converts were set to spinning, weaving and ploughing in order to maintain themselves, but further development plans were interrupted by the illness of Daniel Corrie who left Agra after working for two years with Abdul Masih. Abdul Masih effectively continued the work. He ran a small school and also dispensed medicine. He suffered from poor health, which in July 1825 forced him to leave Agra. Subsequently he was able to return to Agra under the care of Dr Luxmore who took him into his own house. He died shortly afterwards.

The Chaplain at Agra, the Revd John Irving, wrote to the Archdeacon of Calcutta about Abdul Masih: 'The more I see of him, the more I have reason to respect him—so unassuming, and yet so steady. I confess I do sometimes lose my patience when I am asked by Englishmen if I think him a sincere convert; for there are few of us who might not, in some point or other, take pattern from him.'

Among the other nineteenth-century Christians who responded to the call to work among Muslims, two are mentioned briefly for their distinctive contributions:

Karl Gottlieb Pfander (1803–1865)

Pfander was born in Wurtenburg and sent out to the Caucasus by the Basel Mission. He spent most of his missionary service with the Church Missionary Society in Agra, Peshawar and Constantinople. He was noted for successfully taking part in the Muslim-Christian debates which were held at that time, also for his apologetic writing. His best-known book, *Misan-ul-Haqq* (Balance of Truth), is still in print and is used by students of Islam.

'Those who knew Pfander considered him not only courageous but of warm disposition and well-balanced temperament. He was undoubtedly of keen intellect, a blend of European pietism and rationalism' (Van der Werff, 1977, p. 41).

Thomas Valpy French (1825–1891)

Born in Burton-on-Trent, French went with CMS first to Agra, where he met and assisted Pfander in his debates. He was later transferred to the north-west frontier and in 1877, after holding the office of Archdeacon, was consecrated the first Bishop of Lahore. He was responsible not only for the building of Lahore Cathedral but also for a number of other churches and Christian institutions. His interest in training clergy led him to found the Lahore Divinity School; his great burden, however, was for evangelism among Muslims. After his retirement at the age of 66, always a pioneer, he went as the first missionary to Oman, where he died.

His obituary notice in the *Civil and Military Gazette*, quoted by Stacey, reads, 'He was indeed a saintly character, utterly self-denying and unworldly, single-hearted, devout and humble, the fire of enthusiasm for the propagation of the Gospel burned as brightly in his breast in those last lonely days in Muscat as it did when he turned his back on Oxford and all it offered, to give himself to India' (pp. 36–37).

During the last decades of the nineteenth century and those of the early twentieth century there are two men who stand out as having made a particularly valuable contribution to the history of Muslim-Christian relations: Samuel Zwemer and Temple Gairdner.

Samuel Zwemer (1867–1952)

Zwemer, who has been variously called the 'Flaming Prophet' and the 'Apostle to Islam', was born in the USA of Dutch-Huguenot parents. During his senior year in college he became linked with the Student Volunteer Movement that was exercising a great influence on college campuses both in the USA and Britain. Zwemer was fired by the challenge of the movement's watchword, 'The evangelisation of the world in this generation', and as his part in this task formed the Mission to Arabia. He spent many years of sacrificial service in the Arabian Peninsular and also worked in Cairo. He founded and edited the magazine *The Moslem World* (now *The Muslim World*), and for many years devoted all his energies to promoting the work of evangelising the Muslim world. First and foremost he was always a personal evangelist. 'Books were a passion with him. But people, especially Muslims, were his first love' (Van der Werff, 1977, p. 227). When he died it was said of him, 'a loving heart which was the reflection of God's love in Christ' (p. 266).

Temple Gairdner (1873–1928)

If Henry Martyn's life work concentrated on the need for the Muslim people to have the word of God in their own language, and Samuel Zwemer's emphasised that the Muslim needs to see a practical demonstration of the life and love of Christ, Temple Gairdner, the third of our nineteenth-twentieth century heroes, used his life to approach the educated Muslim through the church in a fresh and positive manner. Born in Scotland, where he spent his early years, he went to Trinity College Oxford in 1892, becoming president of the Oxford Inter-Collegiate Christian Union in 1895. He gave his whole life to the service of Christ among the Muslims of Egypt, attempting to use contemporary Arabic musical, poetic, and dramatic forms in reaching them. During his early days in Cairo he wrote:

> It takes faith believing in Christ, His Church and ministry, here in this Moslem city. But on my word, it takes more faith to believe in these when one thinks of the Church itself as it exists here—sect

upon sect, each more intolerant than its neighbour, each practically excommunicating the others in the name of the one Lord—and that in the face of an Islam which loathes all alike. (Van der Werff, 1977, p. 199)

The unity of the church of Christ was one of the major passions of his life, and in this he challenges us today. Yet he had no use for any synthesis reached by ignoring the facts; he saw the intense importance of our denominational distinctions which, he thought, by adding their special insights contributed to the truth as a perfect whole.

Activity 12:2

Look again at the lives of these six people. Can you list some of the problems and also the opportunities of work among Muslims in the eighteenth to twentieth centuries?

6

The church today in Muslim societies

Although it is becoming increasingly difficult for Western churches and organisations to get permission to send their workers to Islamic countries, the Christian presence has certainly not disappeared. In the Middle East, for example, twelve to fourteen million indigenous people call themselves Christians. The great majority of these belong to one or other of the three Orthodox groups:

1. *The Oriental Orthodox Churches*, including the Coptic (Egyptian) Orthodox Church;

2. *The Eastern or Greek Orthodox Church*, including the Russian Orthodox Church; and

3. *The Assyrian Church of the East*, or *The Church of Persia*, which exists in Iran, Iraq, Syria and Lebanon alongside the other Eastern Churches.

In addition to these there are two other groups of churches:

4. *The Catholic Churches of the Middle East*, which accept the authority of the Pope, but use the Eastern not the Latin Rite; and

5. *The Anglican and Protestant Churches*, which are the result of missionary activity in the eighteenth to twentieth centuries. (cf *Turning Over a New Leaf*, 1992, pp. 14–15)

A concluding thought:

> Much of our ability to relate successfully with Orthodox believers depends upon our attitude and personality. There may be things we encounter which will upset us. But if we look beyond our individual world to discuss the whole picture, the little we do, if we do it well can help influence the direction of Christian cooperation in the Middle East Church. (Teague, p. 114)

Notes

Muslims, as we saw in Chapter 9, do look back at history (see notes on Chapter 9). As they look back at Muslim-Christian relationships, they see the Crusades (Activity 12:1) in what to them seemed utterly unprovoked attacks, by hordes of Westerners, on land which was rightfully theirs. They see the ruthlessness and cruelty of the Crusaders, who believed they were fighting a religious war. The scars are very deep and sometimes they can still wreck relationships between Muslims and Christians. Raymon Lull's life was one of total commitment (Activity 12:2). He was prepared to suffer and to be killed in trying to win Muslims to Christ. He was also prepared to forgo worldly status and achievements and to use his talents wholly in his missionary work. The same was true of the other six people listed in the chapter (Activity 12:3). They had to overcome loneliness, in the case of Henry Martyn even to the point of leaving a fiancée behind. They often had to battle on with little support of any kind. They also had problems of rejection and misunderstanding from those they had come to serve. You probably have a lot of other things on your list.

Books referred to in the chapter

Browne, Laurence, *Eclipse of Christianity in Asia* (Oxford University Press: Oxford, 1933).

Attr. Caetani, quoted in Addison, J. T., *The Christian Approach to the Muslim* (Columbia Univ Press: NY, 1942).

Nazir-Ali, Michael, *Frontiers in Muslim-Christian Encounter* (Regnum Books: Oxford, 1987).

Stacey, Vivienne, *Henry Martyn* (Henry Martyn Inst. of Islamic Studies: Hyderabad, India, 1980).

Stacey, Vivienne, *Thomas Valpy French, First Bishop of Lahore* (Christian Study Centre: Rawalpindi, Pakistan, 1982).

Turning Over a New Leaf: Protestant Missions and the Orthodox Churches of the Middle East. Final Report of a multi-mission study group on orthodoxy (Interserve/MEM: London/Lynwood USA, 2nd edn 1992).

Van der Werff, Lyle, L., *Christian Mission to Muslims: The Record* (William Carey Library: S. Pasadena, California, 1977).

For further reading

Turning Over a New Leaf: Protestant Missions and the Orthodox Churches of the Middle East. Final Report of a multi-mission study group on orthodoxy (Interserve/MEM: London/Lynwood USA, 2nd edn 1992). Gives a clear account of the Orthodox Eastern Churches from a sympathetic Protestant mission point of view.

Van der Werff, Lyle, L., *Christian Mission to Muslims: The Record* (William Carey Library: S. Pasadena, California, 1977). A detailed history of mission to Muslims and an investigation into Anglican and Reformed approaches.

PART IV

Islam at the End of the Twentieth Century

13

Global Islam

Study guide

We come now to attempt a contemporary view of Islam throughout the world. You may have a particular interest in one area and will want to study this in detail. Do however, read the whole chapter; although it is necessarily rather long, it provides an overall view. It is no secret that the relationship between Christianity and Islam has often been, and still may be, one of conflict. We have tried to tell it as it is, not exaggerating the differences, the oppression, the desire for expansion; nor pretending that the two religions are living happily together everywhere in the world.

Our team of writers all have recent experience of the areas about which they write. We recommend that you read the case studies carefully, making sure you have grasped the significant points. In this chapter some names are deliberately omitted. This is to protect those of both communities who are involved in sensitive areas.

Although this chapter is primarily about global Islam, it also indicates something of the Christian response to Islam in the world of the end of the twentieth century.

When you have completed the chapter you should:

1 Have an overall view of Islam in the world today;
2 Begin to understand the interaction between Muslims and those of other faiths in different areas of the world; and
3 Begin to formulate your Christian response.

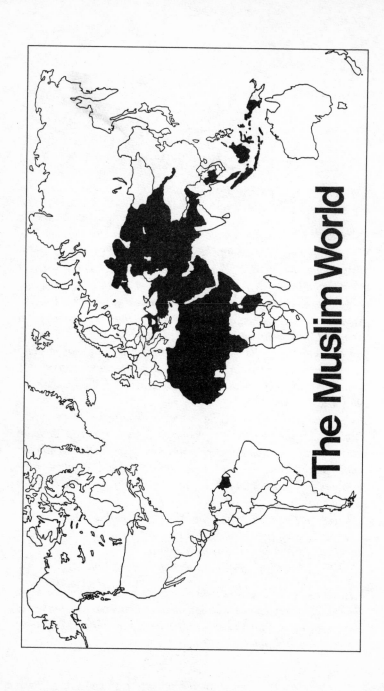

The Muslim World

1

Islam and global strategy

Islam, now the majority religion in thirty-seven nations, has about one billion followers in the world. To the Muslim, Islam is essentially global. As the first Sura of the Qur'an, often called Al-Fatiha or 'the Opener', says, Allah is *Rabb alamin*—'Lord of the Worlds'. We have already noted that Islam divides the world into two sections—*dar al-islam*, that is, the House of Islam or that part of the world which submits to Allah; and *dar al-harb*, that is, the House of War or that part of the world which has yet to be brought into submission or obedience to Allah. Where the ruler is a Muslim and his state based on the Shari'a, that is the House of Islam. Everywhere else is the House of War.

For the Muslim there is no sacred and secular; religion and politics can never be separated. Historically Islam started not at the birth of Muhammad around AD570, nor when he started to preach his revelations of the Qur'an in 610, but in AD622 when, puzzling at his lack of acceptance as a prophet, he led the Hijra from Mecca to Medina and established a city state (See Chapter 5, section 5, p. 106). Islam quickly became a success story. In ten years Muhammad united Arabia; within a century, Islam had spread to three continents (See Chapter 7, maps p 169). With its vision of the world as becoming Muslim it is not surprising to find that Islam is a missionary faith.

The concept of mission is called in Islam by the Arabic word *da'wa*. Muslims do engage in spreading their faith and practice. In the past, trading and preaching often went together, but these days Islam expands mostly through population increase. In heavily populated Pakistan and Bangladesh, the annual population increase is around 3%

In considering Islam's global strategy it may be helpful to look at its plans for one continent. In 1973, at a conference of Islamic cultural centres held in London under the auspices of the Islamic Secretariat, the Islamic Council of Europe was set up. This was the implementation of two resolutions adopted by the Second and Third Conferences of Foreign Ministers, which had been held in Jeddah (Saudi Arabia) and Benghazi (Libyan Arab Republic) respectively.

The Islamic Council of Europe is the supreme co-ordinating body for Islamic centres and organisations in Europe. It is independent, but it works in close co-operation with both international Islamic organisations and governments of all Muslim states. Its headquarters are in London with constituents in almost every country of Europe.

Among its stated objectives are:

To assist, support and supplement the activities of the member organisations in different fields of da'wa, including establishment of mosques and Muslim cultural centres, dissemination of Islamic education, and fulfilment of other Islamic duties and obligations.

To make necessary arrangements for the establishment of new centres for organised Islamic activity wherever necessary.

To seek the co-operation and assistance of Muslim states, national governments and national and international organisations, in the promotion of the activities of the Council and its constituents.

Muslims have similar plans for each continent and most nations. There are other influences to be taken into account which provide some of the fervour behind the strategy. Since the abolition of the Khalifate in 1924 Muslims have sought new focuses for their unity. The most obvious focus is shari'a law as the basis for national life. The growth of Sunni fundamentalism has increased the pressure for the acceptance of Shari'a by Muslim governments. Another focus is the remarkable revival of Muhammad veneration in the last twenty years (See Chapter 11, section 3, p 202). Regard for the Prophet of Islam is something which unites all Muslims. As Muhammad Iqbal wrote in one of his famous poems: 'Love for the Prophet flows like blood in the veins of the community'. A desire for increased unity amid much division is perhaps the main reason for the growing revival of Muhammad veneration in so many areas where Muslims live.

Islam and other faiths

In parts of Asia where Muslims are in a majority, Western countries are seen as 'the Christian West' and actions taken by Western political leaders can affect the way in which Christianity is seen. For example, when the Gulf War was in progress, it was seen by many as the Christian West attacking 'our Muslim brothers'. Effigies of President George Bush hanged by the neck were put up by local people. There were also isolated cases of hostility against Christian institutions. However, a little later in these same areas, when a gigantic cyclone had caused large scale devastation and death a contingent of the US navy arrived and provided a lot of practical help. Then public attitudes towards 'the Christian West' reversed.

In a similar way churches and Christian organisations in these areas have a large number of humanitarian and educational projects. They also provide help and relief in times of special need as well as ongoing development and aid for the poorest. There are many local Christian hospitals and community health programmes caring particularly for the poor, and Christian schools and colleges which have such a reputation for integrity and high educational standards that many of the leaders of local communities prefer to send their children there. This creates a background of goodwill; yet many Muslims cannot understand why Christians do these things, and many are suspicious of ulterior motives. Yet when local people see that help and service to the community are often given unconditionally they show great appreciation.

In such areas of Asia, Muslims and Hindus often live side by side and according to the area one or other religious group can be greatly in a majority. In the areas where Islam is the predominant religion the Christian church has largely come out of a lower caste or sometimes a no-caste Hindu background, and although the gospel has greatly changed the Christian's lifestyle the culture and the language of worship of the church still quite naturally bear marks of its ancestry. There are isolated cases of long-established Christian families whose forbears were Muslims, but over the years these also have assimilated the culture of the church. In areas where there is no Christian presence, many Muslims would have no idea what a Christian is, whereas in areas where churches are established, the church seems to be something like a Hindu sect. This is especially true where there are pictures of Christ in homes and images in churches. Equating Christianity with a Hindu sect is, of course, strongly resented by the Christians. It does mean, however, that most Muslims would think that for one of their number to become a Christian was not much different from becoming a Hindu, and therefore an idolater—a very horrible thing!

One area where such cultural differences are particularly noticeable is in the matter of language. Muslims very often have words and turns of phrase which differ from those used by Hindus. This is because a number of Urdu and Arabic words have been imported into the language, and quite naturally Muslims use the Quranic forms of names of people and places that are found both in the Qur'an and the Bible. They have also consciously excluded Hindu worship words. But the classical form of the local language has come from a Hindu background and this is the form that the Christian will use. Therefore the Bible and any other religious publication in the classical language may well be much admired particularly by the educated Muslim, but he will see it as something that is not for him—it doesn't touch his heart. Because of this, many of those who wish to bring the gospel to Muslims put out publications using the language that Muslims would use. And of course pictures, especially of Jesus or any prophet, are not used, for that would be offensive to the Muslim.

But this goes further. Where there are groups of Christians who have come from a Muslim background, they will not want to appear culturally odd in any way to their Muslim neighbours, friends and relatives. In fact they will want to maintain their cultural identity (See Chapter 8). So although they have now received salvation through Christ, in their style of worship as well as the language they use, their dress and social behaviour, they have retained those elements of Islamic culture which are consistent with the gospel. In practice this means, for example, that they will pray using bodily postures similar to a Muslim at prayer and will use language that Muslims would use. When they meet together there will be no women present in the prayer meeting, and the Bible will be kept on a wooden stand.

But this causes problems for the local Christian church. When they see those claiming to be Christians still looking like Muslims, they sometimes doubt that they are really following Christ. This is complicated by the fact that evangelising Muslims attracts more overseas financial support than maintaining existing work does. This may mean there is money to be made by the unscrupulous 'convert' and the immature can easily have their witness compromised by money. So by this means Satan is once again sowing tares among the wheat, and the Muslim community is confirmed in its belief that it is only financial inducement from unscrupulous foreigners that leads to conversions. This is why many who seek to bring the gospel to Muslims are very careful not to provide money or other material aid to new believers, but to encourage them to provide for their needs from their own resources as they learn to trust the Lord for themselves.

2

The Central Area

This area covers the Arabian Peninsula and extends out from it. It contains the holy cities of Mecca and Medina. The Ka'ba in Mecca is, as we have seen in Chapter 10, pp 175–176, the focal point for Islam towards which every Muslim prays five times a day. For this reason the area is known as the heartlands of Islam.

Survey

Whatever happens in the heartlands of Islam affects Muslims all over the world. Saudi Arabia is the religious centre of Islam with the two most holy cities—Mecca and Medina—to which increasing numbers of Muslims come from each continent and many lands each year on pilgrimage. The unifying effect of the experience of pilgrimage and the other opportunities it offers for international exchange increase year by year. Modern travel and developing facilities within Saudi Arabia and elsewhere permit an annual increase in the number of pilgrims. The present estimate is that well over 2,000,000 come each year.

Egypt, especially Cairo with its Al Azhar University, is the intellectual centre of Islam. Muslim missionaries from many countries are trained there and return to spread the faith in their own countries. Since the widening of the Al Azhar syllabus and the increase of faculties in 1961, Muslim lay people are also trained there. Many then take jobs, particularly in other Arab countries. The influence of Cairo and the Al Azhar goes out through people, radio, TV, cassette and the printed word to the twenty-one Arabic speaking countries of the Middle East; and far beyond the Arab world the ripples are felt.

The Arabian Gulf States, especially Saudi Arabia which has over 25% of the known oil resources of the world, are the economic centre. Kuwait, Iraq, Qatar, the United Arab Emirates with Iran, and Yemen with its more recent oil strikes yet to become viable, account for another 25%. So one can say that nearly half the world's known oil resources lies here. Saudi Arabia especially uses much of its wealth strategically, to spread the faith of Islam. New mosques and Islamic cultural centres have been built in (for example) London, Constantine in Algeria and Hong Kong. The most powerful radio transmitter, the 'Voice of Islam', is in Saudi Arabia. The world's largest printing works is also located there. It publishes 28,000,000 copies of the Qur'an in various languages each year. International gatherings of various kinds are often held in Saudi Arabia—for example, the Conference of World Muslim Organisations was held in Mecca in February 1974. Muslim summit conferences financed mainly by Saudi money are held in various cities of the Islamic world, for example Rabat in 1969 and Lahore in 1972.

Muslim fundamentalism and the reformist Wahabi influences come from Egypt and Saudi Arabia, but Iran is the third giant in the Middle East and vies with Saudi Arabia for control of the Arabia/Persian Gulf. Its 1979 Revolution, although strongly

Shia, appealed to Sunni Muslims especially in the Gulf where the rapid transition from a mainly nomadic society to the modern cities and infrastructures permitted by oil bewildered both the young and old. They were often glad to respond to the clear voice of Ayatollah Khomeini and his revolutionary movement. Iran sees her message as a call to the world.

The Muslims view the new freedoms rightly gained from imperial rules and the oil wealth in their lands as the blessing of Allah. Oil wealth has created another phenomenon; the economic migration of millions of people, including Arabs from poorer Arab states to the oil lands of the Middle East, and the influx in the late sixties and seventies of Indians, Pakistanis and Bangladeshis from their subcontinent. This influx was followed in the 1980s by one from the Far East, with Koreans and Filipinos coming in large numbers to the Arabian Peninsula. Some of the oil states like Qatar and the UAE have drawn over three-quarters of their work force from abroad, even though there is now a stress on indigenisation. Thousands of these workers are Christians. For example, in the town of Abu Dhabi alone there are over 30,000 Indian Christians. One can compare this economic migration and its influence with the Jewish dispersion around the Mediterranean in the inter-testamental period, and the role of the dispersion as a preparation for the first coming of Christ.

The other very significant strategic point in the Middle East is that while in most oil countries there is hardly as yet an indigenous Christian church, there are ancient churches in over seven other countries in the area. The largest of these is the Coptic Orthodox Church in Egypt to which perhaps over 15% of the population belong. It is currently experiencing some revival. In Syria 9.29% are Christian, in Jordan 5.65%, in Iraq 2.48%, in Iran 0.62% and in Turkey 0.28%. Then there is Lebanon with a very large Christian population. These churches were mainly established before the rise of Islam. They are worshipping, structured communities which God can renew by his Spirit; and in some places this is happening (see Chapter 11, section 6, pp 224–225.)

So the Middle East, where three great religions and three continents meet, is a focus for prayer.

Christians in the Middle East

Sandlands is a strongly Islamic country in the Middle East; Sandlands is not, of course, its real name. It is a major oil-producing country, and this has given rise to rapid development of infrastructure and industry within it. Sandlands has had an acute labour shortage and has imported hundreds of thousands of foreign workers. In the mid-1970s there were no known believers among the national population. The Sandlands government follows shari'a law and does not permit non-Muslims to have places of worship. The importation of Christian literature is forbidden. In the past fourteen centuries almost no missionary work has been allowed in Sandlands.

I went to teach biochemistry in one of the university medical schools. My wife and three children accompanied me. We lived in Sandlands for seven years. Before going to Sandlands we had prayed for several years that God would open the door for us to go to that country. We strongly sensed God's call to serve him there. It was that sense of his call and appointment that sustained us through the many difficulties that we faced, especially in the early years there. We had spent five years in other Arab countries before going to Sandlands, so we were not new to the Arab world.

My wife, in addition to a BA degree, has a Teaching English as a Foreign Language certificate. During our first year she taught English in a private school attended by many of the royal family. She was dismissed at the end of the year—as were all the other Christian teachers. For the next six years she taught at the International School attended by our three children.

Difficulties we experienced as 'tentmakers'

There were many frustrations related to teaching in the Medical School. Lack of cultural awareness often caused us to understand something different from the intent of the person speaking.

We felt that promises were being broken (perhaps they were never intended to be promises, but we could not detect the fine differences). There was uncertainty as to when we would be paid. From our viewpoint, ethical standards were not very high and the Middle Eastern style of leadership often appeared to be dictatorial. It was very hard to maintain an academic standard of excellence. Journals were often lost and there was little interest in the university in research. It was very important for us to have the kingdom of God and not biochemistry and career development as our motivation. If I looked for recognition from the university for work done well I would be sorely disappointed. I needed to be content to receive my affirmation from God alone.

It was hard to pursue Arabic study. I attended three semesters of classical Arabic and found that I could pass Arabic exams without learning a great deal of Arabic!

Opportunities

There were daily opportunities to witness to faculty colleagues and to my students. I decided right at the beginning to be open about my commitment to Jesus Christ. Conversations usually only made progress if in private. I followed a moderately contextualised approach. I was interested that at a faculty farewell party when we left, the dean thanked me publicly for being a 'Godly person'. I was clearly an enigma to most people and this generated many questions.

It was difficult in this particular culture to visit nationals as a couple, because of the strict codes of segregation of the sexes among the national population. Of course we could visit in the normal way the many ex-patriate Arabs who were also 'foreign' workers like ourselves. We had many opportunities through a recreation centre—segregated of course—that opened on our compound. My wife made friends with the ladies by teaching conversational English at this centre in the evenings. Together with another believer she also enrolled in Islamic classes for ladies which gave opportunities for many focused discussions. The swimming pool was a great meeting place. This was a new experience for many of the local ladies and our teenage daughter was much in demand to teach both them and their children to swim!

Support structures

We went to Sandlands before missions had developed strategies for reaching such places. A very experienced worker among Muslims strongly advised us to pray about forming our own 'team' when we arrived. We quickly formed an *ad hoc* 'tent-makers' group. It began with ourselves and one other family and we numbered twenty over seven years as folks came and went. We met weekly for worship, prayer, discussion and fellowship. People joined at our invitation after we had got to know them as friends and discovered that they had experienced the same call of God to see a national church come into being. This group was our primary support group. Had there been the possibility of a suitable mission support structure, we would certainly have wanted to be part of it.

We were also part of an ex-patriate fellowship in our city. Most of the time we met as small groups in homes, although at times it was possible to meet in a larger group and at one point almost 1,000 were meeting together. The attitude of the authorities to Christians meeting for worship went through cycles. At times there was a fair degree of freedom, followed by intense periods of clamp down. This made life and witnessing very interesting!

Lessons learned to pass on to others

1. *Make sure you have a clear call of God to go to your target country.* In the case of a married couple, both husband and wife need to have this call individually.

2. *Be part of a mission agency that has 'tentmakers' in the Middle East.* They will help you in preparation, orientation and sustaining you in the country. Choose an agency that works in 'team'—ie places you in a city where you 'team-up' with other tentmakers.

3. *The heart of your preparation should be experience as a 'personal worker'* It's an old-fashioned word; an even older term would be 'soul-winner'. These terms and concepts might seem outdated in the church at home, but they are the heart of evangelism in the Middle East.

4. *Have as your 'team goal' church planting among the local people.* In areas where there is a local national church, explore the possibilities of achieving this goal together.

5. *Make a commitment as a team to learn the language and adjust to the culture.*

6. *Do not have too high an expectation of being able to maintain your professional competence at the same level as in your home country.* While doing the most excellent professional job you can, your fulfilment must come from your obedience to God's call on your life to be his ambassador in that place.

7. *Do not have a preconceived stereotype of how the national church will be formed or will grow.* It is often slow work. Do not judge your effectiveness by the number of those who come to faith! Progress is largely by prayer and intense involvement in the spiritual warfare raging in these lands. Your responsibility is to hear from God and obey him in that place to which he has called you.

8. *Work as hard as you can to build a good understanding of the task and your situation with your prayer base at home.* This is not always easy, as there is not a wide understanding in the churches of the concept of tentmaking as a valid, biblical method of mission. Your mission agency should be able to help you in this.

3

The continent of Asia

When we turn from the Middle East and the heartlands of Islam to which so many come from all over the world every year for work or on pilgrimage, our gaze should follow that of the

Muslim—to Pakistan. As Bishop Kenneth Cragg in *Counsels on Contemporary Islam* has said,

> Pakistan, as concept, policy and fact, must be seen as the surest Muslim index to Islam in our time, doing for its contemporary definition what the Hijra did in the seventh century.

> (Cragg, 1965, p 29)

Wilfred Cantwell Smith in *Islam in Modern History* noted that,

> The ardent emphasis on this new 'Islamic' State attracted the attention of outsiders . . . They were puzzled by the fervour for an Islamic state seemingly accompanied by a vast obscurity as to its nature, or at least an inability on the part of those involved to declare what they had in mind. They failed to realize that fundamentally it was the fact that Pakistan existed, not its form, that had such stirring significance.

> (Smith, 1957, pp 214–215)

The Pakistani Muslim philosopher and theologian Ghulam Ahmad Parvez called Pakistan 'the laboratory of Islam'. It is a twentieth-century experiment the success of which is very important to Muslims everywhere. To sustain its sagging economy Saudi Arabia pours in aid. A state founded in the name of Islam must not fail. Its greatest crisis came in the civil war of 1971, when it became evident that the two wings of Pakistan divided by nearly a thousand miles of hostile Indian territory could not survive. Out of this agony East Pakistan became Bangladesh. The nightmare still haunts Pakistan. If one part of the country can drop off, what about other parts—a Pakhtunistan perhaps—or where else? The early governments of Pakistan were content to maintain the country rather than define it, but President Zia ul-Haqq started to define what a Muslim state is. He began by introducing *Nizam-e-Mustafa*, the organisation of society according to the way of the Prophet of Islam. Muslim banking was introduced forbidding usury, Arabic became the second language of state schools in place of English, women faced more restrictions and certain matters came under the newly introduced Shariat Bench Ordinance. The next two governments under Benazir Bhutto and then

Nawaz Sharif tried to please the more liberal sections of society as well as the fundamentalists. Shari'a law was stressed even more and the minorities began to feel more threatened.

Bangladesh is 86% Muslim compared to Pakistan's 96%. In March 1988 Islam became the state religion of Bangladesh. Like Pakistan it has also elected a woman Prime Minister. In Bangladesh, as in Pakistan, about 70% of the Muslims go to shrines or belong to religious brotherhoods. The most famous of these brotherhoods or orders are the Chisti, the Naqshbandi, the Surhawardi and the Qadiri. One can call this popular or folk religion (See Chapter 11). It is denounced by the fundamentalists—Wahabis and Jama'at-e-Islami followers.

Afghanistan, having been strongly Muslim for so many centuries, is not so consciously Muslim as the newly created states of Pakistan and Bangladesh. The communist influence in recent years has probably reduced the number of those practising folk Islam by about 10%. If it is able to re-establish its viability as a country and become politically stable, Afghanistan will become an important crossroads for both trade and the affirmation of Islam between Pakistan and the new Muslim republics of Central Asia.

Although Indonesia is the largest Muslim country in the world as far as population is concerned (more than 80% of its 187,000,000 people are Muslim), Islam is not the state religion. Indonesia is a secular republic. The Constitution of Indonesia, based on 'Pancasila' ideology (see case study below), provides conditions for religious peace and freedom by acknowledging equal rights for Islam, the Catholic Church, the Protestant Church, Buddhism and Hinduism. At the same time Pancasila requires every citizen to belong to one of these five recognised religious systems. Members of all the five systems have the same right and duty to participate in the political, social and economic life of the nation (see the case study below for further details).

Again we meet up with folk religion. Islam in Indonesia has been strongly influenced by popular religious beliefs and practices including Javanese mysticism, animism and the matrilinear system of law together with Hinduised Islam which came centuries ago from India. Orthodox Indonesian Muslims are very critical of this folk Islam. Muslim modernists have tried to purify Indonesian Islam by rejecting the *Thariqah Nasyabaniyah* and the inheritance (*warith*) law, the matrilinear system of law (in Minangkabau), and visits to the tombs of saints. In Indonesia the divorce (*talaq*) rate is unusually high at 52% of the marriage rate. Indonesia is the only country in the modern era where there have been large numbers of people from Muslim background joining the Christian churches.

Malaysia, on the other hand, with a strict Muslim government and a 53% Muslim population, exercises considerable influence on its neighbours in South East Asia.

We now look at two case studies from Asia. The first is on Indonesia which, as you have just read, has developed in a different way from most Islamic countries. We move on then to Central Asia, where, since the break up of the USSR, the mainly Muslim republics have become independent.

Indonesia: a case study

Indonesia is the largest Muslim country in the world. Islam entered with merchants in the fifteenth century and soon replaced Hinduism as the dominant religion of the rulers. Now the majority of the 187,000,000 population would have 'Islam' as their religion on their identity card. However there is a sizable proportion of the population (10–20%) who would claim some Christian allegiance.

Christianity arrived in Indonesia with the colonial powers in the sixteenth century. First the Portuguese and then the Dutch sought to Christianise the pagan people of the profitable Spice Islands. Today many people in North Sulawesi and the Molluccan Islands would say that they have been Christians for more than 300 years. As Dutch people settled in different parts of the archipelago, chaplains were appointed for their spiritual well-being. However, until the British interlude under Governor Raffles (1811–16), there was no permission granted to evangelise the native people. By this period Islam was well established in Java and in parts of Sumatera, Sulawesi and the Molluccan

Islands. In East Java in the nineteenth century Christian converts found it hard to remain in their traditional village communities, so Christian villages were established. In the Molluccan Islands traditional relationships (*pele*) between the villages led to tolerance between Christians and Muslims. Such mutual respect however often curbed evangelism. The entry of more missionaries in the early twentieth century led to the conversion of pagan tribal groups in the Outer Islands who had never embraced Islam.

As the pressure for independence grew, Christians were not aloof from anti-colonial aspirations even though many in Molluccan Islands and North Sulawesi had developed close cultural and family ties with Holland. The participation of sufficient Christians in the 'generation of '45' that established independence, contributed to the decision of the leaders to establish a religious state that was not specifically Islamic. The foundation document of the 1945 constitution, Pancasila, contains as its first point belief in one God. The Department of Religion has sections for Muslims, Catholics, other Christians, Buddhists and Hindu-Bali. There is a tradition of tolerance and freedom to change religion that has matched the countries' motto of 'Unity in Diversity'. It is the acceptance of tribal, cultural and religious diversity together with a growth of national identity as Indonesians that has made possible rapid church growth since the mid-sixties.

This rapid growth began after the abortive communist coup in 1965, when those whose hopes had been centred on communism responded to the government insistence that they should have a religion. They did not return to Islam, but wanted to be instructed in the Christian gospel. At that time village communities would decide that they wanted to become Christian. The pressure on limited church resources meant that many were not fully discipled. In the late seventies some of these 'converts' were renouncing Christianity to embrace Javanese mystical sects, which they claimed spoke to their hearts in a way that the Christianity they had embraced had not. In the eighties there was a slower growth of the Church and some difficulties in maintaining existing churches, but there was still sufficient openness to the gospel for one Bible school to decide only to accept graduate students who had planted a congregation of at least 30 adults. The figure now stands at 20 adults.

The presence of indigenous Javanese mysticism presents one explanation of the open response to the gospel among Javanese Muslims. Their Islam has affinities with the Folk Islam that has been described previously. The attachment to Islam for many is formal. For the important daily needs there is recourse to traditional sacrifices. For heart satisfaction there is an effort to feel at peace with the whole universe through following the teaching of a Javanese mystical sect. Some recent converts recognised this when they decided to become Christians, on the ground that Islam did not cover all their needs in the same way as Christ does.

Conversions within Javanese village communities seem to take place as a series of steps rather than a continuous process. The first converts, who have been attracted to the gospel by Christian relatives, colleagues, education, exorcism/healing or a dream, will often succeed in bringing a few others in their village to faith in Christ. The new group is then observed for a time by the rest of the community. Its distinctive character will be noted, but continuing activity as normal members of the village is the key to future growth of the church in the village. Those who exhibit the peace of mind that Javanese desire and are not disruptive of village traditions will prove effective in bringing others into the church. The danger is that the national stress on unity waters down the Christian distinctiveness until it is just one more element in the syncretic 'Religion of Java' that has already successfully absorbed Animism, Buddhism, Hinduism and Islam.

The migration of Christians from tribal heartlands to the cities and towns of Java within the context of a developing united nation has presented the opportunity for the conversion of many Muslim individuals. Although there are occasional tensions, there has been little difficulty for ex-Muslims in joining existing churches. Their common Indonesian citizenship has facilitated a change of religious community. In towns and cities, growing individualism allows many to make a personal religious choice. Even some from the more fanatical Islamic areas in West Java, Sumatera and Sulawesi have come to Christian faith away from their tribal areas. Some of this growth has occurred in inter-religious marriages, where the converted partner has exhibited a greater desire to know God and Jesus than the nominal Christian she/he has married. Some in city life regard Christianity as more progressive than the Islam they have known in their villages.

In recent years there have been new pressures to reduce freedoms to proselytise. External and internal pressures towards an Islamic state will always be present. As long as the national emphasis is on diversity as well as unity and the Christian churches remain committed to a converting and Biblical gospel, the conversion of Muslims to Christ will continue in Indonesia.

Central Asian case study: an example of the changing nature of mission to Muslims

Peter the Great (1672–1725) was the founder of today's modern Russia. Through him the Russians were drawn into conflict with the Muslim states of Central Asia which were largely Turkic in origin. A number of wars were conducted against them, trying to curtail their raids into Russian territories.

This expansion was continued by successive governments including the communists until the Central Asian states became an integral part of the communist regime.

From Moscow economies were tightly planned and controlled with the result that Uzbekistan was assigned to be the cotton producer of the regime. In consequence it became the producer of one-third of the world's cotton. This required heavy use of nitrate fertilisers and access to the waters of the two rivers that run into the Aral sea.

Minority nationalities were sent to run these enterprises, with the result that Russians, Ukrainians, and other nationalities were assigned to live and work in these desert areas. Among them were many Christians.

In 1979 one of the first forays to assess the possibilities of working among the Muslim groups resulted in the long-term aspirations of some of us who had worked in Afghanistan and Iran coming to fruition.

Several doors were seen to be open although in a small way.

First, we found that *there were German- and Russian-speaking churches in the area*. The Germans had been brought there by Stalin and would have starved had not the Muslims assisted them through the first winter. Some were evangelical and evangelistic. All they needed were materials in these Muslim languages. A literature-smuggling ministry down to these far-away places was initiated.

Second, *radio was seen as an important tool in reaching over the Hindu Kush into these areas*. A German who had been adopted by a Kazakh family became the first voice on the airwaves to bring them the message of Christ.

Third, *believers, although living among the Muslims, knew little about their beliefs and practices*. They only learned what little language they needed to buy food in the markets. A series of seminars was planned and carried out in order to train these believers to share their faith. This was all under a very tight KGB atmosphere and many a time we were followed, hassled, and even attacked physically.

Slowly reports of church growth filtered out. Translation and radio work was speeded up, and more got involved in the training aspect. It was interesting to note that those first followers of Jesus that stood firm were those married to Russian wives.

With the fall of the communist regime more opportunities opened up. Newer groups got involved and translation work became very much easier. Russian missionary societies came into being, some for the express purpose of reaching Muslim areas, others of a more general nature.

The long years of Russian domination has also meant a legacy of hatred. Many of the believers have left the area, or even left Russia for the West; this is specially true of the German community. The lifting of oppression has also affected the children of believers, who feel more free to question the rather conservative attitudes of their parents. Muslim animosity has become apparent towards these former colonisers and threats against them have been issued.

The single-product economy means that they are still very dependent upon other states for their survival. The ecological disaster is now very apparent in that the Aral Sea water level has dropped leaving miles of nitrates on the beaches, to be whipped up into the desert air causing many illnesses and stillbirths. This, also, adds to the resentment of the peoples.

Ethnic tensions between the Slavs, the Turkic peoples, and amongst the Central Asians themselves is another feature of life in the area. Old political alliances clash with new aspirations of freedom and democracy.

Since the future is seen to be in the area of trade and education many opportunities have come about for 'tent makers' to assist in teaching European languages, opening up market forces and training the young people in technical subjects. Aid and development programmes are now being allowed.

Believers from a Muslim background are coming together but are still having to find their own ethnic expression of their faith in Christ, apart from European and Russian worship patterns.

Naturally other Muslim nations are anxious to draw these new republics into their orbit. Iran is signing trade agreements with these states and is beaming programmes in from an 800,000-watt station in the Caspian Sea area. Turkey is best situated to bring aid, with its administrators, teachers and political links based upon a common Turkic heritage. Of course Libya and Saudi Arabia are also seeking to influence the future. This means that a wide variety of Islamic attitudes are present. Much prayer is needed that the door may remain open, even open wider, for the gospel to have effect in the area.

The desire for a clean break with the Russian culture has resulted in each of these republics seeking to establish its own identity. This is especially seen in the change of the alphabet to Latin and Persian scripts. It also may mean that there is only a small window of opportunity for the future of the church in the area; if fundamental Islam wins the race, the window will be closed.

4

The continent of Africa

Both Islam and Christianity are spreading in Africa. In some
African countries the adherents of the two religions are living
happily side by side, but in others there is conflict, amounting
in some cases to civil war. The survey which follows shows how
Islam has spread southwards from the North African countries.
In the north of the continent Islam is numerically strong, but in
the south Muslims are found mainly in communities living
around the major cities. In these areas there is some interaction
between Muslims and Christians.

Survey of Islam in Africa

Islam entered Africa on the northern coasts through conquest
that eventually reached Spain. It took over from the former
Eastern and Western Roman powers, who had imposed a
Western and Latin, or Eastern and Greek form of the Christian
faith upon their peoples. We should not forget that Saint
Augustine of Hippo wrote from North Africa about what
seemed to be a catastrophe—the fall of Rome—and that he
wrote in Latin.

The Arab powers also tried, and still try, to force Arabisation
upon the subject peoples. Some responded by adopting dissident
forms of Kharadjite or Shiite Islam in order to maintain their
dignity. One of the significant differences between the regimes
is that the Arabs were and are at home in the desert, whereas
to the Romans the desert was a fearsome place.

Jihads in the Western Sahara have caused the indigenous
people in that area to adopt a type of Arab culture. They no
longer wear the distinctive veil, or speak their own language,
but a dialect of Arabic known as Hassaniya. Nor do they inherit
through the line of the women in the family, as they did in their
own culture.

But for most of Africa Islam spread through intrepid traders,
in the East directly by sea from Arabia, in the West along trade

routes established through the desert over the centuries. They were followed by Arab geographers like Ibn Battuta, whose written accounts form a lot of our knowledge about earlier times. We forget, however, that we are seeing these events through foreign, Islamic eyes. The underlying African culture is not visible in these written accounts.

In the days of Western colonialism, there was a steady influx of traders from the Indian subcontinent. In addition, a labour force was introduced to build the railway, because it was thought that the local people would not be able to do this. These labourers were both Muslims and Hindus.

Much of the trade was in slaves, and Islam shares with Christianity the indictment of its inbuilt policies towards African peoples. One difference was that the Muslims took wives from the local people. The whole problem of whether they should also have given wives to the local people is a sore point up to this day. Among the Christians, the Southern Europeans intermarried, but the Northern Europeans tended not to do so.

Freedom from European powers has taken place in this century. This has been slow and painful in East, West and South Africa. In North Africa the position is more complex. The Arabs have a privileged place in society. There is a battle going on over whether French or Arabic is to be the language of university education, which is significant in the ongoing debate. In some African countries an even more significant and tragic battle is being fought. Black Arabs, descendents of the Arab traders above, are fighting with ruthless determination to de-Africanise stretches of territory and their political systems. There is bound to be reaction from Africans. In Uganda, for example, the action of ex-President Idi Amin in expelling the Asians, so getting rid of Asian domination, received a great deal of support.

The upsurge of Arabism through the great oil wealth, and the position of the Saudis at the centre of the pilgrimage world, is spreading through the whole Muslim world. Reaction to this has not only come from the Persians of Iran. How far one can be African and genuinely Muslim is a question debated both openly and privately among Africans.

The great movement to revive the customs (*sunna*) of the Prophet and to remove innovation (*bid'a*) from Islam is continent-wide. Innovation, by which so many Muslims have lived in the past in an easy harmony, is now seen as a threatening African cultural trend.

The spread of Islam through the desert was anchored in the lives of members of the Sufi fellowships, notably of the Qadari order. Their great Shaikhs exercised a religious authority upon the warring tribal chiefs of the desert. They also provided a haven like the Old Testament cities of refuge, for political refugees from the different factions. They do so to this day, especially in the centres in and near Senegal.

The power of these movements often consisted in their division of life into that of this world (*al-dunya*) and the world to come (*al-akhira*). This allowed a secular view of this world which is transient and will pass away. It also allowed comparison between this world, in which sinful or un-Islamic practices take place, and the vision of an Islamic paradise in the world to come. The freedom in this world, for example, to embrace socialist ideas, to make alliances with Christians and even pagans in politics, presided over by the genial shaikh of the order, will only last as long as the system does. The great orders of Senegal elected a Christian, Leopold Senghor, poet and founder of the black cultural movement of negritude, to be their first president, but this did not last.

Just as in Europe, Christian socialists founded political parties, yet their followers have often kept their socialism, but not their faith in God, so, too, the spiritual heirs of the shaikhs may keep nominal allegiance to their orders, but only to emphasise their political stance.

Christians need to be aware of these things; to sympathise, but not to condone; to make the power of the Holy Spirit their true weapon.

North Africa

Since this book was first published in 1985 there have been significant political developments in the lands of North Africa.

These lands known in the Arabic-speaking world as 'The Maghreb' (Lands of the Setting Sun) have all in some degree or another been faced with the challenge of an extreme form of Muslim activism which has assumed revolutionary proportions. The governments of some of these countries are opposed to this fundamentalist Islamic movement.

The Romans first brought the Christian religion to North Africa. By AD148 Christianity began to spread in what is now Libya and Tunisia, penetrating Algeria during the second century. Tertullian and Cyprian were early church fathers and in AD396 Augustine was appointed bishop of Hippo, now Annata in Eastern Algeria. The Roman church did not last. As Roman power declined, first the Vandals and then the Byzantine Church took over. The Eastern Church did not last long and by the end of the seventh century it collapsed when confronted by the spread of Islam. The new monotheistic religion founded by Muhammad, Islam, remains to this day the religion of perhaps 99% of the population. Egypt does still have a Christian community of approximately 20%.

Recent surveys indicate that there is an active Roman Catholic church which has attracted North African converts. The same is true of the Protestant church in North Africa. Both conduct their worship in French. There are also English language Anglican churches in some of the major cities. The Bible Society still operates in North Africa and although the sale of Scriptures in Arabic is forbidden, the Bible is available in other languages.

That there are Christians of North African origin is without dispute. Many of the major cities have groups of national Christian believers who meet regularly for worship in various centres. Governments seem to have relaxed the more extreme forms of persecution of Christians while the fundamentalist Islamic movement has intensified its opposition to known national Christians. Some have received death threats and have fled the country.

Many of the indigenous Christians are of the Berber race. Some anthropologists believe the Berber people to be descendants of the original inhabitants of the lands of North Africa.

Some Berbers claim they were Christians until Islam came. This may be one factor which explains, in part, why a group of them have responded eagerly to the Christian gospel. It is certainly a moving experience to worship with these North African believers and to see the church beginning to reach people, young and old, of both Arab and Berber race.

It has to be stressed that this church is truly indigenous, being led by the Holy Spirit through North African believers; is entirely self-supporting; and is making exciting plans to reach out to others. Plans have been made to establish a graphics studio in addition to recording and video production facilities. A printing press is also being planned. Centres for Bible teaching and Christian fellowship are being established.

Nigeria: a case study

Nigeria like Gaul can be divided into three main geographical parts, and the spread and development of Islam differed in each area.

In the north, Islam was spread by Arab traders gradually influencing the chiefs of the Hausa and Kanuri tribes up to the eighteenth century. In the nineteenth century it grew more violently, encouraged by holy war and enclavement. Islam spread from the top down.

In the west, Islam spread up to the nineteenth century through the slavery of Muslims from the north and pockets of northern traders. It spread from the bottom up.

In the east, apart again from pockets of Hausa traders, indigenous Muslims were mainly Ibo traders who had Islamised in the north. Then in the 1960s with the beginning of civil war these traders had to flee south.

Colonial Britain had used the existing Islamic framework in the north to rule indirectly and had kept the old Fulani emirates that had existed from the time of the holy wars. This old framework was represented by the facade of the Fulani chief's palace, the Islamic law court, and the Friday mosque, which stood at the top of the hill in Zaria. But the power lay with the Resident at the bottom of the hill. It was there that Babban

Dodo, 'the Big Bogey Man', as the Resident was called, lived. This was a truth that was only gradually learned in society, and how it must have annoyed the Emir.

Islam in the north was centred on the celebration of its festivals, one at the end of Ramadan, the sacrifice feast, and the Hajj seasons when the people came to salute the emirs. One perceptive imam spoke up: 'The people used to flock to the Friday mosque in Kano to see the chief. If the chief was there alive and well, so too was Islam.'

In another area, such as the west, Islam flourished in the great traditional Yoruba states without the support of a medieval aristocracy. So when the power of the chief was seen to decline, the influence of Islam remained the same.

But the question was, where could the physical force be found in the north to impose Islam to take the place of the emir? Would it be in the shari'a law imposed by selected judges? Would it be in the slow weeding-out of all Christian leaders from government, army, and the civil service? Young fanatics translated their creed 'There is no traditional chief except Allah', to the alarm of their elders. In the west the question did not arise like that.

The Christian gospel was flourishing in the rural areas. 'The Muslims came with burning of our villages and enslaving our forefathers,' one shaikh declared. 'The *Nasara* [here European Christians] came with medicine and education. We should know where the truth lies from this.' Christian communities flocked to the large towns, and this upset the old political balance.

In the north, Islam then felt the need to be seen to be in a state of triumph. This seemed to mean periodic burning of Christian churches.

Popular Islamic movements also flourished in Nigeria. The Tijani brotherhood was based on Kano, and from there it moved to the west. It provided both an ethical and moral anchor to young Muslims who had lost the discipline of the village, and also a religious fellowship. The initiator, or shaikh, became the centre of their moral lives. But what would happen when the Saudi influences would declare that *tajdid* renewal could not be found through confessing one's sins to a shaikh?

The Qadari brotherhood followed the Tijani in becoming a popular faith for many Muslims, cut off from the village community to be lost in the suburbs.

The Saudi influence has spread, raising questions about how Islam is practised, causing matters to be re-examined and bringing some unrest. How far could a man be a Muslim and keep to his tribal customs of drumming and dancing? Some children called their parents who practised such *kuffar*, pagan unbelievers.

How far can a traditional *mallam* (religious teacher) continue his own African customs, of blessings and cursing and blood sacrifices, if he is supposed to give these up for a pure legal Islam? The power to do this rests in only one Name, as Christians know, the name of one who appears in dreams to strengthen the believers. The Qur'an has been re-opened to see what that name means. This too has brought both glory and unrest.

The old Katsina Emirate fetish, wrapped in skins, was torn apart by the jihad leaders in the nineteenth century. It was found to contain a copy of the Qur'an. In this century the Qur'an is again being re-opened to see if it contains the miracles of modern science.

The re-opening of the Qur'an by the people has been encouraged by the emergence of the Ahmadiyya movement, whose idea that 'this is the age of the Qur'an' galvanises those who want to return to the customs (the *sunna*) of the Prophet alternately to rage and to imitation.

Where should the de-tribalised descendant of the Fulani slaves find a Muslim community to accept him? Should it be with their family tribe, now often Christian, or should it be with a dreadful Mahdi to rebuild Islam from scratch in a society that had cut them off?

'Search for knowledge even as far as China', says the Tradition, and many have quoted this in order to justify their sending their children to Western schools. But where could a student, divorced from his tribal roots, in secondary school or university find

comfort? Should it be in the arms of the Muslim Brotherhood
or Ayatollah Khomeini, or in the fulsome praise of God in the
Pentecostal movement?

Former Christian patterns were changing. In one way all
Christian tribes, however small, now wanted to worship in their
own language and to look after their own affairs. In another,
Christian revival was breaking down tribal barriers with deep
healing of the soul in a middle-class and university revival.

'He who has ears to hear, let him hear.'

5

Muslim minority groups

Survey

India has the largest Muslim minority in the world—over
100,000,000, about 12% of the total population, accessible but
often forgotten. Many of them speak Urdu at home but find
this problematic, as it is not a state language. So Hindi, English
and the state language take precedence over Urdu in the
schools. Even with the rise of indigenous missions, Muslims
tend to be neglected.

The Philippines with a population of 65,000,000 has about
8.4% Muslims. They live mostly in South West Mindanao,
Sulu Islands and Palawan. They are the largest unreached
religious grouping in the country. Work among them by Filipino
Christians and foreign believers is made more difficult by the
variety of languages used and the 'militant' liberation organisations which engage in anti-government activities, kidnappings
and other forms of terrorism.

In China, Muslims form 2.4% of the population. Out of 55
ethnic minorities, ten are Muslim and number about 27,000,000.
Nine of these minorities reside in the autonomous region of
Xinjiang Uygyre Zizhiqu (Sinkiang) in the north-west of China.
The most numerous are the Uighur with about 6,660,000 and
then the Kazakh with 1,000,000. The 8,000,000 Hui Chinese
Muslims are spread all over China with the largest number

in Ningzia. There are now 14,000 functioning mosques and Islam is one of the resurgent faiths filling the present spiritual vacuum. Communism has given Muslim women in China a greater sense of worth, independence and equality with men.

The Republic of Korea gives us an example of how a Muslim minority is established in a country which had no Muslims. In 1955 there were no Korean Muslims. Two Turks who were with the UN forces started to preach. The stages as outlined by the Muslims have been: the introductory stage, the preparatory stage, the settled stage and now the take-off stage. There are now 32,500 Muslims with mosques in six major cities.

In South America Muslims only exist in minority, the largest being in Brazil. The first Muslims arrived in Brazil at the start of the sixteenth century, as part of the group of settlers who discovered the country. In the early nineteenth century, many of the slaves were Muslim and there was even an attempt to set up an 'Islamic Khalifate'. Most of the Muslims at present in Brazil are Arabs, who have come for economic reasons from some of the poorer Islamic countries. Out of Brazil's population of 150,000,000, about 2,000,000 are Muslims. Most of the Muslims live around the big cities. There are about 40 mosques in the country. There is as yet very little Christian response to the growing number of Muslims in South America.

While we think of Muslim minority groups like the ones mentioned above we should not forget those other groupings of Muslims in minority—Muslim students studying outside their own countries (e.g. 120,000 in USA), wealthy Arab tourists in the capitals of Europe, Muslim refugees whether from Afghanistan, Iran, Bosnia or elsewhere. Then there are the Muslim migrants and immigrants who have sought and found work abroad, for example, Turkish 'guest workers' in Germany and Holland, or North Africans in France. Also in the West, as in Korea, there are citizens who have become Muslims. Finally there is that growing number of Muslim citizens in such countries whose children and grandchildren are born Muslim. Muslims tend to have large families and so the growth rate among Muslims is generally higher than among many other groups.

In the 1960s and 1970s one of the largest groups of immigrants was of South Asians. They came both from their own countries and from East Africa. Many of them settled in Britain where their links through the former British Raj made them think they would be more at home. Many of the East Africans had British passports. Other South Asians went to the United States, Canada, or the Continent of Europe, even a few to Australia.

Israel is a unique and complex situation. As Christians we have a natural empathy with the Jewish nation. We worship the God of the Jews and our Old Testament is the Jewish Scriptures. We remember God's promises to his people concerning the promised land. At the same time we see the human rights situation and desire justice for the Palestinians. As Colin Chapman has said, 'We walk on a tightrope'. We cannot condone the militancy of some Palestinians who struggle to regain their homeland through violence and believe that they are engaged in jihad. There are however some Palestinians who want to live peaceably and some who are our fellow Christians.

A Town in north-west England

There is a town in the north-west of England with a population of 216,500 people. 6.5% are Muslims of South Asian origin.

Although it is an independent town it is joined to a much larger metropolitan area. It is also one of about a dozen towns situated on or near a major motorway which crosses the country from east to west. Each of these towns has an above-average number of ethnic Asians, most of whom are Muslims. They come from two different South Asian countries. Many of the features described here would also be found in the other towns.

This ethnic minority group started settling in the town nearly thirty years ago. During the 1960s large numbers came, mainly for economic reasons. They found employment in the mills. Many of these mills have now closed, but some new industries have been established. Even so, unemployment is higher than average, particularly among the Asians. Although the immigration laws have become more restrictive, there is still a trickle of new people arriving.

The Asians have settled in four districts in the town. In the two main districts they are in the parishes of lively churches, which are keen to reach out to them. Over the last ten years, God has been calling Christians who have experience of working among Muslims into the two churches. The work has developed rather differently in the two parishes, perhaps because of the different vision and gifts of the workers. There is, however, close co-operation between them and as the parishes adjoin it is easy for them to work together.

Parish A

The parish church is on the edge of the Asian area, looking out into it. There is a daughter church in another non-Asian part of the parish. Both these churches have around two hundred members. The curate-in-charge of the daughter church worked among Asians in another of the towns before he was ordained. He and his wife have visited the country from which the Asians in the parish have come and can speak their language. The curate advises and visits in the Muslim area from time to time. His wife does part-time voluntary work in the office of the Bible correspondence school which is described below.

A Church Army officer is attached to the parish church. He leads the outreach into the Muslim area. His vision and energy have enabled him to get to know the imams in the mosques and other Muslim leaders in the community. There are three mosques in the parish: one follows orthodox Sunni teaching, another is a more fundamentalist group and the third is attached to a cultural centre, which follows a more popular expression of Islam. There are regular discussion meetings between the first mosque and the church, with either a Christian or a Muslim leading on a subject chosen by those who attend. Although discussion may get quite heated, there is a good atmosphere, with each side prepared to listen. There have also been social gatherings at times when religious festivals are being celebrated. This gives opportunity for both Muslims and Christians to explain the meaning behind such festivals. They are also a time when the two communities can meet in a relaxed atmosphere and people can relate to one another across religious and cultural boundaries. There are no plans for inter-faith services of worship as neither side would be happy to take part in these. The Church Army officer considers that some progress towards a better understanding between the two groups has been made, although he and a number of others would love to see this being faster and more specific. As he remarked, 'In other parts of the world Christians and Muslims are killing one another; we call each other by nicknames!'

An important Community Development Project has been set up in the parish through the efforts of the church, the mosque and the community primary school. It is run by a management committee composed of both Muslims and Christians, who employ people with professional qualifications to assist the community with welfare rights, family support, pre-school development and work among women. The office, situated centrally in the area, attracts many who need counselling and help. Classes are held in language learning, both English and the language of origin. There are also social events, sewing classes and Keep Fit instruction. Financial help has been received through the social services and the Church Urban Fund, but other requests for support have not yet been successful. The project relies heavily on voluntary help.

Parish B

The church is situated in the middle of the Asian area. The area was originally built to house the managerial and 'white collar' staff of the mills, and there are restrictions concerning its development. Public houses are not allowed and this has made it an attractive area for Muslims. The church primary school has 100% Asian enrolment and the other primary schools about 85%.

The work in this parish is developing through the people who are working among the Asian community rather than through any specific project. They have all had experience in one or other of the Asian countries and speak the languages fluently. The church is involved through these people, who are members of it, rather than through initiating activities or organising outreach. Originally built for the families living in the area, it has seen much change. Some of the present congregation live

outside the parish, but continue to take part in the life
and worship of the church. After a long period without a
vicar, an appointment was made about a year ago. The
present vicar and his wife worked for a number of years
in South Asia and speak the language. The vicar believes
that his primary task is to build up the present congregation. Apart from involvement in the church school and starting
a service in an Asian language with the two Asian Christian
families in the church, his contact with Asians is spontaneous
and unofficial. The vicar's wife works as a practice nurse
in a practice run by Asians, which is next door to the
church.

The head of one of the two Asian families in the church is
from a Muslim background. He is supported by a Christian
organisation and directs the Bible correspondence school. The
school is his brainchild. Although it has only been going a few
years it has made good progress and is being used not only in
this town, but throughout the country, even reaching Muslim
enquirers in other countries. As well as writing courses, advising
students and counselling enquirers, this key worker has a
ministry to Muslim leaders, writing, speaking and debating as
opportunities arise. He is also a member of the Asian Christian
Fellowship which is active in all the towns near the motorway,
some of which have many more Asian Christians than this town
has.

The organisation that supports this Asian Christian and his
work also supports another couple who are attached to parish
church B. They have worked in both of the South Asian
countries, so are able to relate well to both language groups.
They are well integrated into the communities and run clubs for
the young people. Their outreach is mainly through personal
contact and the husband runs a stall in the local markets, selling
general goods as well as Christian literature. The children
attend one of the local primary schools and the wife gives
them extra tuition while they are there. This allows them
to mix with the local community without being educationally
disadvantaged.

Another member of the church assists the Bible correspondence school as administrator, while his wife works as a health visitor with many Asian clients.

The husband in a third couple is in charge of the teaching of those with special language needs in the town and the wife is a practice nurse in another of the Asian practices.

A single man is also a language teacher. He has taught an Asian language as well as English to the Asian community.

A single women is a health visitor. She has worked about ten years in the area and is a guide, counsellor and friend to many of the Asian women in her care. The health visitors meet Asians living in the other two Asian districts of the town as well as those in the two parishes.

'Why have you chosen our town for your case study? There is a lot more going on in some of the other towns,' said one of the workers. That may be so, but the work in this town is being built up gradually and only God knows what the future will hold. The impression given is that the encouraging growing points will eventually bring much fruit. The town is also an example of Christian teamwork, a subject which is taken up again in Chapter 15.

A concluding thought:

From a worker among Muslims,

> Our stress is that Jesus is Lord of the Church and he is in the process of building his Church.
>
> 'Who do you say I am?'
> Simon Peter answered, 'You are the Christ, the Son of the living God.'
> Jesus replied, 'Blessed are you, Simon son of Jonah, for this was not revealed to you by man, but by my Father in heaven. And I tell you that you are Peter, and on this rock I will build my church, and the gates of Hades will not overcome it.' (Mt 16: 15–18)

Notes

We hope that you have now got some sort of overall picture of what is going on in the world of Islam. It may be helpful to try to separate Islamic countries and governments from Muslim people. It is the latter to whom we relate and interact. However, particularly if we live in an Islamic country, we will also be very much aware of the laws and the need to keep them. Islamic fundamentalism has been mentioned a number of times. It is a key factor. The next chapter explains it in some detail.

Books referred to in the chapter

Cragg, Kenneth, *Counsels on Contemporary Islam* (Edinburgh Univ Press: Edinburgh, 1965).

Smith, Wilfred Cantwell, *Islam in Modern History* (Mentor: NY, 1957).

Information concerning Islam in Brazil was obtained from a leaflet produced by World Horizons.

14

The Political Face of Islam

Study guide

The rise of Islamic fundamentalism in the latter part of the twentieth century is, perhaps, the most significant development to occur in the recent history of Islam. The adoption of shari'a law by a number of Islamic countries is changing the political face not only of Islam, but of large parts of the world. This chapter describes the movement, starting from the furore over the publishing of Salman Rushdie's book, The Satanic Verses *(1988). It goes on to show how Islamic fundamentalism can be seen as the realisation of all that Muhammad taught, and the setting up of Islamic states as the fulfilment of his vision.*

This chapter includes some material already covered earlier. However, the repetition was thought worthwhile, as different contexts and emphases come into play as we discuss the political aspects of Islam.

When you have completed the chapter we hope you will:

1 *Understand why the writing of* The Satanic Verses *led to Ayatollah Khomeini's fatwa;*
2 *Begin to understand the vision of fulfilling the teaching of the Prophet Muhammad; and*
3 *Begin to see the political results of the spread of Islamic fundamentalism.*

Talk of the devil

I inform the proud Muslim people of the world that the author of *The Satanic Verses* book which is against Islam, the Prophet and the Qur'an, and all involved in its publication who were aware of its contents, are sentenced to death. I ask all Muslims to execute them wherever they find them. (Shabir Akhtar, 1989, p 64)

The message which came out of Iran on St Valentine's day 1989 deeply shocked the free-thinking Western world. By contrast Muslims, including many of those who refused to condone the imposing of the death sentences, felt that Imam Khomeini had restored honour to Islam. He had exposed the severity of Rushdie's insult. The stern pronouncement (*fatwa*) warned of the dangers of printing 'blasphemy'.

Salman Rushdie had focused on a sore point in the history of the revealing of the Qur'an. A brief investigation exposes the inflammatory nature of his book. At the heart of his novel he questioned the inspiration of Prophet Muhammad. As he discovered to his cost, that was a very provocative thing to do.

1

A Prophet's preparation

As we have seen (Chapter 5), Muhammad was born into the tribe of the Quraysh, part of the clan of Hashim. He lived in Mecca, an economic and religious centre in Arabia in the sixth and seventh centuries.

Trading interests and guardianship of religious places went together in the tribal society. Mecca was a centre of both with a cultus of idol worship which brought pilgrims into its environs especially at times of trading festivals. Some 360 idols were housed in Mecca, reflecting the allegiances of various residents and visitors to the town.

Four of these gods and goddesses had special significance. The god, al-Llah, was vaguely recognised by the tribes as a high god. More visible and important in the minds of the bedouin were the three goddesses known as 'the daughters of al-Llah'. They were al-Lat, 'the goddess', whose major shrine was Taif; al-Uzzah, 'the mighty one', (most popular of the idols) whose major shrine was at Naklah; and Manat, goddess of fate, whose shrine was at Qudayd. Each of these goddesses had minor shrines in Mecca, maintained by one privileged clan.

By the time of Muhammad, the tribal structure of the Quraysh living in and around Mecca had reshaped into three major groups of alliances. Muhammad's own clan, the Hashim, had had its heyday but was now very much on the decline.

Muhammad began receiving revelations in AD610. It was some time before he comprehended what was happening to him. His meetings with Gabriel were frightening at first. Muhammad eventually realised that he was to be the recipient of God's word, 'sent down' via the angel. He learned to recite what came to him.

During AD612 the revelations took on new momentum. People from different clans began to be deeply affected by the message Muhammad was passing on.

Gradually, Muhammad's preaching split families and clans. In AD615 he received a revelation commanding him to declare himself openly to his whole clan and invite them to enter Islam and worship al-Llah (Sura 26:210–220). Muhammad put on a meagre meal for forty leading men of Hashim and invited them to enter Islam. A relative interrupted the meal and broke it up. The meeting was repeated the following day, but when Muhammad issued his invitation there was silence. No one converted.

Whispers from hell?

During the next year a crisis arose. It revolved around a potential compromise. The details are recorded by al-Tabari (Rodinson, 1989, p 106).

> When the Messenger of God saw his people draw away from him, it gave him great pain to see what a distance separated them from the word of Allah which he brought to them. Then he longed in his heart to receive a word from Allah which would bring him closer to his people. Because of his care for them and the love he had for them, he would gladly have seen those things that bore too harshly on them softened a little, so much so that he kept saying it to

himself, and desiring it and wishing for it. It was then that Allah revealed to him the sura of the Star . . .

'Did you consider al-Lat and al-Uzza
And al-Manat, the third, the other?
Those are the swans exalted: (They are the Exalted Birds)
Their intercession is expected: (And their intercession is desired indeed)
Their likes are not neglected.'

When these verses were declared, acknowledging inclusion of the three major idols of Mecca in the new religious hierarchy, the Meccans reputedly prostrated themselves.

Soon God took Muhammad to task, and the verses were replaced by what now appears as Sura 53:19–23. Both versions were proclaimed publicly, and the explanation given for the change was that Satan had managed to slip in the false verses of the first version without Muhammad noticing it. An exoneration appears later in Sura 22:52:

> Never did we send
> An apostle or a prophet
> Before thee, but, when he
> Framed a desire, Satan
> Threw some (vanity)
> Into his desire: but Allah
> Will cancel anything (vain)
> That Satan throws in,
> And Allah will confirm
> (And establish) His signs:
> For Allah is full of knowledge
> And wisdom.

Down through the centuries, this incident has been known to Muslims by the catchphrase 'The Satanic Verses'. The abrogation of the 'satanic verses' marked the beginning of violent opposition to Muhammad.

Only human?

Salman Rushdie, in his rewrite of this incident in Muhammad's life, concludes that neither God nor the devil are involved in the process of 'sending down'. The Qur'an is rather the product of Muhammad's own wishful thinking. As Mahound (Rushdie's pejorative nickname for Muhammad) returns to Mecca with the corrected sura, Rushdie describes the angel Gabriel's secret joke:

> . . . but Gibreel, hovering-watching from his highest camera angle, knows one small detail, just one tiny thing that's a bit of a problem here, namely that it was me both times, baba, me first and second also me. From my mouth, both the statement and the repudiation, verses and converses, universes and reverses, the whole thing, and we all know how my mouth got worked. (p 380)

Gibreel (Gabriel) 'gets his mouth worked' by Mahound in wrestling matches, during which the Prophet forces Gibreel's face open and makes the voice pour out of him 'like sick'. It is Mahound's own voice, it is self-projection, nothing to do with either God or the devil.

Rushdie names his whole novel after this incident in Muhammad's life.

Filth or fiction?

The impact of *The Satanic Verses* upon Muslims from Bradford to Bombay, and the incredulity of Western secularists at the ensuing *fatwa*, illustrates the huge chasm between opposed concepts of what life is all about.

Why can't a twice-married, lapsed-Muslim, gifted British author write what 'fiction' he likes 'in good faith'? (Rushdie, 1990, p 18–20). Such is the angry question of poets, politicians and publishers in Western capitals.

Why does it prove impossible for educated and responsible Muslims to find a sympathetic hearing in democratic societies, for the sense of anguish and outrage at what they can only feel is 'a calculated attempt to vilify and slander the Prophet of Islam'? (Shabir Akhtar, 1989 p 1). Such is the frustrated demand of Muslims the world over.

Book burnings and death sentences portray a face of Islam largely unrecognised by Western onlookers. How is it that politics and religion are so closely entwined? In what ways do prayer and protest together invigorate modern Muslims?

Activity 14:1

At the height of the 'Rushdie affair', a group of protestors against the *fatwa* set up a stall in a London street. They invited passers-by to write a letter to the author.

What would you write in a letter to Salman Rushdie?

2

Realisation of a dream

If you see the whole of life as revolving around submission to God, and if the way of pleasing God in such submission depends fundamentally on a book (the Qur'an) and a prophet (Muhammad), then subtle underminings of the integrity of book and prophet constitute attacks on ultimate convictions.

For all Muslims, and especially for reformist (or 'fundamentalist') Muslims, a concern for 'doing God's will' is primary. That divine will has been faithfully declared, though not so faithfully preserved, in succeeding generations through revealed 'books' made known by prophets. Finally the authentic, original and correcting revelation has been sent down in the form of a recitation in Arabic. The Qur'an, mediated via the archangel Gabriel through Prophet Muhammad in the twenty-two years following AD610, brings to mankind the definitive statement of how life is to be lived on earth.

When Prophet Muhammad shifted to Medina, he was given the opportunity of putting into civic effect the instructions received from heaven. He formed a society (Umma) of Muslims intent on living out the implications of submission to God. Further revelations came, defining how to behave in all kinds of situations, public and domestic, personal and political. A record grew (the *sunna*) of how the Prophet responded to God's burdens in speech and action. That record came to be codified and compiled after Prophet Muhammad's death. It is contained in the various records of Traditions (Hadith). See Chapter 7, pp 130–131.

Framework for submission

One of the strongest movements going on in the contemporary world of Islam is a concern for renewed faithfulness to the seedbeds of the Islamic faith: Qur'an and *Sunna*. After decades of humiliation under Western, 'Christian', colonial powers and years of disillusionment under Western-influenced national leaders of 'independent' Muslim states, many Muslims are today clamouring for an alternative expression of polity. They want to give God a chance in their societies. They want to see the establishment of an Islamic state.

The setting for an Islamic state, unlike a secular state, is determined by peoples' self-inclusion as part of the community or Umma. It is not primarily defined in terms of nationhood, race or territory. The concept of Islamic community is rather like the Christian sense of belonging to the kingdom of God, a commitment that recognises no earthly, political, geographical or temporal allegiances as ultimate. In true Islam the faithful, the submitted, comprise the Umma. The aspiration, therefore, is to become a universal state. The Islamic Republic of Iran does not see it as a matter of 'exporting' its 'government of God' to Saudi Arabia or Iraq. Rather it sees itself as calling true Muslims in those (falsely defined) political entities to join the one true community, the Umma of renewed Islam.

In an Islamic state, ultimate sovereignty belongs to God. He is Lord. He determines the appropriate way to construct societal life, individual mores, family relationships and so on. He has a view on everything. That view, more or less, is declared or discernible within Qur'an and prophetic tradition (*Sunna*). It is not a question of human beings getting together to work out a philosophy of life. Laws made through human

**COMPONENTS OF
THE ISLAMIC STATE**

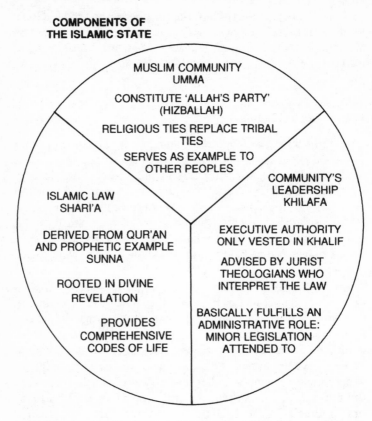

MUSLIM COMMUNITY
UMMA

CONSTITUTE 'ALLAH'S PARTY'
(HIZBALLAH)

RELIGIOUS TIES REPLACE TRIBAL
TIES

SERVES AS EXAMPLE TO
OTHER PEOPLES

COMMUNITY'S
LEADERSHIP
KHILAFA

ISLAMIC LAW
SHARI'A

DERIVED FROM QUR'AN
AND PROPHETIC EXAMPLE
SUNNA

EXECUTIVE AUTHORITY
ONLY VESTED IN KHALIF

ADVISED BY JURIST
THEOLOGIANS WHO
INTERPRET THE LAW

ROOTED IN DIVINE
REVELATION

PROVIDES
COMPREHENSIVE
CODES OF LIFE

BASICALLY FULFILLS AN
ADMINISTRATIVE ROLE:
MINOR LEGISLATION
ATTENDED TO

reason are an irrelevance. It is a matter of deducing what God's will is:

> The entire system of government and administration, together with the necessary laws, lies ready for you. If the administration of the country calls for taxes, Islam has made the necessary provision; and if laws are needed, Islam has established them all. There is no need for you after establishing a government, to sit down and draw up laws, or, like rulers who worship foreigners and are infatuated with the West, run after others to borrow their laws. Everything is ready and waiting. All that remains is to draw up ministerial programs, and that can be accomplished with the help and cooperation of consultants and advisers who are

experts in different fields, gathered together in a consultative assembly.

(Khomeini, 1981, pp 137–8)

In his major work on Islamic government, written in exile in Iraq, Khomeini thus states the reformist case. Islamic law (Shari'a) is to be the order of the day, because that law comprises a discerning of God's will. Those who are expert in the understanding and interpretation of Islamic law should be overseers of the Islamic state. They are qualified to make sure that all human life comes to agree with God's way for it to be lived. They can also determine where human beings have gone astray from that way.

Leadership, or authority, in the community of Islam is consequently a shared affair. There may be a titular head, a Khalif, or even a king or politician. The important point is that only executive authority is vested in that part of the leadership. He executes the divine pleasure. The ones who determine what the divine pleasure might be are the jurist-theologians, the experts in Islamic law. The ones who evaluate the leader's faithfulness in carrying out the divine pleasure are the judges—further specialists in Islamic law. That is why, during the second half of the twentieth century, specific leaders or regimes have been such pointed targets of Muslim reformist anger. The reformists feel that the political leaders of Muslim states have not been faithful in incorporating Islamic law. Instead they have concentrated on aping the West in consolidating their nation states along secularist, humanist lines. What mockery that the Shah of Iran should go poking around with the constitution of Belgium, when what was needed for a Muslim country was already in Iranians' hands!

The focus of the fundamentalists' dream is the Islamic state. It is in the Islamic state that true 'submission' (*islam*) finds proper expression. Such a state-without-walls comprises the genuine community of believers. God himself is the ultimate sovereign, his law is the basis for how life should be lived and religious scholars are the guardians of the tradition. The health of a Muslim government is measured by its commitment to upholding the Shari'a.

Apart from the Islamic revolution which occurred in Iran in the late 1970s and 1980s, other significant efforts have been made throughout the twentieth century towards the establishing of an Islamic state. They include the strivings of the Muslim Brotherhood (al-Ikhwan al-Muslimun) in various countries of the Middle East, the development of the Islamic Organisation (Jama'at-i Islami) in the Indian subcontinent, the agendas of the National Salvation Party (Milli Selamet Partisi) in Turkey and the Masjumi Party in Indonesia.

Activity 14:2

'The concept of Islamic community is rather like the Christian sense of belonging to the kingdom of God' (p. 271). From your own understanding of the kingdom of God, list ways in which you think it is similar to the Islamic community and ways in which they differ.

3

Onto the streets!

Reformist slogans, paraded in successive decades through the boulevards of Delhi, Islamabad, Tehran, Cairo and Algiers, have all had the same tenor: 'Back to the Qur'an and *Sunna*!' 'Give us the political system (*nizam*) of Mustaga!' Recent elections in Jordan, Egypt and Algeria have seen major gains by 'fundamentalist' groups. Aggressive lobbying in Nigeria and Tanzania has marked the strong politicising of Islamic concerns in the sharing out of power in those African nations at the end of the twentieth century. Pakistani and Sudanese minority religious groups are learning the pain of being irritations in the sides of governments determined to impose a shari'a-informed status on non-Muslims within their nations. In many Muslim countries, in a variety of ways, the 'fundamentalist' agenda is finding an increasingly high profile as part of the current expression of Islamic resurgence:

> During the latter half of the 1970's, Islam dramatically re-emerged in Muslim politics across the Islamic world; in General Zia ul-Haq's coup d'etat in Pakistan in 1977 and his call for establishment of an Islamic system of government (Nizam-i Islam); in the Iranian 'Islamic revolution', in the seizure of the Grand Mosque in Mecca, in the assassination of Anwar Sadat in Egypt, and in the bloody suppression of the Muslim Brotherhood in Hama by the Syrian government. Islam has played a more active and widespread role in Muslim politics from North Africa to Southeast Asia. However, this political phenomenon has been rooted in a deeper, widespread and more profound religious revival which has encompassed both the personal and the political sphere. The personal aspect of the Islamic revival is reflected in increased emphasis upon religious observance (mosque attendance, Ramadan fast, outlawing of alcohol and gambling), religious programming in the media, the proliferation of religious literature, the rebirth of the Muslim Brotherhood, the rise of new Islamic associations, the success of Muslim student associations in university elections, and the vibrant dawah (missionary) movements which seek not simply to convert non-Muslims but to 'Islamize' the Muslim population, ie to deepen their knowledge of and commitment to Islam.
>
> (Esposito, 1983, pp. 10–11)

Behind the widespread acceptance of many of the goals of the Islamists, focused so often in demands for a return to the Qur'an and the authentic traditions of the first Muslims, lie two other concerns.

Unshackling Islam

The first burden is a fight for liberation from Western influence. Earlier in the twentieth century, this meant a battle for real, political independence. The reformist Muslims were strongly involved with many other Muslim groups in those struggles. More recently, this concern has metamorphosed into an attempt to neutralise continuing political, economic and cultural domination of Muslim countries by Western-controlled international bodies (such as the United Nations security council, the International Monetary Fund and the World Bank). Imam Khomeini and his Islamic revolution in Iran may not have been welcomed throughout the Sunni, non-Persian Islamic world, but he was certainly applauded by millions of Muslims for his success at standing up to a Western superpower and coming out on top. Saddam Hussein, despised as he is by most non-Baathist, non-Iraqi Muslims, is nevertheless credited as the one man who has successfully managed to focus world attention on the injustices suffered by Palestinians in the State of Israel. The dominant, secularising culture of the West, with its loose morals, political prejudices and massive influence, is a continuing focus of much Islamist invective.

The second major concern has been the necessity of fighting Muslim rulers who reject reforms designed to reflect a more faithful living under shari'a law. The Shah of Iran was forced from throne and country in January 1979 by a popular revolution predominantly guided and guarded by reformist Muslims. Amongst other issues, the Shah's deliberate emphasis on his inheritance of the mantle of Cyrus the Great, rather than his identity as a Muslim, provoked ordinary Muslims in Iran to a very great degree. Two and a half years after the Shah's demise, President Anwar Sadat was assassinated by members of the Jihad Organisation in Egypt. This was despite Sadat's deliberate cultivation of his image as 'the Believer President'. In the view of the Islamists in Egypt, Sadat was an 'apostate' Muslim rather than a believer. In a desperate act of faith, urged on by a young visionary who would later be executed together with the soldiers who had fired the weapons, Sadat's killers believed that if they did their part, God would do his. If they disposed of the great apostate leader of Egypt's Muslim community in a literal holy war (jihad), God himself would intervene on behalf of the true Muslims and change everything. An Islamic state would come immediately into existence in their beloved country. As demonstrated most graphically in Iran and Egypt, compromised leaders of half-hearted Muslim societies are high on the list of Islamist concerns.

Striving always

Through independence movements, through advisory posts (to the Free Officers after their revolution in Egypt in 1952, or via Mawdudi's influence on General Zia ul-Haq in Pakistan), through education at national and provincial levels, through the ballot box, through popular revolution, armed insurrection and assassination, the reformists have taken their agendas onto the streets of the Islamic world.

It is hard today to gauge the depth of penetration of the Islamists' perspective on life, but it has to be admitted that it constitutes one of the major driving forces for reform at both societal and individual level throughout the Muslim world at the end of the twentieth century.

What is more, the 'fundamentalist' perspective is increasingly being carried onto the streets of Western nations urging room, in democratic societies, for Islamist concerns to be met.

The agendas of reformist Muslims in Western societies cohere around injustices felt by minority faith-holders in a secular world. There are issues of racism and discrimination. There are sensitivities about childrens' education, the provision of ritually slaughtered meat and the conceding of time and space for Friday noon prayers. For the more radical, there is the imperative of monitoring British law-making from a perspective that is informed by shari'a law. The current 'Muslim Parliament' in the United Kingdom is born of this imperative.

4

Friend or foe?

In certain respects, committed Christians have considerable ground in common with Islamic reformists. Is it not significant that some of the earliest, public presentations to the British parliament about the wickedness of British abortion laws came from concerned Muslims? More recently, it appears that British television presenters take stronger note of Muslim objections to misrepresentations of Jesus on *Spitting Images* than of others' problems with the programme.

In terms of its critique of rampant secular humanism, many Western Christians would want to concur in much of the reformists' grief about the paganism, greed, selfishness and family breakdown rife throughout our societies. We might well be challenged by the Islamists' burning zeal for pleasing God, for fulfilling his will, for living as representatives of him in every aspect of life. Not for them the split between the secular and the sacred, nor the hiving off of religious allegiance as some kind of private option for those who choose to be pious.

Identification . . .

In Britain, we accommodate a million and a half Muslims within our shores. Sadly, we have largely failed to fulfil our responsibilities as hosts to them. Instead, lines of hostility have been drawn. Public book-burning has been deemed the only way to make a point about 'blasphemy' by those denied a legal privilege available to others. Surely it is time for Christians to be in the forefront of those seeking to understand the pressures and pains of second- and third-generation immigrants—British Muslims—in their midst? It is not good enough for church schools with a majority of Muslim pupils to refuse to co-opt or encourage Muslim parents to become governors, out of a feeling that such an action would constitute unfaithfulness to Christ. It is time for Christians to be perceived as interpreters of Muslim concerns to structures and bureaucracies that operate in a manner foreign to those from a non-secularist background. Those of us who are Christians need to be seen to understand the anger and revulsion felt by Muslim readers of Rushdie's dream-charade, whether or not we think it good literature.

I am haunted by that incident in Christ's life where he is accused by the Jews of being a Samaritan and demon-possessed (Jn 8: 48). One can well understand that the only explanation in the observers' minds for all the works of power which Jesus performed were either divine or devilish. But what an impact is implied in this Jewish accusation about Jesus' friendship with Samaritans: the leprosy sufferer, the woman at the well, the real 'neighbour'? The Jews felt that Jesus had really let the side down there: 'You are a Samaritan at heart,' they sneer, 'and a demon gives you your power'. Incredibly perhaps, Jesus leaves the accusation half-hanging. He replies: 'I am not possessed by a demon' (v 49). The identification with Samaritans is allowed to stand. Jesus has obviously walked a long extra mile! Is the Lord asking Western Christians to identify a little more closely with Islamic 'fundamentalists' in our midst?

. . . at a cost

At the same time, our witness for Christ must embrace the risk of rejection or alienation by those we seek to serve. At its heart, the reformist perspective derives from a view of God radically different from the glimpses afforded in the Bible. The reformists' world is quite clearly divided between the House of Islam (*dar al-Islam*) and the House of War (*dar al-harb*). Within the rule of Islam, their concern is to make that rulership more faithful to the original revelation in Qur'an and *sunna*. Christian brothers and sisters in Pakistan, Iran, Afghanistan, Egypt, even (outwardly secularised) Turkey and many other countries pay the price for this contemporary programme. They increasingly suffer the insecurity and ignominy of supposed *dhimmi*, or secondary status. In the case of those who, from a Muslim background, have declared their allegiance to Christ, persecution has often been intense, continuous and lifetaking. (This matter is taken up again in Chapter 15, section 2, pp. 294–295) Such intolerance needs to be challenged. Private intercession and public lobbying at international level can each play their part in the process of learning to bear the burdens of those suffering for Jesus' sake in Muslim contexts. Issues of justice and freedom compel us to speak out, even if that is perceived by Muslim authorities as interference or modern-day 'colonialism'.

In the area of struggle, the 'House of War', it is the Islamists' conviction that God has given them economic wealth and political clout on an international scale to influence the world for Islam. Often their attitudes and language bespeak coercion, persuasion, even outright abrogation of individuals' human rights—as in the sentencing of Salman Rushdie. What response is appropriate in those for whom the way of their servant-Master is to be their way also? Instead of our adopting the counter-mentality of warfare, crusade and enmity, maybe the 'slave girl approach' of 2 Kings 5 would be more timely and appropriate. At one stage the great Syrian army commander, Naaman, dared to reveal that he had a life-threatening problem lurking beneath his superior uniform. The slave girl obviously liked the man, her mistress' husband. For years she had served quietly and with integrity in the general's household. Now came the heaven-sent opportunity. She urged her mistress to persuade Naaman to visit prophet Elisha in Samaria. There might he learn that there is no God in all the world except in Israel (v15)!

With those who are so sure of God and themselves, those who seem in so many cases to be in the ascendancy, those who look down on Jews and Christians, those who despise secular humanism, can we become friends, servants, advocates, interpreters, helpers in the tasks of living? When the day comes that our reformist friends dare share with us unanswered prayers, gnawing bitterness, unhealed hurts, let-downs by their sovereign God—perhaps we could then be on hand to introduce them to Jesus Christ, the one who knows best about human suffering?

Notes

How would you have answered the supporters of Salman Rushdie in Activity 14: 1? You might have wanted to say that it is not right to cause offence to any established religious group by publishing material which they would call blasphemous. As Rushdie himself comes from a Muslim background, he must have realised what he was doing. Of course he has a right to his own views, which he is free to pass on to others privately. You might also have wanted to express concern over the *fatwa*, which amounted to a death sentence. One would like to think that Christians have better ways of dealing with those who blaspheme.

From one point of view Islamic Umma and the kingdom of God do have similarities (Activity 14: 2). All the members of each are committed to the community and believe that God is in control and that he rules completely justly, and they are obedient to him. Christians believe that in this life we catch a glimpse of the kingdom of God, but in the life to come it is fully revealed and we can enter into it fully. Muslims have a much more here and now understanding of Umma. How do we become a part of either the Umma or the kingdom of God? Muslims believe that it is through keeping the shari'a Law, following the Traditions and engaging in jihad. Christians come as forgiven sinners, by faith in the Lord Jesus Christ into the kingdom which God by his grace has prepared.

Books referred to in the chapter

Shabbir Akhtar quote in *Be Careful with Muhammad: The Salman Rushdie Affair* (Bellew: London, 1989).

Esposito, John L., 'Islam and Muslim Politics', in *Voices of Resurgent Islam* (Oxford Univ. Press: NY, 1983).

Khomeini, Imam, 'Program for the Establishment of an Islamic Government' from *Islamic Government*, in Imam Khomeini (tr. Hamid Algar), *Islam and Revolution: Writings and Declarations* (KPI: London, 1981).

Maxime Rodinson quote in *Mohammed*, tr. Anne Carter (Penguin: London, 1971). See also W. Montgomery Watt, *Muhammad at Mecca* (Oxford University Press: Karachi, 1953).

Rushdie, Salman, *The Satanic Verses* (Viking: London, 1988).

Rushdie, Salman, 'In Good Faith', an article written in his own defence: *Independent on Sunday*, 4 February 1990.

For further reading

Anderson, Norman, *Islam in the Modern World* (IVP Apollos: Leicester, 1990). Chapter 4 discusses Islamic fundamentalism and its astonishing power in the world today.

Hiro, Dilip, *Islamic Fundamentalism* (Paladin Grafton: London, 1988). A non-partisan view which helps in understanding the political consequences of Islamic fundamentalism.

Musk, Bill, *Passionate Believing* (Monarch: Tunbridge Wells, 1992). Written by the author of this chapter. The book discusses the subject of fundamentalism from a Muslim perspective, then describes how it is functioning politically and finally discusses the subject in both its Islamic and Christian forms.

15

A Call to Prayer and Action

Study guide

As you start reading the final chapter of this book you might like to look back. How have you got on? Some of you may have skipped passages which have not seemed interesting or relevant. As was indicated in the study guide to Chapter 1, distance learning is designed so that you can do this. However, do get an overall view of Islam and be prepared to look back later as you meet Muslims and have discussions with them. Another reaction to this book may well be, 'It's too superficial. I would like to know more about the subjects which interest me.' That is why there are lists of books for further reading at the end of each chapter. However you have reacted so far, we hope you will read this chapter, which deals with the subject of how we can all be involved in making a Christian response to Islam.

When you have completed the chapter we hope you will:

1 Want to be more involved in praying for the Muslim world and for your Muslim friends;

2 Have thought about ways in which you might help your Muslim friends to be less resistant to the good news; and

3 Have resolved to play a part in making a positive Christian response to Islam.

1

Prayer

How should Christians react to Islam and to the actions and ambitions of Muslims throughout the world? It is important not to run away from this issue or behave negatively in a spirit of fear because of the growth and outward successes of Islam. Our response must be founded in faith. We are to believe God's promise that people from every nation, ethnic group, tribe and language will be found among the innumerable company of those redeemed by the blood of Christ. So our outlook must be one of hope, never of despair because the task of reaching the Muslim world with the gospel seems so enormous. And our approach must be in love, with spiritual weapons alone. We can show the compassion of Christ and the nature of his kingdom by healing and teaching ministries, relief work and other sacrificial service combined with the declaration of the Good News.

Only these weapons can cast down strongholds, deal with false teaching and misunderstanding, and bring the thoughts of Muslim people into captivity to obey Christ. While we recognise that there is a spiritual battle involved, we must avoid any attitude of crusading and militancy. This may not be easy when confronted with the aggressive tactics or hardness of some Muslims. The Christian messenger has to present truths to them that their religion denies, prayerfully seeking that light may shine in their darkness and knowledge dispel their ignorance. But the truth must be spoken in love, or it will accomplish nothing.

So 'the prayer of faith' is an urgent priority for all who are concerned for Muslims. The practising Muslim prays five times a day, and we can pray for the progress of the gospel in the Muslim world in five ways:

1. 'Ask the Lord of the harvest . . . to send out workers,' (Mt 9: 38).

Who can fully understand why we are told to ask the

sovereign Lord to act? In his love he gives us the privilege of being involved in the fulfilment of his great purposes, by praying to him about the situation. There is a harvest waiting to be reaped in Muslim lands; and there are fewer labourers than there are opportunities waiting to be taken.

2. 'I urge, then, first of all, that . . . prayers . . . be made for everyone—for kings and all those in authority, that we may lead peaceful and quiet lives in all godliness and holiness,' (1 Tim 2: 1–4).

We should pray for rulers and local authorities in Muslim lands, that churches in the areas they govern may freely worship and witness. This includes freedom from laws they cannot in good conscience respect and obey, and from persecution or subtle pressures. Pray for the day when in every Muslim land it will become a real option for Muslim hearers to respond openly to the gospel and join a Christian community.

3. 'Remember those in prison as if you were their fellow prisoners,' (Heb 13:3).

Pray for all who are suffering any loss of liberty (or work) because of their faith; and for their families who may be left in severe need, in addition to their personal grief and suffering. Pray for their friends and church fellowships, that they may not be intimidated.

4. Matthew 9: 35 'Teaching . . . preaching the good news of the kingdom and healing every kind of disease and sickness,' (Mt 9: 35).

Pray for Christians engaged in any form of ministry to Muslim men, women and children, that they may have continual love, grace, wisdom and spiritual power.

5. 'The thing you have heard me say . . . entrust to reliable men who will also be qualified to teach others,' (2 Tim 2: 2).

Pray that all those who know the Good News will continually pass it on and urge their hearers to do the same.

Several groups now supply regular information about what is happening in the Muslim world, the needs of Christian churches, and how the gospel witness is progressing or being held up. Without giving details that might endanger workers or local Christians, they can often also report examples of what has happened in answer to prayer. It is still true that prayer changes things, or rather that God changes things when his people pray.

Consider for example what has happened in Albania. The 1986 edition of *Operation World* (published by OM Publishing) introduces it as 'Europe's most closed and least evangelised land'. Operation Mobilisation included it among the 'most needy countries' when printing a set of special pocket prayer cards. While there are still many problems and needs, the land is now open and the whole situation is very different. Christians can be sure that this is the result of prayer focused on this land during the past few years.

One well-established source of prayer information is the Fellowship of Faith for the Muslims. This was founded at the Keswick Convention in 1915 after a stirring message from Dr Samuel Zwemer (see Chapter 12, section 5, p 223). He challenged the Christians of Britain to give themselves to a more definite ministry of intercession for the Muslims. Representatives of many missionary societies were present and have continued their relationship with FFM through the years. The Fellowship is international and inter-denominational. Membership is open to any Christian who is willing to pray regularly for Muslims and for those who are seeking to win them.

With the primary aim of stimulating informed prayer, a regular confidential prayer bulletin is sent to members. This contains news from all over the world. Members also organise prayer days and an annual prayer conference. The FFM publications department produces booklets on Muslim belief and practice, and issues a book list to guide those interested in knowing more about Islam and how to reach Muslims with the gospel. There is also a reference library of classics on Islam and some newer books.

Independent FFM groups have been formed in Scotland, Northern Ireland, some European countries, Canada and USA, Australia and New Zealand. Some of these have their own publications.

FFM is a 'fellowship', not a missionary society. It does not appeal for workers, or funds to support them, though it continually urges prayer that more Christians will be sent to Muslim areas, in their own countries and overseas.

God has called us to believe, to pray and to work that Muslims may become followers of the Lord Jesus Christ. Dr Lionel Gurney, founder of the Red Sea Team International, spoke at Keswick on the seventieth anniversary of FFM. He challenged those present not to pray for 'cracks in the walls of Islam', but to look for its walls to fall down flat, like those of Jericho after they had been marched around for seven days.

> O God, to whom the Muslim world bows in homage five times daily, look in mercy upon its people and reveal to them thy Christ.
>
> (Zwemer, 'Call to Prayer')

2

Action

A group of students was studying the six main world religions. In the last tutorial before the exam, their tutor was going over likely exam questions. 'What about Christianity?' he was asked. 'Revise the Reformation', the tutor replied. When someone expressed surprise he added, 'Well, there isn't really anything else they can ask you!'

Nothing else? How sad! How sad that all the riches that we have in Christ Jesus seemed to have passed him by. And he was a specialist in religions. No wonder our Muslim friends have difficulty in understanding what our Christian faith is all about. What a challenge to us to present the gospel in a way which can be understood!

Pat Cate writes in an article in the *Evangelical Missions Quarterly*,

One of the keys to reaching Muslims is relationships. It takes time for relationships to develop, and repeated visits. On the other hand, we need to be careful of only developing friendships but never sharing Christ.

(Cate, 1992, p 231)

In Chapter 2 we looked particularly at forming relationships and also at how we may begin to share Christ. The importance of relationships cannot be over-emphasised. They go hand in hand with a second key, that of appreciating cultural differences. John Stott writes,

We have to divest our gospel of the cultural clothing in which we have received it and sometimes even of the precise cultural garb in which Scripture presents it. We also have to reclothe it in cultural terms appropriate to the people to whom we proclaim it.

(Stott, 1991, p 187)

The subject of Islamic culture runs throughout the present book, but it is described in detail in Chapter 8.

Colin Chapman, speaking at a conference recorded in the book *Muslims and Christians on the Emmaus Road* says, 'Wherever there is resistance to the gospel, it is easy to find reasons *on their side* for such rejection. But what if some of the responsibility *is on our side*?' (Chapman, 1989, p 105). He goes on to quote from the 1981 Pattaya Consultation:

As soon as we begin to listen to Muslims and try to share the gospel, we begin to realize how difficult it is to express ourselves in a way that Muslims understand. The painfulness of this experience ought to drive us back to the Bible, in order to learn new ways of understanding our faith and relating it to the Muslim mind.

(Lausanne, 1981, p 13)

In Chapter 1 section 4 (p 33), four principles for the study of other faiths were defined. The second of these was, 'Any activity of reaching out to others should be expected to deepen our own spiritual understanding.' As you have studied Islam and have met and related to Muslims, we hope that you have found this to be true. Bishop Kenneth Cragg has put it this way, 'Trying to relate, to rethink, or simply to understand our own gospel is immensely facilitated and sobered by a real desire to encounter the alternative patterns of another religion' (Cragg, J11/5). This chapter tries to show how these various concepts can be worked out in action both personally and collectively. It encourages us to move on from a study of Islam and of Muslims to a lifetime of meeting Muslim friends and sharing with them what following Jesus means to us.

As God's fellow-workers (2 Corinthians 6: 1)

We have seen what a powerful concept community (Umma) is in Islam. Perhaps we need to strengthen the Christian concept of community. We have seen how believers in Islam are Muslims first and foremost, to the point that they may refuse to identify their other loyalties (Chapter 10, section 1, 175–176). We need to recapture a sense of Christian togetherness, not ignoring our doctrinal differences, nor trying to build unifying structures, but establishing the Christian community in our hearts and lives.

John Stott comments on 2 Thessalonians 2: 15 ('So then, brothers, stand firm and hold to the teachings we passed on to you, whether by word of mouth or by letter') as follows:

> The context in which they were to 'stand firm and hold to the teachings' was the Christian fellowship, the family of God. In other words, we need each other. The church is the fellowship of faith, the society for sacred study, the hermeneutical community. In it we receive teaching from pastors who are duly authorized to expound the tradition of the apostles. We wrestle together with its contemporary application, and we teach and admonish each other out of the same Scriptures. (pp 178–179: hermeneutical = 'concerned with interpretation')

'We need each other' if we are to reach out to Muslims. This means that wherever possible our work will be church-based. Where this is not possible, Christians will normally work in groups or teams linked together in fellowship. As we have seen from the case study in Chapter 13, section 1, 238–241 in many Islamic countries Christians will usually be witnessing through their lives and their work rather than through public proclamation and debate.

Phyllis Tring shares her experiences of this kind of ministry. She recognises that there are two main problems in forming teams. Christians who hope to live and work in Muslim countries need visas and work permits. They also need to have suitable jobs. Jobs are dependent on the job market and cannot necessarily be obtained in places where there are other Christians with whom to have fellowship. Even if a job is found where there is a Christian fellowship, it is not easy for secular Christians to join the group. In fact their presence may endanger the other worshippers. It seems that God calls some to be involved in Christian groups and others to be on their own, with only loose links with other Christians, perhaps through their home churches. This needs initiative and flexibility. The following is an extract from a prayer letter written by a Christian working in an Islamic country, to his supporters:

> The key to effectiveness . . . is to be flexible: to have aims and goals but to have no plan (slightly scary for me) or to have at least two plans in mind as to how to achieve.
>
> The second key is to go slowly—giving time always to people rather than plans, however good they seemed during the morning quiet time!

It may not always be possible to give 'time to people rather than plans'. It depends on circumstances. Most Christians have their own life-pattern. They have responsibilities, they are answerable to or for other people. We can safely say, however, that in Western cultures we tend to give far too much weight to plans and far too little to people. As Christians, we may face dilemmas and need to ask God to guide us. Here is an example:

> Travelling to speak at a Christian meeting in a Government hospital, I was with a group of Muslim village women. We got talking about our beliefs and I was able to share something of what it meant to me to be a follower of Jesus. One woman, who had shown considerable interest, asked me to go back with her to her village and meet the rest of her family. Another older woman

announced, 'Yes, you should go!' Others joined in pressing me to do so. I remembered my friends waiting at the station. I imagined the disappointment and frustration when the meeting had to be cancelled and I thought that if my culture had anything to offer in this country it would be to do with reliability and keeping one's promises. I explained to my fellow travellers as carefully as I could and went on to the meeting. I often wonder what would have happened if I had gone to the village instead!

We need to remember that there will always be two sides to our life and work; and we need to ask God to help us keep a right balance between them. We can call them the 'care' side and the 'flair' side. We must be wholeheartedly committed to doing our best, even if it feels like a boring routine at times. It is important to be accurate and painstaking and this will involve extra effort and extra care. At the same time, if we want to avoid getting stuck in a rut, when any change is threatening because we 'have always done it this way', we shall need new ideas. We must ask God to give us initiative and flair; to be prepared to take risks, to have fresh vision. Again, balance is necessary. We have all suffered from those with too many bright ideas and not enough practical wisdom! We need each other. We need to be able to work together. We need to remember,

> Whatever you do, whether in word or deed, do it all in the name of the Lord Jesus, giving thanks to God the Father through him.
>
> (Col 3: 17)

For we are God's workmanship (Ephesians 2: 10)

Sometimes the 'team' which is used to show someone the Way is not one organised by a church or Christian organisation. Phyllis Tring gives an example from her own experience. It is about a young woman F in a Muslim country in the Middle East. These are the steps which led to her becoming a follower of Jesus.

1 A tract was put into her school books while she was studying in a government school. This was probably done by a Christian schoolfriend, who was too frightened to speak about her faith.

2 She read the tract and then she had a dream about Jesus Christ. No other human agency was involved here. She read—God showed.

3 Later she became a student at a women's college. This college had been started by a foreign church, but, in order to give degrees, had become secular. When she went to the college she met Christians and talked with them.

4 She went with them to a Bible study group which was held in the college, with one of the Christian teachers as leader.

5 This led to her accepting the Lord Jesus Christ as her Saviour.

6 She bought a New Testament to study for herself.

7 She started going regularly to a weekly meeting which was run by a Christian students' organisation, outside the college.

8 She told her fiancé about her new faith and he agreed that he would not object.

9 During the vacation she kept contact and also learnt about the churches in the city.

10 At this point there was a political upheaval in the country. All foreign workers had to leave. F's family and her fiancé were on different sides politically.

A year later it was known that she had remained faithful. There has been no news since then.

There were many people involved in her conversion and they would not have thought of themselves as a team; they did not even know each other. Yet each one was important in the life of that woman. Phyllis Tring herself was important, although the conversion would never have reached the reports of the Christian organisation to which she belonged. She was a teacher in the college where F was a student. She arranged the first of the Bible study groups for Christians to which F came; sometimes Muslims were brought along. She also arranged a prayer meeting every day before work. At first there were often only two praying and for several years it lapsed. As the numbers at the Bible studies grew, so did the prayer meeting; and there was also a desire for more active outreach. In her free time, one of the Christian students used to take her guitar and sit outside, playing Christian songs—the only songs she knew. She, too, was a young convert from a nominal Muslim home and was full of love, joy and enthusiasm, filled with the Spirit. It was through her that F was reminded of her dream and started going to the Bible study. The New Testament F bought was one Phyllis kept in her office for just such a purpose. It had recently been translated, so the translators and the Bible Society were also part of the 'team'. So was the Pakistani who led, and the Americans who helped in the meetings F went to outside the college.

And what of the dream? God often uses dreams and visions in the conversion of Muslims, something that Westerners do not expect, but Easterners find quite natural. We believe too, that God was working through other members of the team and that the Holy Spirit was speaking to F as she read the Bible. God drew together all the various elements that he not only set up, but also led.

Activity 15: 1

There are three basic factors that are almost always present when a Muslim becomes a follower of Jesus. From the story of F, can you suggest what they might be?

Do not worry about what to say or how to say it (Matthew 10: 19)

A Muslim man had been talking to the nurse working in the doctor's surgery. Suddenly he said, 'You know our language. You have worked in our country. You are a religious person [she is the vicar's wife!]. Why don't you become a Muslim?' Quickly an answer came to her mind, 'Because there is no salvation in Islam'. The man thought for a minute, then he said, 'No, we cannot know about salvation.'

The nurse was able to answer in this way because she remembered N, a young Muslim girl who had become a disciple of Jesus. On one occasion N stood in front of a Muslim judge in a Muslim court. The judge asked her, 'Why did you leave Islam?' She answered, 'Because there is no salvation in Islam.' The judge turned to his advisors, experts in Islamic law, and asked them, 'Is this true?' After consulting together they answered, 'It is true.' The judge turned to N and said, 'There is no case. You are free to go.'

What an illustration of how we can learn from one another! What an illustration of the truth of the promise of Jesus, 'But when they arrest you, do not worry about what to say or how to say it. At that time you will be given what to say, for it will not be you speaking, but the Spirit of your Father speaking through you' (Mt 10: 19–20).

We read in Chapter 14, section 4, 279 'In the case of those who, from a Muslim background, have declared their allegiance to Christ, persecution has often been intense, continuous and lifetaking.' As Islamic countries adopt the shari'a law and implement the death penalty for apostacy, those who have left Islam are accused of dishonouring their prophet. The word of a Muslim will always be accepted before that of a Christian, so a fair trial is almost impossible. There are many modern martyrs.

An Asian friend from an Ahmadiyya background (see Chapter 10, section 7, pp 188–189) is now a Christian leader and teacher. Although not living in an Islamic country, he realises that he is in a dangerous position. He says, 'I could cut myself off, living alone with my family, never speaking about my faith, but I don't think God wants me to do that. I don't take foolish or unnecessary risks, but I look for opportunities to declare my faith and to talk with Muslims about it. I try to lead my life under God's guidance and protection.'

He also said, 'When Muslims say to me, "What is wrong with Islam that has made you leave your religion?" I say, "I could discuss that, but I would much rather tell you why I have become a follower of Jesus."'

We can learn much about evangelism from this positive approach. Our aim should be not to engage in sterile argument, but to show how much following Jesus means to us. Many of us do not have personal experience of being Muslims, but we can all know what it means to follow Jesus and can talk about him. The apostle Peter gives us such good advice:

> But in your hearts set apart Christ as Lord. Always be prepared to give an answer to everyone who asks you to give the reason for the hope that you have. But do this with gentleness and respect . . .'
>
> (1 Pet 3: 15–16)

Against this background of persecution, the support and discipline of those coming to Christ from a Muslim background becomes extremely important.

In the Lausanne Occasional Paper No 13, *Christian Witness to Muslims* (p 18) we read:

> Many Muslim converts experience the same difficulties which Saul experienced as a new convert among Christians in Damascus and Jerusalem . . .
>
> We therefore need to give special care and attention to discipleship training for new believers, since this can sometimes be more difficult than the initial teaching of the gospel which brought them to faith. As far as possible, this teaching should be done in the context of the family.

Gwendy Anderson writes that costly practical implications surround the matter of receiving converts into the church. Whether we are in the West or in an Islamic land, we face searching questions.

Firstly, what is our attitude to Islam as a religion? If we believe that Islam is totally demonic, and Allah an idol, we will not receive a convert's background, but try to remove him totally from it. If we believe Islam contains elements of truth and beauty, we will encourage him to retain the good elements from his religious and cultural background. We should note (in context) the comment by a Pakistani that 'Protestants seem to come here because they hate Islam and Catholics because they love God' (Murphy, 1965, p 167).

Secondly, what is the convert's background? Is he an illiterate farmer? Is he or she from a less educated urban society? Is he or she a highly intellectual man or woman? Our gifts and calling need to be matched, to be more appropriate. Dialogue is important, and awareness of each person's background. 'Sitting where they sit' means orientation to the way a Muslim thinks, and where possible to his poetry, his proverbs and his sense of humour.

Thirdly, can we avoid polarisation regarding the form of church gathering into which a convert is to be welcomed? Missiologists have two different emphases—two scripturally-based approaches—which will go on being debated.

1. ***Converts are brought into the fellowship of the local church.*** Are we praying that the ancient Christian churches still found in Muslim lands may yet become the receivers of Muslim converts? Are we seeing the welcome of the local church less as the endeavour of one teacher with one seeker/convert, and more as the house group/open family/team relationship? Is not 'you' in the New Testament predominantly plural, not singular? Wherever possible in a local church, are we encouraging a long period of education towards becoming sensitive to Islamic culture and being positive about some of the ways in which Muslims live and worship? Are we aware of the convert's difficulty with non-Muslim elements? Why should a Bengali convert have to use the name Ishwar (the Hindi word for God) instead of Allah? (Or *khuda*, the Urdu word for God, for that matter.) We must listen to the testimony of converted peoples and individuals, so that there is continuity between faith in Allah and faith in the God and Father of Jesus Christ.

2. ***Converts are organised separately into a 'Muslim church'***, defined as a company of people committed to Jesus Christ and the teaching of Scripture, yet remaining within the community of Islam and retaining many of the cultural forms of Muslim society. Can we identify with a 'Muslim church' in areas where there is no local church, or where temporarily at least the local church still shows too much resistance to positive involvement?

Activity 15: 2

It may be helpful to look back to the case studies in Chapter 13. Can you identify these two types of church growth in any of them? List what you consider to be the pros and cons of each type.

There are different kinds of gifts (1 Corinthians 12: 4)

And How does this passage go on?

> . . . but the same Spirit. There are different kinds of service, but the same Lord. There are different kinds of working, but the same God works all of them in all men. (1 Cor 12: 4–6)

God unites us by his Spirit for service and for work. As we have seen, God may use many Christians in bringing just one Muslim to know the Lord Jesus. God calls many people with many different gifts to serve him and do his work. When we say that a person is 'gifted' we usually mean intellectually or artistically gifted, and these are wonderful gifts to have. It is important to remember, however, that those whom we might describe as 'less gifted' also have an important contribution to make. We may relate to Muslims in the unemployment queue and at the baby clinic as well as, perhaps better than, in the university or the solicitor's office. Perhaps the 'gifts' which will be used most in relating to Muslims are two which we might not call gifts at all: gender and ethnicity. It is important, however, that we accept these as gifts from God and use them in our service for him.

Because of the differing roles and status of men and women in Islam, relationships will be formed in single-sex gatherings. This may seem strange to Westerners, but it does mean that as men meet in coffee shops, clubs and professional groups and women in homes, schools and clinics, there will be opportunities not only for friendship but also for finding out the things

Muslims talk about, the things they think are important and what their worldview is.

Ethnicity is another gift which can be used in God's service. Christians who belong to the same ethnic group as Muslims may feel themselves at a disadvantage, a minority within a minority. But having the same culture and heritage as Muslims brings advantages as well. An Asian Christian friend pointed out the advantages not only of a common language, but also of common experiences. He gave as his illustration of this, being able to say when speaking to a fellow Punjabi, 'You're sitting on the number four bus!' The number four bus terminates at Lahore Mental Hospital, so this is a nicer and more familiar way of saying, 'You're not thinking straight'!

In a conversation with another Asian Christian friend, she agreed that there are mixed loyalties and a lack of a sense of belonging and identifying with any one group. This does not encourage outreach to Muslims. There is, however, tremendous potential for well-informed Christians to get to know their Muslim neighbours. My friend herself visits in the neighbourhood. Some of the families live in the same road as she does. She believes that Christians should learn to pray for their neighbours, perhaps two or three praying together regularly, for their own and each others' contacts. Christians should be known as good neighbours, giving hospitality, being there to help in times of need and being generous with little gifts, especially at Christmas. They should also be prepared to join Asian clubs, not confining their activities to the Asian Christian Fellowships.

Generations of Asian Christian children are now growing up in Western societies. They have their own special problems of adjustment, but they also have great potential which must be realised. They need to have easy access to Christian organisations which work among young people and be encouraged to play their full part in them.

It is not only Asians, Africans and people from the Middle East whose gift of ethnicity can be utilised. As we saw in Chapter 8, we can gain much through finding out some of the riches found in cultures other than our own. In cases where

Muslims are an ethnic minority group we can all learn from one another and the indigenous majority should not feel that they have no part to play, especially if they are Christians.

So, to summarise, skills, status, gender and ethnicity are precious gifts from God and should unite rather than divide those who are in Christ. As the apostle Paul wrote to the Galatian Church,

> There is neither Jew nor Greek, slave nor free, male nor female, for you are all one in Christ Jesus
>
> (Gal 3: 28)

A concluding thought, taken from the conclusion of William Miller's book, *A Christian's Response to Islam*:

> What then should be the attitude of us Christians toward the task of making Christ known to the [millions] of Muslims of the world? It should be one of faith and hope and love: faith in Almighty God, the 'God of the Impossible', who moves mountains and is today working out his eternal purpose in the Muslim world; hope in the promises of God, the 'God of Hope', that the day will come when every knee will bow to Christ, and every tongue confess that he is Lord: and love that never fails toward the people of Islam who have not known the love of Christ, a love that is Christlike and is poured into our hearts by the Holy Spirit, a love that will create in us a passionate longing for Muslims to know and love Christ crucified and risen from the dead, a love that will constrain us to labor for their conversion, and to say with all sincerity, 'Our hearts' desire and prayer to God for them is that they be saved!'
>
> (Miller, 1986, pp 174–175)

Notes

Those interested in joining FFM or learning more about the Fellowship are invited to write to the General Secretary, PO Box 58, Wakefield, West Yorkshire WF2 9YD.

The three basic factors usually present when a Muslim becomes a follower of Jesus (Activity 15: 1) are: friendship with Christians; reading Scripture; and having some manifestation of

God's power, such as dreams, visions, or healing. Sometimes one, sometimes another seems to be the key factor.

In Chapter 13 (Activity 15:2), you probably found that the case studies on Indonesia and North Africa show the first type of church growth and those on Islam and other faiths and Central Asia the second type.

Books referred to in the chapter

Cate, Pat, *Evangelical Mission Quarterly*, July 1992.

Chapman, Colin, *Rethinking the Gospel for Muslims* (MARC: Monrovia, California, 1989), ch. 6.

Cragg, Kenneth, from an address obtainable from the Tape Library, All Souls Church: London (tape ref. J11/5, see Educational Materials, 309).

Lausanne Committee for World Evangelization, *Christian Witness to Muslims* (Lausanne Occasional Paper No 13, LCWE: Wheaton, Illinois, 1980).

Miller, William, *A Christian Response to Islam* (1976: UK edn, STL/ Kingsway: Bromley/Eastbourne, 1986).

Murphy, Dervla, *Full Tilt: From Ireland to India With a Bicycle* (Pan: London, 1965).

Stott, John R.W., *The Message of Thessalonians* (IVP: Leicester, 1991).

Woodberry, J. Dudley (ed.), *Muslims and Christians on the Emmaus Road* (MARC: Monrovia, California, 1989).

For further reading

Reading one or two books by those from a Muslim background who follow Jesus will be very useful. Here are some suggestions:

Esther, Gulshan and Thelma Sangster, *The Torn Veil* (Marshall, Morgan & Scott: Basingstoke, 1984) [new edn Marshall Pickering: London, 1992]. Imprisoned in an orthodox Muslim family and suffering from a severe physical disability, she found healing and freedom through faith in Jesus Christ.

Esther, Gulshan and Vita Toon, *Beyond the Veil* (Marshall Pickering: London, 1992). Continuing the story, this book describes Gulshan's visiting and speaking ministry in England and other countries, sharing her experiences of healing and faith in Christ.

Masood, Steven. *Into the Light* (Kingsway: Eastbourne, 1986) [2nd rev. edn, OM Publishing: Carlisle, 1992]. The journey of a young Muslim who wanted to be a faithful Muslim, but found what he was looking for in Jesus Christ.

Naaman, Ghulam Masih, with Vita Toon, *The Unexpected Enemy* (Marshall Pickering: Basingstoke, 1985). How a zealous Muslim freedom-fighter found Christ and has himself suffered persecution as an ordained Episcopalian minister.

Sheikh, Bilquis, *I Dared to Call him Father* (Kingsway/STL: Eastbourne/ Bromley, 1978). A Pakistani woman of noble birth, looking for peace in her own faith, found Jesus through a series of dreams and through studying the Bible.

Tafti, H. Dehqani-, *Design of my World* (United Society for Christian Literature [Lutterworth Press]: Guildford and London, 1959) [2nd rev. edn, Lutterworth 1982]. The story of a young Iranian schoolboy who becomes a Christian, and eventually the first Iranian bishop in modern Iran.

Tafti, H. Dehqani-, *The Hard Awakening* (SPCK Triangle: London, 1981). Describes the persecution of the church in Iran, the murder of his son and the imprisoning or killing of some of his fellow clergy.

Bibliography

The bibliographical details provided are those of the editions referred to in the text. Where a later edition has been published, details are added in square brackets. New editions are by the same publisher unless otherwise stated. In order to provide the best help possible in finding books, alphabetisation and spelling of names follow the forms in British and American national bibliographies. This may differ sometimes from the forms used in the main text.

Ahmed, Akbar S., *Living Islam: From Samarkand to Stornoway* (BBC Books, 1993).

Ahmed, Akbar S., *Postmodernism and Islam: Predicament and Promise* (Routledge: London, 1992).

Abdul-Haqq Abdiyah, Akbar, *Sharing Your Faith with a Muslim* (Bethany Fellowship: Minneapolis, 1980).

Al-Ahsan, Abdullah, *Ummah or Nation? Identity Crisis in Contemporary Muslim Society* (Islamic Foundation: Leicester, 1992).

Ali, Abdullah Yusuf, *The Holy Qur'an: Text, Translation and Commentary* (Islamic Foundation: Leicester, 1975).

Ali, Abdullah Yusuf, *The Meaning of the Glorious Qur'an: Text Translation* (Nadim and Co, London, 1975).

Ali, Muhammad Maulana, *A Manual of Hadith* (Curzon Press: London, 3rd edn 1978).

Anderson, Norman, *Islam in the Modern World* (IVP Apollos: Leicester, 1990).

Anglican Inter-Faith Consultative Group of the Board of Mission and Unity, *Towards a Theology for Inter-Faith Dialogue* (Church Information Office: London, 1984).

Arberry, Arthur J. (trs), *The Koran Interpreted* (Oxford University Press: Oxford, 1983).

Bowker, John, *Worlds of Faith* (BBC Ariel: London, 1983).

Brewster, E. Thomas and Elizabeth S., *Language Acquisition Made Practical* (Lingua House: Toronto, 1976).

Burness, Margaret, *What Do I Say to my Muslim Friends?* (Church Missionary Society: London, 1989).

Burnett, David, *Clash of Worlds* (Monarch: Eastbourne, 1990).

Butt, Gerald, *The Arab World* (BBC: London, 1987).

Carey College, three series of booklets: *A General Introduction to Islam; Comparing the Doctrines of Islam with Christianity; Islam in the Modern World* (1987, Carey College Publications: PO Box 109, Doncaster DN4 6UL).

Chambesy Dialogue Consultation Report (Islamic Foundation: Leicester, 1982).

Chapman, Colin, *Cross and Crescent: Responding to the Challenge of Islam* (IVP: Leicester, 1993).

Chapman, Colin, *You Go and Do the Same* (CMS/BMMF/IFES: London, 1983).

Committee for Relations with People of Other Faiths, *In Good Faith: the Four Principles of Inter-Faith Dialogue* (CCBI: London, 1992).

Cooper, Anne (comp), *In the Family of Abraham* (People International: Tunbridge Wells, 1989).

Cooper, Anne, Chapter 14 in: Keay, Kathy (ed.), *Women to Women* (MARC: Eastbourne, 1988).

Coulson, N. J., *A History of Islamic Law* (Edinburgh University Press: Edinburgh, 1964) [new edn 1979].

Cragg, Kenneth, *The Arab Christian in the Middle East* (1991: 1st UK edn, Mowbray: London, 1991).

Cragg, Kenneth, *The Call of the Minaret* (1956: 2nd rev. edn, Collins: London, 1986).

Cragg, Kenneth, *Muhammad and the Christian* (Darton, Longman & Todd: London, 1984).

Dawood, N. J., *The Koran Translated from Arabic with Notes* (Penguin: Harmondsworth, 4th edn 1974) [rev. edn 1990].

Douglas, J. D. (ed.), *Let the Earth Hear His Voice* (World-Wide Publications: Minneapolis, 1975).

Esposito, John L., *Islam the Straight Path* (Oxford University Press: Oxford, 1988) [rev. edn 1991].

Esther, Gulshan and Vita Toon, *Beyond the Veil* (Marshall Pickering: London, 1992).

Esther, Gulshan and Thelma Sangster, *The Torn Veil* (Marshall, Morgan & Scott: Basingstoke, 1984) [new edn Marshall Pickering: London, 1992].

Evangelical Alliance, *Christianity and Other Faiths* (Paternoster Press: Exeter, 1983).

Fitzsimons, Lionel, *Not at Home: British Muslims and the Gospel* (Private publication).

Gilchrist, John, *The Christian Witness to the Muslim: Vol. 2* (Jesus to the Muslims: Benoni, S. Africa, 1988).

Gilchrist, John, *Jam'al-Qur'an: the Codification of the Qur'an Text* (Jesus to the Muslims: Benoni, S. Africa, 1989).

Goldsmith, Martin, *Islam and Christian Witness* (Hodder & Stoughton/ STL: London/Bromley, 1982) [3rd rev. edn, STL: Bromley, 1991].

Goldsmith, Martin, *What About Other Faiths?* Hodder & Stoughton: London, 1989).

Haneef, Suzanne, *What Everybody Should Know About Islam and Muslims* (Kazi Publications: Lahore, 1979).

Hiro, Dilip, *Islamic Fundamentalism* (Paladin Grafton: London, 1988).

Horner, Norman A., *A Guide to Christian Churches in the Middle East* (Mennonite Board of Missions: Elkhart, Indiana, 1989).

Hughes, T.P., *The Dictionary of Islam* (Asia Publishing House: London, 1988).

International Institute for the Study of Islam and Christianity, *The Status of the Church in the Muslim World* (IISIC, 1992).

Kateregga, Badru D., and David W. Shenk, *Islam and Christianity* (Uzima Press/Eerdmans: Kenya/Grand Rapids, Michigan, rev. edn 1981).

Keay, Kathy (ed.), *Women to Women* MARC: Eastbourne, 1988). Anne Cooper contributes Chapter 14.

Koran: *see* Qur'an

Lausanne Committee for World Evangelization, *Christian Witness to Muslims* (Lausanne Occasional Paper No 13, LCWE: Wheaton, Illinois, 1980).

Lings, Martin, *Muhammad* (Islamic Texts Society/Allen & Unwin: London, 1983) [2nd rev. edn ITS: Cambridge, 1992].

Lings, Martin, *What is Sufism?* (Islamic Texts Society/Allen & Unwin: London, 2nd edn 1981) [new edn ITS: Cambridge, 1993].

Masood, Steven, *East to West* (Interserve: London, 1992).

Masood, Steven. *Into the Light* (Kingsway: Eastbourne, 1986) [2nd rev. edn, OM Publishing: Carlisle, 1992].

McCurry, Don M. (ed.), *The Gospel and Islam: A Compendium* (MARC: Monrovia, California, 1979).

McDowell, Josh, *Evidence That Demands a Verdict (2 vols)* (Here's Life: San Bernadino, California, 1979) [UK edn, Scripture Press: Amersham, 1990].

McDowell, Josh, and John Gilchrist, *The Islam Debate* (Here's Life: San Bernadino, California, 1983).

Maududi, Sayyid Abul A'la, *Towards Understanding Islam* (Islamic Foundation: Leicester, 1980).

Miller, William, *A Christian's Response to Islam* (1976: UK edn, STL/Kingsway: Bromley/Eastbourne, 1986).

Molteno, Marion, *A Language in Common* (The Women's Press: London, 1987).

Mottahedeh, Ron, *The Mantle of the Prophet* (Penguin: Harmondsworth, 1985) [new edn 1987].

Moucarry, Chawkat Georges, *Islam and Christianity at the Crossroads* (Lion: Tring, 1988).

Musk, Bill, *Passionate Believing* (Monarch: Tunbridge Wells, 1992).

Musk, Bill, *The Unseen Face of Islam* (MARC Monarch: Eastbourne, 1989).

Naaman, Ghulam Masih, with Vita Toon, *The Unexpected Enemy* (Marshall Pickering: Basingstoke, 1985).

Nasr, Seyyed Hossein, *Ideals and Realities of Islam* (Allen & Unwin: London, 2nd edn 1975) [3rd rev. edn 1985].

Nazir-Ali, Michael, *Frontiers in Muslim-Christian Encounter* (Regnum Books: Oxford, 1987).

Nazir-Ali, Michael, *Islam: A Christian Perspective* (Paternoster: Exeter, 1983).

Nehls, Gerhard, *Christians Answer Muslims* (Life Challenge: Capetown, South Africa, 1980).

Nehls, Gerhard, *Christians Ask Muslims* (Life Challenge: Capetown, South Africa).

Neill, Stephen, *Crises of Belief* (Hodder & Stoughton: London, 1984).

Neill, Stephen, *A History of Christian Missions* (Pelican: Harmondsworth, 1964).

Newbigin, Lesslie, *The Gospel in a Pluralist Society* (SPCK: London, 1989).

Parrinder, Geoffrey, *Jesus in the Qur'an* (Sheldon Press: London, 1965).

Parshall, Phil, *Beyond the Mosque* (Baker: Grand Rapids, Michigan, 1985) [reissued 1991].

Parshall, Phil, *Bridges to Islam* (Baker: Grand Rapids, Michigan, 1983) [reissued 1991].

Parshall, Phil, *The Cross and the Crescent* (1989: 1st British edn, Scripture Press: Amersham, 1990).

Parshall, Phil, *New Paths in Muslim Evangelism* (Baker: Grand Rapids, Michigan, 1980).

Pfander, C.G., rev. and enlarged W. St Clair Tisdall, *The Mizanu'l*

Haqq (Balance of Truth) (Persia 1835; rev. and enlarged 1910; rev. and enlarged edn, Light of Life: Villach, Austria, 1986).

The Qur'an: Ali, Abdullah Yusuf, *The Holy Qur'an: Text, Translation and Commentary* (Islamic Foundation: Leicester, 1975).

The Qur'an: Arberry, Arthur J. (trs), *The Koran Interpreted* (Oxford University Press: Oxford, 1983).

The Qur'an: Dawood, N.J., *The Koran Translated from Arabic with Notes* (Penguin: Harmondsworth, 4th edn 1974) [rev. edn 1990].

Raza, Mohammad S., *Islam in Britain* (Volcano Press: Leicester, 1991).

Ruthven, Malise, *Islam in the World* (Pelican: Harmondsworth, rev. edn 1991).

Saal, William J., *Reaching Muslims for Christ* (1991: US edn, Moody Press: Chicago, 1992).

Schlossberg, Herbert, *A Fragrance of Oppression: the Church and its Persecutors* (Crossway: Wheaton, Illinois, 1991).

Sell, Edward, *The Historical Development of the Qur'an* (1st pub. 1893) (People International: Tunbridge Wells, 1990).

Sheikh, Bilquis, *I Dared to Call him Father* (Kingsway/STL: Eastbourne/ Bromley, 1978).

Shorrosh, Anis A., *Islam Revealed: A Christian Arab's View of Islam* (Nelson: Nashville, Tennessee, 1988).

Stacey, Vivienne, *Henry Martyn* (Henry Martyn Inst. of Islamic Studies: Hyderabad, India, 1980).

Stacey, Vivienne, *Practical Lessons for Evangelism Among Muslims* (Interserve: London, 1988).

Stacey, Vivienne, *Thomas Valpy French, First Bishop of Lahore* (Christian Study Centre: Rawalpindi, Pakistan, 1982).

Stott, John R.W., *Understanding the Bible* (Scripture Union: London, 1972) [2nd rev. edn 1984].

Tafti, H. Dehqani-, *Design of my World* (United Society for Christian Literature [Lutterworth Press]: Guildford and London, 1959) [2nd rev. edn, Lutterworth 1982].

Tafti, H. Dehqani-, *The Hard Awakening* (SPCK Triangle: London, 1981).

Taheri, Amir, *The Cauldron: The Middle East Behind the Headlines* (Century Hutchinson: London, 1988).

Taheris, Amir, *Crescent in the Red Sky: The Future of Islam in the Soviet Union* (Century Hutchinson: London, 1989).

Tisdall, W. St Clair, *The Sources of Islam* (rev. edn, T & T Clark: Edinburgh).

Trimingham, J. Spencer, *Christianity Among the Arabs in Pre-Islamic Times* (1979: 2nd edn, Librairie du Liban, 1990).

Turning Over a New Leaf: Protestant Missions and the Orthodox Churches of the Middle East. Final Report of a multi-mission study group on orthodoxy (Interserve/MEM: London/Lynwood USA, 2nd edn 1992).

Van der Werff, Lyle L., *Christian Mission to Muslims: The Record* (William Carey Library: S. Pasadena, California, 1977).

Watt, W. Montgomery, *Muhammad, Prophet and Statesman,* (Oxford University Press: Oxford, 1961) [new edn 1974].

Woodberry, J. Dudley (ed.), *Muslims and Christians on the Emmaus Road* (MARC: Monrovia, California, 1989).

[Wootton, R.F.W.], *Understanding the Sects of Islam*. Rev. edn of Wootton, *Understanding Muslim Sects* (FFM/CPO: Worthing, 1992).

Wright, Christopher, *What's So Unique About Jesus?* (Monarch: Eastbourne, 1990).

Zakaria, Rafiq, *The Struggle Within Islam* (India, 1988: Penguin: London, 1989).

Zwemer, Samuel M., *The Moslem Doctrine of God* (American Tract Society, NY, 1905) [repr. as *The Muslim Doctrine of God* (Darf: London, 1987)].

Zwemer, Samuel M., *The Muslim Christ* (Oliphant, Anderson & Ferrier: Edinburgh & London, 1912).

Educational Materials

All Souls Tape Library (2 All Souls Place, London W1N 3DP) has a series of seven tapes by Bishop Kenneth Cragg entitled *The Muslim and the Christian*, reference J11.

Carey College Publications (PO Box 109, Doncaster DN4 6UL) publishes three series of study materials, details of which are provided in the Bibliography (p 304).

The tape library of the organisation *Jesus to the Muslim* (St Andrews Bookshop, St Andrews Road, Plaistow, London E13 8QD) contains the following items:

John Gilchrist:	How to Witness to Muslims
	The Religion of Islam
	The Crucifixion, Fact not Fiction
	Muslim Objections to the Gospel
	Jesus in the Qur'an
	The Qur'an, the Scripture of Islam
	The Gospel and Islam
Bilquis Sheikh	A Testimony
Debates:	
McDowell/Deedat	Was Christ Crucified?
Gilchrist/Peerbhai	Jesus in the Qur'an and the Bible
Gilchrist/Buckas	Is the Bible God's Word?

Interserve (325 Kennington Road, London SE11 4QH) has a study pack and video entitled *Through Their Eyes*, and can provide other videos on Islam.

London Bible College (Green Lane, Northwood, Middlesex HA6 2UW) has a teaching video entitled 'Islam', and also runs a course on Islam.

Glossary of Arabic Words

These Arabic words are transcribed approximately, as there are not English equivalents of each Arabic sound. As a guide to pronunciation, the (') is a glottal stop. The letter 't' is often the plural ending, but many Arabic words are now frequently used in English, and often with the English plural ending 's', e.g. Sufi, Sufis. The Arabic language is constructed from roots, which consist of three consonants. Vowels are added in different ways to make different parts of speech (adjectives, nouns, etc.). For more detailed discussion see chapter 3, note to section 2, p 61.

Ahmadiyya	a sect of Muslims following the teaching of Mirza Ghulam Ahmad
akhira	life after death
Allah	God
Allah Akbar	God the Greatest
ansar	helpers, the people who in Medina welcomed the people from Mecca, when they came on hijva
'ard	honour
Ashura	The first ten days of the month of Muharram, For Shiites, a celebration of the death of Hussain at Karbela
asr	afternoon prayer time
aya	a verse in the Qur'an, also a sign or miracle. Pl. Ayat or ayas
Ayatollah	most senior title for Shia scholar
Baqara	The Heifer, the cow: the name of Sura 2 in the Qur'an
bid'a	innovation
bismillah	in the name of God
burqa	long veil, drape worn by women

caliph	see Khalifa
Dar al Harb	name given to those who are not Muslims, outside the family of Islam
Dar al Islam	name given to those who are in the family of Islam
da'wa	mission, calling people to join Islam
Dawud	David
dhuhr	also Zuhr; the midday prayer
Dhu L'Hejja	the twelfth month of the Islamic calendar
din	religion, the practices or duties of religion
din el fitra	natural religion
du'a	prayers of supplication (not the formal prayer, Salat)
Eid ul Adha	the feast of the sacrifice, in the 12th month
Eid ul Fitr	the breakfast feast which ends Ramadan
fajr	the dawn prayer time
Fatiha	the first Sura in the Qur'an
Furkan	another name for the Qur'an
Hadith	the collection of stories about what Muhammad did and said; the traditions
hajj	the pilgrimage to Mecca
hajj or hajja	name given to man or woman who has gone on the pilgrimage
Hassan, Hussain	sons of Ali
hijva	the Emigration to Medina from Mecca, AD 622
imam	leader of the mosque; leader of the Shiite community
iman	faith
imra'a	woman
Imran (Al Imran)	Sura 3
Injil	The Gospels, or New Testament, the book brought by Jesus
insan	man; al insan al kamil, the perfect man
inshallah	God willing, if God wills
iqraa	read, recite, or proclaim
Isa	the name used of Jesus in the Qur'an
Islam	to submit; submission; surrender to the will of God or to the law of God. See Muslim
isha	evening prayer
jihad	holy war; to struggle to the best of one's ability to accomplish a job
jizya	tax
al Ka'ba	the black stone at Mecca
kafir	unbeliever, infidel, blasphemer
Al Kitab	The Book, the Qur'an
Khadija	the prophet's first wife

Khalifa	a ruler, a deputy
Khalifate	the rule of the Khalifa
kufr	to cover up, to conceal, to deny God
Lalatas al Qadr	the night power, the night of the Qur'an came down
Al Lat	a goddess, pre-islamic idol
maghrib	the prayer at sunset
Al Manat	a goddess, pre-islamic idol
el Mas'haf	a name for the Qur'an
mi'raj	when Muhammad is said to have ascended to heaven
Muawiya	first ruler of Ummayad dynasty
mu'azzin	the prayer caller
muhajirun	the migrants, who went on the hijva
mullah	in charge of local mosque, also maulvi and maulana
murabit	pl. of marabout, religious leaders who exercise occult powers
Musa	Moses
mushahara	month, used in popular Islam of the months surrounding childbirth
Muslim	person who follows Islam
nabi	prophet
Naqshbandi	a Sufi order
nasikh	abrogation
nisaa	women, and the name of Sura 4
niyya	purity of intention
AL Qadr	All-Powerful, a name of God
qibla	the direction facing Mecca, for praying
Qur'an	the book of the revelations to Muhammad, sometimes spelled Kor'an
Quraysh	Muhammad's tribe
Rabb	Lord
Rabb al Amin	Lord of the faithful
radda	apostacy
rahim	gracious
rahiman	merciful
raka'	bowing up and down in praying; prostrations
Ramadan	the fast month, ninth month of the Muslim calendar
rasul	apostle, messenger
sadaqa	charity, alms
sajda	to bow down in worship
salam	peace
salat	prayer
sawm	fasting
shahada	the creed, the confession: there is no God (or

	deity) but Allah and Muhammad is Allah's messenger
shafi	intercessor
Shari'a	the religious law based on the Qur'an
Shawal	the 11th month of the Islamic year
Shaykh	(also spelt shaikh, sheikh), elder, leader, chief
shirk	to associate or share partnership, and used of association of Jesus with God, making them partners, to be a polytheist, an idolator (another noun: mushrikun, the polytheists)
sura	a chapter in the Qur'an, Pl. Suras
ta'aruf	knowledge, etiquette
tanzil	come down, the coming down of the Qur'an
tawaf	the first part of the Hajj ceremony, in Mecca going round the Ka'ba, and running between the mountains
tajdid	renewal, revival
tariqa	the path, the way, the pattern a Sufi follows
tawhid	the oneness of God
Tawrat	the books of Moses
Umma	the community, the family of Islam, the nation of Islam worldwide
Al Uzza	pre-islamic goddess, Sura 53
wahy	inspiration
Yunus	Jonah
Yusuf	Joseph
Zabur	Psalms
Zaid	Muhammad's adopted son
Zakariya	Zechariah, John the Baptist's father
zakat	legal alms from every Muslim
zakat ul Fitr	the alms given at the end of Ramadan
Zamzam	Hagar's well, in Mecca

Index